D0616140

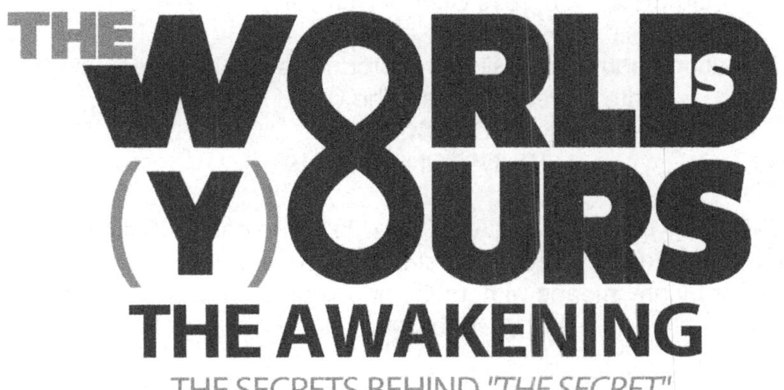

SECOND EDITION

Kurtis Lee Thomas

Printed in the United States of America
Second Edition

Library of Congress Control Number: 2014904227

Cover Credits:
Michael Catabia, Corey Robert, Ross Maq, William Bain, Michael Pontarelli, Lineup Ink and Picture Mosaic.

JOHNSTON, RI 02919
www.BrainyActs.com
ISBN NUMBER 978-0-9913797-0-5 (Hardcover)
ISBN NUMBER 978-0-9913797-1-2 (Paperback)

ON THE COVER

"A birth certificate shows that we were born, a death certificate shows that we died, images show that we lived!"

—Gerry Curry

On the cover of this book you will see an image of what seems to be (y)OUR world. Although this is (y)OUR Mother Earth, this image is composed of hundreds of smaller pictures of my friends and family members, as well as myself. This image of Earth, seen from outer space, illustrates viewing our world as a whole, made up of all the beautiful souls that personify it. As human beings we are all related and we are all divinely connected to ONE another. Therefore, we represent the Earth at this time, because we are the Earth! A picture captures a moment, cherishes a memory, and is said to be worth a thousand words. So when we collectively compile hundreds of pictures into ONE global image, what does it say? It says...THE WORLD IS (y)OURS!

COVER CONTEST!

Would you like to win tickets to my next workshop or seminar? Would you like to be on the mosaic cover of my next book? Then submit a picture of yourself showing the world your uniqueness; and don't be shy! Top 100 photos are chosen (must own copyrights to your image).

ADDITIONAL PRIZES

CATEGORIES: Funniest Photo, Bravest Photo, Best Nature Shot, Most Loving Moment Captured, Cutest Couple, Cutest Baby, Coolest Pet, Best Humanitarian Pic, Pic with Your Favorite Celebrity, Wildest Pic, and Most Creative Photo Win! Visit www.IamAwakened.com to submit your photo.

Dedication

This book is dedicated to my dear brother, the late and great Kevin L. Thomas. I cannot thank you enough for assisting in my awakening and helping guide me through a world filled with illusions and deception. I wrote this book for you, big brother! Thank you.

Special Thanks

To the true loves of my life, my beautiful daughter Kaila, and my Mother, Linda J. Cole, an extraordinary lady filled with great wisdom. A mother who single-handedly accomplished a woman's greatest feat by teaching a boy how to become a man. I thank you, mother, for believing in me at such a young age and teaching me *how* to think, and not *what* to think.

Acknowledgements

Elizabeth Luft Desrochers, G.W Hardin, Sophia Lugo, Christine Johnston, Maggie Bakhtiari, April Sheerin, Ron Ash, Lina Bain-Giarrusso, Nicolas Lonardo, Felicia Costa, Tina Lonardo-Shepard, Shirley Louise Cole, Miss Betty Grimes, Kevin Thomas Sr., Manil Suri, Joseph D'Arezzo, Nicole Silva, Jessica Xavier, Amanda Assante, Migdalia Gonzalez, April Andrews, William Bain, Marissa Yazidjian, Roy Colebut-Ingram, Wendy Beauchene, Sarah Vega, Sarah Hynes, The Masello Family, and to all of my Crowdfunders, especially Greg Takesian and James Sahady.

This book could not have been possible without all of your help and inspiration. I thank every one of you from the bottom, to the top, and throughout every part of my heart, with love and light.

Namaste!

TABLE OF CONTENTS

Chapters < Subchapters

CHAPTER 9

CHAPTER 10

CHAPTER 11

CHAPTER 12

CHAPTER 13

CHAPTER 14

CHAPTER 15

CHAPTER 16

UNDERSTANDING THE LAWS OF THE UNIVERSE

Glossary < Universal Laws

PREFACE | THE AWAKENING...

You might have heard that 90 percent of an iceberg exists below the surface of the water while only 10 percent protrudes above the water's surface. Just like an iceberg, the universe is showing you that something is here, but it's not allowing you to see it all at once. The universe is merely showing you the "tip of the iceberg"; in other words, "What you see is what you get." However, there is much more to discover in life, if you choose to take that leap of faith into uncharted waters.

Many are afraid to explore the unknown because they fear what they may discover. It's finally time to venture out of those shallow comfortable waters and explore greater depths of truth. It's time to dive into a deeper level of consciousness and discover all the secrets about the human race and our universe, once and for all. The time has finally come to reclaim the secret treasures hidden deep below the surface, and for the world to find out WHY these secrets and treasures have been kept from us in the first place.

Enjoy the ride!

CHAPTER

0

THE INTRODUCTION YOU SHOULD NOT SKIP

A big shift is taking place as you read this. This change is in the air, and you can feel it resonating deep within your soul. It's subtle because it's a change of awareness, a change of consciousness, and the unveiling of long-awaited truths. You can feel in your bones that there is more to life than just what you have been experiencing or have been told: go to school, get a job, get married, have kids, and die. This planet is filled with ancient wisdom, hidden knowledge, and many amazing truths that are right here for us to discover if we just take the time to look.

What To Expect...

This book will be a dynamic tool for anything you are trying to obtain: money, empowerment, confidence, love, forgiveness, success, hidden knowledge, universal truths, and much more. This is the dawn of uncovering all of life's secrets and tools—the same tools and abilities we've always had but just didn't know how to tap into. We all have them and they are ready for us to start using. Once you start to *awaken* and unveil all of the astounding hidden secrets I describe, I promise you'll never want to go back to sleep!

Your new journey begins right here, right now! It's time to wake up and take hold of the reins in your own life and start co-creating your own outcomes instead of just accepting what's presented to you. Learn how to manipulate energy and use the laws of the universe to your advantage. You're using them anyway, right now, whether you like it, know it, believe it, or not, so it's time to know and harness the power of co-creation that you possess within. If you change the way you think and feel, you can change your life any way you want, and attain all that you've ever desired. How do you do this?

In our broken system of education, we aren't being taught our true abilities as human beings or how powerful the human mind, body, and spirit really are. Unfortunately, we must discover this on our own and begin asking ourselves questions such as: Is this really it? Is there more to life than I know? You can start right now by answering this simple question for yourself, "BESIDES MY NAME, WHO AM I?" You should try asking that question to family, friends and co-workers as well, just to see what they say. You will notice that many will hesitate or even get stumped by this simple question because most people tend to define themselves by their name or by their occupation. This is mainly because most people don't know who they are or why they are really here. Others may attempt to answer this question by stating that they are a mother, a wife, a father, a sister, etc. However, no other person can define who you are but YOU.

We have been living in a state of oblivion for far too long, and it's time for us to reclaim our powers and remember who we really are and why we are here. As soon as you start to ask questions such as "Why am I here? What is the purpose of my life, and life itself?" It usually marks the beginning of your greatest discovery… YOU!

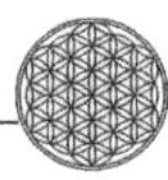

You Don't Know What You Don't Know

You must believe that there are no coincidences in life and that you have manifested this book into your hands somehow, someway. *How* you did this is irrelevant at this moment, what matters is "Why?". So without further ado, let me tell you why you are here…

> "*You're here because you know something. What you know you can't explain, but you feel it. You've felt it your entire life, that there's something wrong with the world. You don't know what it is, but it's there, like a splinter in your mind, driving you mad. It is this feeling that has brought you to me. Do you know what I'm talking about?*"
> ~ Morpheus (Laurence Fishburne), The Matrix 1999 film

They say when the student is ready, the teacher will appear. So, per your request, let this book become your new guide for the time being. Of course all authors want their readers to read through to the very last chapter. However, I am only recommending you do so because if you have this book in the grasp of your hands, and are reading this very sentence right now, then you must trust me when I tell you it's for a greater purpose than what you're imagining at the moment.

You will only discover what this greater purpose is after you have completed the first half of this book (chapters 1-9), revealing your true powers while simultaneously preparing you for the second portion of the book (chapters 10-19), where the real story begins to unfold as I tell you how and when to use your new powers.

Consider what you are about to read to the comparison of going into surgery, eye surgery let's say. You wouldn't just get up in the middle of surgery and go home, would you? Of course not! You must wait until the entire process is complete and trust that when all is said and done, you will see with much better clarity and wonder why you didn't get it over with sooner. This "consciousness surgery" that you are about to undergo is no different. You will soon view the world with an entirely new perspective, as a new pair of eyes awaits you as well!

Before We Begin

Take a moment and allow your mind to open up. Free it from any worry, stress, or bothersome thoughts. Take this time to temporarily neutralize all your current beliefs, assumptions, and previous knowledge just for the duration of this book. Allow what you read to sink deep within your subconscious where the truth always resides and will never steer you wrong.

You are about to quench your thirst, satisfy your hunger, and indulge in some profound food for thought that your being has longed for. Now, prepare yourself for a five-course meal of some real "soul food," and enjoy the buffet...

Bon appétit!

CHAPTER

1

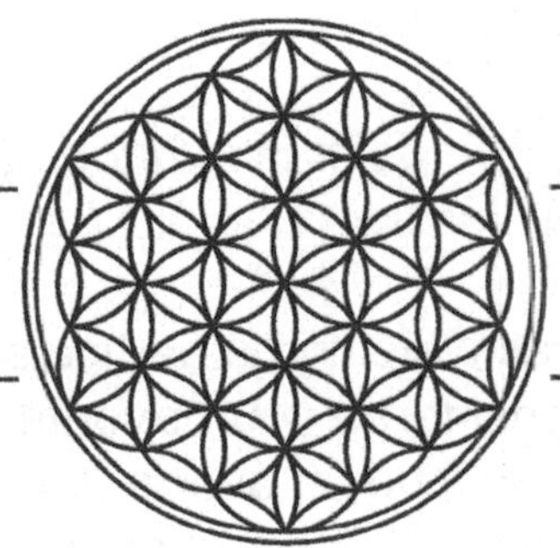

CONSCIOUSNESS

"*Consciousness, in some sense, is the most precious commodity in the multiverse of universes.*" ~ Dr. Michio Kaku

In baseball they say leadoff hitters are the most well-rounded and reliable players on the team. So, why lead off with the first chapter of this book discussing consciousness? Because the understanding of human consciousness is the only prerequisite to getting the most from this book. As an intelligent businessman would understand the difference between being rich and being wealthy, truly understanding consciousness would be the equivalent to knowing the difference between knowledge and wisdom.

Consciousness: What is it exactly? Consciousness is the state of being conscious, aware, and awakened to your environment. It's the perception of one's own personal existence or collective identity of an external object or situation. Consciousness is being inwardly attentive to your attitudes, beliefs, thoughts, and surroundings. It's your ability to pay attention to the subtle signs in life while perceiving places, people, or events in order to understand what's really being said or done. There's always a bigger picture in life that we cannot see until we reevaluate things, or see those things from a higher perspective.

"Any fool can know, the point is to understand."
~ Albert Einstein

Can you recall watching a particular Disney movie as a kid that you considered your favorite movie? You loved it so much that you watched it over and over again until you knew all the lines and could even act out the scenes. Maybe now you have a little brother or sister, or even your own children that you can watch your favorite movie with for old times' sake. But this time when you watch your favorite movie, you notice that the script includes adult content and there are certain lines and gestures that a kid couldn't even understand. Of course you never noticed this while you were a kid, but it sure sticks out like a sore thumb now that you're an adult.

It's not that the movie changed; it's that your awareness has been raised to the point that your consciousness' capacity for understanding the movie has increased. Since your level of awareness is solely contingent upon your consciousness level at that time, you will always have a deeper understanding the more you watch any movie or read any book than the previous time.

In his groundbreaking speech "Consciousness, Creativity and the Brain," American filmmaker David Lynch explains consciousness in the following way:

> *"If you have a golf-ball-sized consciousness, when you read a book, you will have a golf-ball-sized understanding…when you wake up in the morning, a golf-ball-sized wakefulness…But if you can expand that consciousness,*

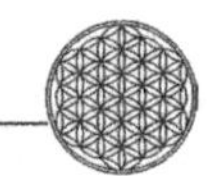

make it grow, then when you read that book, you'll have more understanding; when you look out, more awareness; when you wake up, more wakefulness...It's consciousness, and there's an ocean of pure vibrant consciousness inside each one of us and it's right at the source and base of mind, right at the source of thought, and it's also at the source of all matter."

As Lynch explains, consciousness is purely our perspective and understanding of the things that our conscious minds have the ability to comprehend. Our consciousness is limited by how we perceive our world and what we understand of it. But our consciousness also has the ability to grow and expand once we develop better instincts, intuition, and awareness of the goings-on around us.

"*Once you realize that there's something to be realized, then your realization has begun.*" ~ 3 Magic Words Documentary

The more you develop your awareness, the more you'll be able to start processing deeper levels of truth and understand what's really going on around you; something that I like to call your *Consciousness Net*. As your awareness grows and your perception enhances, your net gets larger and your holes get tighter, allowing you to *catch* things that would have normally gone under or over your head, or through your net!

Alcohol is a substance that lowers our level of consciousness, while cannabis, also known as marijuana, is a drug that raises ones level of consciousness. This is why when people smoke marijuana they seem to notice the most intricate details in things they normally wouldn't be conscious of (including objects, people, and situations). They look at life with a completely different perspective while under the influence. This rapid influx in consciousness can sometimes result in deep spiritual insight, revelations and epiphanies.

While at other times, smoking marijuana can result in paranoia because the person tends to "overthink" and look too deeply into a situation. This paranoia is caused by something I like to call "Consciousness Overload". Our consciousness will allow itself to stretch and bend, but will never break. One thing I must say is that although smoking marijuana may raise our level of consciousness temporarily, there are other significant side effects besides 'couch-lock' and 'the munchies' that are rarely talked about. The key is to remain in higher levels of consciousness at all times, but how so?

Some might think our consciousness expands automatically as we grow older and "smarter," but this is not completely true. One must understand that intelligence and higher levels of consciousness are like apples and oranges, a bit similar, but mostly different. Brain surgeons may tend to be what one might call smart, but this doesn't necessarily mean that they have higher levels of consciousness as well. In fact, the more training and conditioning one might have in a particular field or specialty, the more it can limit or constrain the expansion of their overall consciousness, if they don't maintain an open mind. Whatever socio-economic status or level of consciousness you currently hold, the one thing you can count on is that your perception of the world will change by the time you turn the final page of this work.

Test Your Consciousness

"*We don't see things the way they are, we see things the way we are.*" ~ Anaïs Nin

Naturally, humans are extremely tactile beings. We need to "see it to believe it." I, too, was once like this. In fact, I was the epitome of this type, living by the phrase "Believe none of what you hear and only half of what you see." If you're one of those people who need to see it to believe it, consider this: What if I told you that you have been seeing

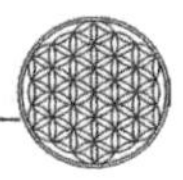

it without seeing it this whole time? What if I told you that everything has been right at the tips of your fingers, right under your nose, staring you right in the face the entire time but you just haven't been able to see it yet? Just because we have eyes doesn't mean we see everything, and just because we don't see something for what it really is doesn't mean it was never there all along.

"*Even with our eyes open, we tend to still be blind.*"

~ The World is (y)ours

Look at the famous FedEx logo for example. You must have seen this logo a thousand times. But were you always aware of the blatant pointing arrow inside of the logo? Take a look at this logo if you're not familiar with this arrow.

If you don't see this arrow at first glance, look for the white arrow in between the bottom half of the E and the X. Did you know that this arrow was there all along? This logo is seen all over the world, yet why are so few able to spot this arrow or even become aware it's there in the first place?

Once we are "aware" that this arrow exists, it sticks out like a sore thumb and it's pretty hard to believe that we've never seen it before. Now that you know where the arrow is, I guarantee that every time you see this logo, it will be the first thing you will notice. The same experience is true once you find yourself awakening to the real world in which you live. But what the arrow-in-the-logo example really does is make you think, "I wonder how many other examples like this are out there that no one ever catches?" The "signs" and "arrows" that have always been there and have always been pointing you in the right direction will begin to seem more obvious now. As you raise your awareness and consciousness levels you will realize there is an entirely new language out there for you to decode and discover. You will look at everything with a new perspective and start to see things you never noticed before, yet seem so evident once they are exposed to you. In later chapters you will see far more mind-blowing examples on a much larger scale that will really make you shake your head in disbelief.

Some of the hardest things to see are the things in plain sight. We tend to overlook many of the things we believe, see, do, or say without much thought. For instance, the majority of people in this country grew up singing the famous ABC Alphabet song like myself. However, most people have no clue they've actually been singing along to the tune of Twinkle Twinkle Little Star their entire lives. You can go ahead and sing both tunes in your head right now and see for yourself if you're not aware of this. Point being made, some of the most common things in life are where we fail to connect the dots. We tend to overlook so many things in life, big and small, but when these things are finally pointed out to us we can't seem to understand how we never caught it on our own.

There is plenty of ancient wisdom, suppressed knowledge, and undisclosed truths right under our noses just ready for us to discover. However, "the truth" is something that we must find first, it will not find us. Not because it is not looking for us, but because it has already found us. We just haven't acknowledged it. Even if the truth did find us per se, we would not recognize it nor would we accept it as our truth. We would either immediately dismiss it or ridicule it as we have in the past. However, once our consciousness levels rise high enough to see things from a new perspective, we will realize these truths have been tapping us on the shoul-

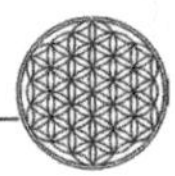

der and were here for us to discover the entire time.

It might seem like a catch-22 if you feel you must see something to believe it. The real truth is that it's the other way around; you must first believe it, in order to see it. Although we feel we need to see something to believe it, we actually don't. We can't see oxygen, but we know it's there. We can't see God, but most people have faith that He/She/It exists. We've never actually seen a dinosaur with our own eyes, but we've seen bone fossils that prove their existence. Well, just like those dinosaur bones, if you continue to dig, you will eventually find your proof too!

Understanding consciousness, how to expand it, and the awakening of humanity, is not just the basis of this book, it is crucial to the world in which you live. You will see how elevating your consciousness not only has the ability to change your reality, but humanity's as a whole. This conscious awareness is essential to the forthcoming mass awakening that's near. It is a powerful tool, and when collectively unified with humanity, this can and will change life on this planet forever! But before we travel down that rabbit hole, we must first explore where the seeds of consciousness originate, and understand how powerful these seeds can be!

CHAPTER

2

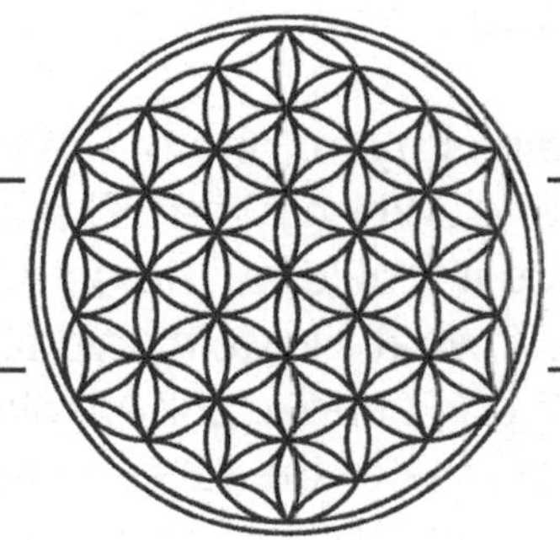

THE POWER OF THOUGHT

"Whatever the mind can conceive and believe, it can achieve." ~ Napoleon Hill

The power of the word is said to be the most powerful tool given to humankind. However, aren't words just thoughts said out loud? Don't we need to have the thought before we make the word? When we pray aren't we sending out thought? When we meditate aren't we looking to receive that life-changing "thought"? Everything in this universe started with a thought. Intention and thought are the most powerful tools given to humans, yet the most unheeded. But why haven't we learned the significance and the power of a thought? Why aren't we being taught how to utilize these powerful building blocks of life while in school?

Although you can't see your thoughts, it doesn't mean your thoughts aren't physically manifesting themselves around you this very second. We already know science can measure the energy emitted from our thoughts, and just because we can't physically see this energy, doesn't mean that something amazing isn't happening right before our eyes.

Living in a Wireless World

"*Our entire biological system, the brain and the earth itself, work on the same frequencies.*" —Nikola Tesla

Albert Einstein is by far one of the most ingenious minds I enjoy studying. When Albert Einstein was famously asked, "So how does it feel to be the smartest man in the world?" Do you know what Einstein said to that person? He replied by stating, "I don't know, ask Nikola Tesla." Tesla was an awakened genius to the fullest degree; he invented wireless electricity by understanding the language of the universe and coming to the realization that everything in this world is energy comprised of various vibrational frequencies.

If you look at where technology is taking us today, everything is becoming wireless. The whole world, including us, is now operating on wireless signals. These invisible signals are everywhere and travel within the same space. We cannot see these signals or frequencies, but they are there and they are communicating/interacting with one another even though we can't see this happening. You don't have to be somewhere to read something, know something, or even feel something anymore.

Similarly, our brain waves emit frequencies created by our thoughts, and those frequencies communicate to the universe through "wireless" signals. These thoughts and frequencies we emit create the world in which we live. Although actual wireless technology is relatively new to humankind, we have had these internal abilities since creation. We are all operating on wireless signals: sending, receiving, transmitting, and encoding every second of every day. If some of these devices that we've created are advanced enough to have the ability to wirelessly communicate with one another, is it so hard to believe that we humans have these same abilities as well?

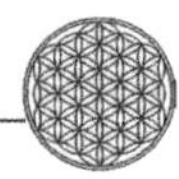

Thoughts Create

"*We are precious; every single one of us. We are magnificent human beings who have been given an almighty gift- the ability to create our own lives, without limits.*"

~ *The Secret,* by Rhonda Byrne

Look around you. Everything in the room you're in right now was created with a thought. This book you're reading, the chair you're sitting in, or the bed you're lying in, EVERYTHING started with a thought! Every embryonic idea in the world was conceived by a single thought. Humans create with tools, thoughts, and imagination!

Even if you're riding in an airplane or in a car right now, or in a home or some sort of massive building, it can all be traced back to just a thought from one person who acted on what she or he called an idea. Somewhere, someone, sometime had a single thought of inventing that car you're driving, computer you're using, or phone that you're texting with. In order for something to be made, it first needs to be invented. So before it's invented, it doesn't exist. Therefore, in order for that item to exist, someone, somewhere, at some point in time had an "aha" moment from a single thought, and eventually created what you see before you. It all emerged from an invisible thought that manifested into the tangible item you see today. They say energy can neither be created nor destroyed. But, if humans can create something with just a single thought, then where are these thoughts and that energy coming from? This should lead us to think, either energy can be created (because we are the creators), or this is proof that our thoughts are indeed energy!

If you're having a hard time grasping the concept that your thoughts shape your reality, or the fact that you emit certain frequencies and energies that communicate to the universe, then let's make a comparison. Today, most of us in the world use a computer or cell phone in our daily lives. These devices send out wireless signals, or frequencies, that we cannot see, but we know they are there. When these signals are emitted, they travel through the atmosphere and communicate with a satellite or some sort of wireless router; which in turn, encodes this invisible message, then sends a signal back allowing our device to unlock all the wonderful gadgets, widgets, apps, and features of the World Wide Web. This is just proof that cell phones and satellites, which we created, have the ability to send out an invisible signal to let another device know that it needs something. If one can understand this, then why would it be so hard to believe that humans have these same abilities to communicate with the universe from which they were created? Aren't we the geniuses that created all these wonderful gadgets and technologies in the first place?

We put too much faith in technology and attach such mystery to it; we forget that we are the ones who invented it. When I say the true power of thought is underestimated, that statement in itself is an understatement. I wouldn't just consider it to be something we take for granted. I think it's something that we forget was granted to us in the first place. Even if you feel you've landed right where you would like to be in life, just know that the power of your thoughts is what got you there. We must understand the power of our thoughts and how they not only affect us, but the entire world around us. We must finally realize that "we" (not the things that we create), are the most intelligent and amazing biomechanical machines on this planet.

Your Thoughts Affect Your Physical World

"*I admit thoughts influence the body.*" ~ Albert Einstein

The placebo effect has been used in many studies in which researchers take one or more groups of people with similar physical conditions and give them "the cure" to fix

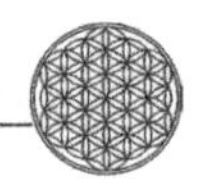

their ailments. However, this cure is not really the cure; it's only a sugar pill, or something natural and noninvasive, irrelevant to their symptoms.

At the end of the study, the subjects have measurable, observable results. The majority of the subjects feel improvement in health or behavior that is not attributable to the medication or treatment that has been administered to them. So why is this? How is it possible that they feel so much better after just taking a pill filled with sugar?

It's because the mind creates the medicine, not the pill. So, by believing and expecting something to work, it actually does. These simple studies blatantly demonstrate how effective our thoughts can be and the effects they have on our bodies. A single thought about our favorite dessert can make a hungry person salivate, just as a single thought is so powerful it can give a man an erection.

Take a polygraph (lie detector test) for example. It's obvious that our body reacts to our thoughts and that they directly affect one another. Just one thought can increase our heart rate, change our temperature, elevate our blood pressure, make us perspire, tense our muscles, and change our breathing patterns. When you tell a lie while strapped to one of these machines, it will pick up on all of the telltale signs of you articulating that lie without you even noticing. That's because your heart rate and blood pressure begin to rise, your breathing becomes faster, your hands start to sweat, and your body temperature begins to change. These kinds of physiological reactions in the body occur in relation to every thought you have, not just when you're lying.

When I Became a Believer

When I was in fifth grade, my neighbor and I had this plan to fake sickness to our parents so that we could cut school and play with our new Christmas toys. I woke up that morning and should have won an Oscar for my performance. However, the plan backfired. I did such a good job at playing sick that my mom actually decided to take the day off work and take care of me. This wasn't good news. I felt perfectly fine, but for the entire day I had to play ill so that my mom wouldn't know that I was just trying to play hooky. What happened next is something I'll never forget.

The next morning I woke up ready to go to school and soon found that I was deathly ill. I had actually made myself sick by acting sick that whole day. All those thoughts, emotions, words, stomach grunts, whines and cries I was faking really tricked my body into thinking I was sick. Normally, I can feel when I'm about to get sick. The day before I was in perfect health, but by the next morning I had become probably the most sick I've ever been in my life. So from this personal experience, I gained a lifelong understanding of how the power of constant thought with intense matching emotions can create anything, good or bad, if I put my mind to it.

Thoughts Can Grow!

I remember watching Leonardo DiCaprio's movie, Inception. In the movie, a technology exists that enables people to enter the human mind through dream invasion. DiCaprio's character is a highly skilled thief that is in the "subconscious security" business. In the very early minutes of this movie, he explains the power of a thought or an idea. He explains that an idea can spread like a virus or cancer until it takes over a person so much that it comes to define that person. He suggests that a single thought from the human mind has the power to build cities, transform our world, and rewrite the rules by which we live.

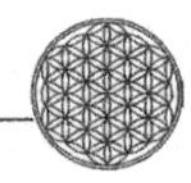

"*You really can change your own reality based on the way that you think.*" ~ Oprah Winfrey

In this sense, a thought is like a virus. It grows and grows. The more energy you give it, the more it will eventually become your reality. We must understand that our outer world is directly created by our inner world…our thoughts, emotions, and inspired actions create our reality! Take the talented celebrities Mariah Carey, Britney Spears, and Tiger Woods as examples. The whole world knew of their marriage struggles, which consequently affected their careers. This was quite obvious to anyone who attended one of their tournaments or concerts during this time. These examples are the epitome of how someone's outer world is a direct reflection of their inner world. If your inner world (thoughts and emotions) is a mess, your outer world will reciprocally manifest.

The power of thought can be life changing. The first step to changing the way we are and the way we live is to change the way we think. There is nothing miraculous about any of this. Once you know how your thoughts affect the way you live, it's up to you to make those changes happen. Thoughts without action are useless. For example, if you tend to be a negative person and you find yourself constantly thinking about how bad your life is, yet you do nothing about it, not much will change. In fact, you will just attract more negativity to you. This is what Einstein meant when he said, "Insanity is doing the same thing over and over again but expecting different results."

But can our thoughts consume us to a point where we can lose ourselves during this journey? If we have enough of the same thoughts, can we slowly transform our identity into someone or something we are not?

Becoming Our Thoughts

"*All that we are is the result of what we have thought. The mind is everything. What we think, we become.*" ~ Buddha

Few people take notice of the fact that our reality is merely a materialization of our thoughts. Hollywood actors and actresses are well aware of how much their thoughts affect them. In fact, they are trained to completely change their normal thinking patterns to something they aren't used to in order to "get into character" for a movie role. I've watched many interviews with actors discussing how they prepare for a tough role. They diligently study their character day in and day out and try to become that person by getting into that character's mind-set. In some cases, actors' or actresses' spouses have urged them to get counseling after the filming has ended because they have become so wrapped up in the character that they've actually lost a sense of themselves and undergone a complete personality change. The actor Heath Ledger is a perfect example. After playing the role as *The Joker* in Batman, it was said that Ledger started to lose touch of reality, eventually leading to his fatal drug overdose in 2008. This is another prime example of how the power of thought and visualization can change any outcome, or even any person, for that matter.

I remember watching an episode of the comedy series Seinfeld in which Jerry was searching for a way to beat a lie detector test and realized that he had access to the master of all liars, George Costanza. When Jerry asks for George's advice, George turns to Jerry with a most serious face and says, "Jerry, it's not a lie, if you believe it." I always remembered that episode and laughed because I felt that George was right. If you truly believe it, then that's your reality. So, who can tell you differently? But what's more powerful; your beliefs/thoughts, or the images you visualize in your mind most?

CHAPTER

3

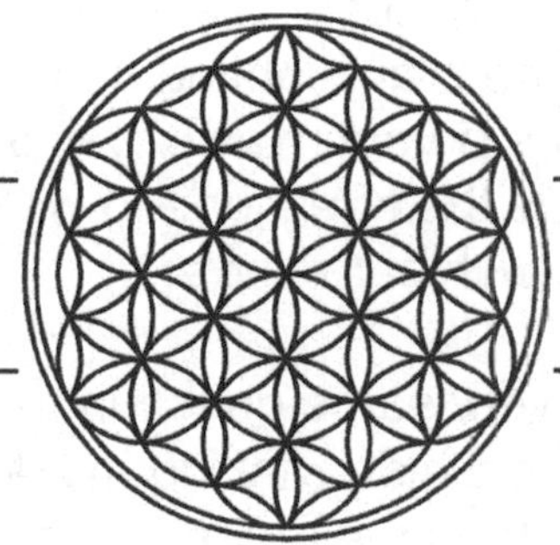

THE POWER OF VISUALIZATION

"*When you visualize, then you materialize. If you've been there in the mind you'll go there in the body.*"

~ Dr. Denis Waitley

Only you are responsible for the thoughts and images that you project in your mind. Your brain can't distinguish whether the images you project in your mind are real or imaginary, and doesn't know the difference between the two. How is this?

Scientific experiments have proven that when we hook a person's brain up to computer technology that monitors her or his neurons and receptors, we can track the activity within the brain.

In 2004, there was an interesting documentary titled What the Bleep Do we Know!?. The documentary hypothesizes a spiritual connection between consciousness and quantum physics through unique narratives, interviews, and computer-animated graphics. The film cites a scientific study in which a subject was asked to stare at a certain object.

Scientists would then watch specific areas of the subject's brain light up. The object was then taken away and the scientists asked the subject to close his eyes and envision that same object he was just looking at. The results showed the same areas of the brain lighting up in the exact same patterns as when the person was physically looking at the object. So this poses the question, do we really see with our eyes, or do we see with our minds?

I posed this very same question to one of my business partners who is a high-ranking military officer. He told me this is how they train their men in the military for combat situations. Troops are trained to play out a variety of different scenarios in their minds so that when the real scenario happens they already know how to respond because they've already envisioned it. The power of visualization is the reason why vision boards are so effective for manifesting and why police detectives use similar boards as an essential tool for their investigations.

Another study, done with Olympic track runners, was highlighted in the movie The Secret. During a race, the runners were hooked up to machines that monitored the biofeedback brain activity and recorded the results. After the race, the runners were then put in a room and asked to run that same race, except this time only in their minds. The results were similar. The same parts of the brain were triggered in the exact same sequence as when the runners were physically running the race.

This means that the daily thoughts and visions you hold in your mind most, end up becoming your reality. Ultimately, your thoughts and your visions make up your inner reality of what your brain believes, eventually making your inner reality manifest into your physical reality. This is proof that you "create" your reality using your thoughts and visions. To your brain, these thoughts and visions ARE your reality,

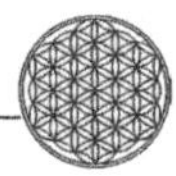

because it cannot tell the difference between the two.

The brain or subconscious can't tell the difference between real experiences, a dream, or what is being visualized or imagined. Therefore, remembering, pretending, imagining, or actually doing something, are all one in the same to the brain. Try this visualization exercise for an example and see what happens. As you read this, it's important to read the words slowly, and equally important to vividly imagine doing this word for word, step by step, as described.

The Lemon Visualization Exercise

Picture yourself somewhere in your kitchen. Imagine wherever you are sitting or standing there is a big bowl of freshly picked lemons in front of you. You look at a few lemons and choose the yellowest, ripest, and best-looking lemon in the basket. As you pick it up you can feel the weight of the lemon in your hand, the dimples on the outer skin, and the smooth waxy skin texture as you slide your fingers across it. You raise the lemon to your nose and smell that faint lemon scent.

You then grab a sharp kitchen knife from the drawer, place that lemon on the table, and cut into the lemon. As the knife slices through the lemon the juices squirt out like a bright yellow flash and lightly hit your skin. An attractive and familiar lemony aroma fills the room. You cut a smaller slice from one half and the citrus smell gets stronger and stronger as the lemon nears your mouth. As you put it in your mouth, you bite down on it and the juice runs all over and under your tongue as it seeps deep into your taste buds and the bottom of your tongue. Your mouth fills with the taste of lemon juice and your eyes almost begin to water and your mouth puckers. So, how does it taste?

If you vividly imagined yourself eating this lemon then

you most likely found yourself beginning to salivate and felt your mouth or eyes start to water. This visualization exercise of eating a lemon is something that creates powerful physical reactions in the body like an involuntary reflex.

Images, whether you see them through your eyes, or project them in your mind, both stimulate your emotions in the same way. These visual images and pictures that we project in the mind are even more powerful than a thought; hence, "a picture is worth a thousand words." You could have merely read the lemon visualization exercise and not visualized it and nothing would have happened. However, when you visualize those words with vivid thoughts, they create images in your brain that can trigger a physical response.

Our ability to visualize and mentally believe in something seems to make it our reality. Not just mentally—but physically, not just imaginary—but in reality, with real physical reactions. The way we think influences our health and well-being beyond belief. If merely thinking about a lemon can make your mouth water, then just imagine what thinking positive thoughts can do to the rest of your body and your well-being? The way we think, feel, and act have been proven to have a direct influence on our physical bodies. Our thoughts alone have the remarkable ability to make us sick and enough power to make us well. It's all a matter of our perception of life. So take full responsibility, be conscious of your thoughts, and don't allow negative images to fill your mind.

We have been taught to believe that our external world (our reality) is more real than our internal world. However, what we create within us—our thoughts, visions, and emotions—dictate what we create outside of us. If you continue to dedicate time and energy to playing out the worst-case scenarios in your mind, then you are automatically emotionally and physically responding to those images and

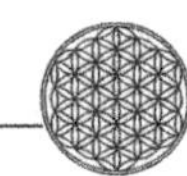

attracting those outcomes into your life. Be aware of the thoughts you create, images you project, and emotions you conjure up. Stay positive by having positive thoughts and visualizing positive images and outcomes.

You must remember that this is your movie; you are the actor, editor, producer, and director. If you choose to create a horror film in your mind and play out the worst-case scenarios, this is what you'll invite. If you choose to create a great story with a happy ending, then that's what you'll attract. Always be aware of your current state and remember, these are your thoughts, your visions. If you don't like the way a scene is playing out, you can "edit" your movie whenever you choose and flip the script by changing your thoughts and visions, because ultimately your thoughts *are* your visions.

In Dr. Michio Kaku's most recent book, *The Future of the Mind*, he explains this in the following:

> "*In the future we will have the ability to have a motion picture of your thoughts, and in fact, a motion picture of your dreams. At the University of California at Berkeley, I went to the laboratory there where they have an MRI machine that takes all of your thoughts and breaks them up into thirty thousand dots, then there's a computer program that interprets the 30,000 dots and creates an image of what you're looking at.*"

This is just additional scientific proof that our thoughts indeed create images within our mind; images that spark visualizations, which spark our imagination!

Throughout the journey of my awakening, I must say I was most upset when I discovered that I have been fooled into throwing out the most powerful tool in my toolbox. In the next chapter, I will attempt to revive the power and significance of this very tool that is the most disvalued and misused magical tool we ever possessed!

CHAPTER

4

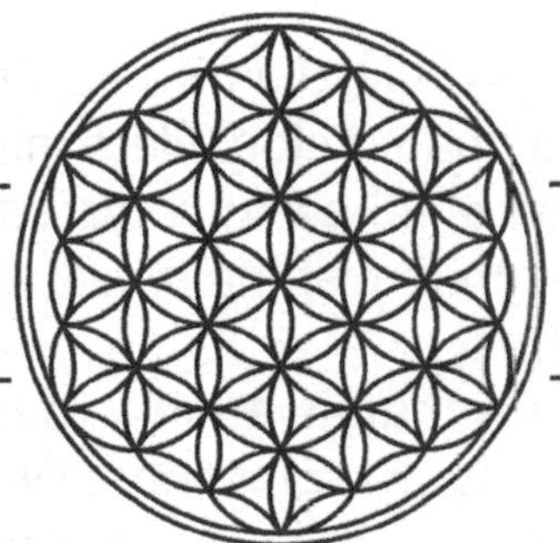

IMAGINATION - THE TRUE SOURCE OF ALL CREATION

"*There is no life I know to compare with pure imagination.*"
~ Willy Wonka

As Albert Einstein said, "*The true sign of intelligence is not knowledge but imagination.*" Imagination is powerful! Everything starts from an idea! We take that idea and imagine a situation coming to life in our minds before it actually happens. We create these emotions and capture the feeling of that scenario as if it is happening or has already happened. By doing this, our imagination activates the law of attraction. Our minds create a thought, our thoughts spark our imagination, and our imagination connects with our hearts. Then, our hearts create intense emotions that match our thoughts, and BOOM! We've just ignited the most powerful force known to man: Co-creation!

The majority of people in the world do not know how powerful the human heart and mind really are. "If the mind can conceive it and believe it, you can and will achieve it." This is merely creative visualization and the natural law of attraction coming together. To take what is only imaginary and make it come to life is a gift that everyone has. Now if that's not true magic, then I don't know what is.

In an interview on Oculus Radio with Bob Wright, he discusses collective imagination. He explains the significance of imagination and how to control it using the heart and emotions rather than just the mind.

Wright explains that as adults we have forgotten how to play and use our imaginations. We worry too much about work, survival, and the monotony of life instead of letting our imaginations create the life we want. In school, we were told not to daydream and to get our heads out of the clouds. Wright states that this was the absolute worst advice that was ever given to us. This is where our power is: in the imagination. The very tools that help us co-create in this life are the same tools we were told not to use since adolescence.

A Magical Trip to La-La Land

Daydreaming is an altered state of consciousness that puts us in a euphoric haze temporarily detaching all sensations from the physical body and allowing our mind to shift and drift into higher levels of consciousness. Daydreaming enables us to bi-locate and teleport our consciousness into a higher frequency (a deeper thought) or into a higher realm that we create with pure subconscious thoughts and imagination. The same imagination that has been referred to as La-La Land during our adolescent years is that same happy place you imagined in your mind's eye from time to time.

This fundamental human feature was given constant reprimanding from our parents and schoolteachers, who told us to "wake up and snap out of it" whenever we got caught daydreaming. Little did they know that we were exercising

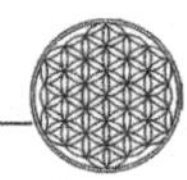

life's most powerful tool and manifesting with our thoughts through visualization and imagination!

We were misled about the powers of this priceless gift along with the knowledge of how to use it. This information was suppressed and humanity was deterred from utilizing this vital ability to create our own reality instead of accepting the one presented to us. It is now clear that this powerful tool of daydreaming is the motherboard for manifesting any life you choose for yourself. We all have this ability (rich or poor) to co-create the life we choose and not the life we were given. But why weren't we taught how to use these powerful tools of manifesting to our advantage? Could it be possible that these abilities were far too powerful that it could potentially jeopardize someone's master plan if humankind actually knew the powers they possessed? Who this someone is and what their master plan could possibly be will soon be revealed as you continue to read on.

How to Create a Magical Child

I watched an interview with famous scientist and inventor Dr. Pete Peterson in which he mentioned a book called Magical Child by Joseph Chilton Pearce. He stated, "Anyone who has a child and doesn't read this book should be jailed—I'm serious!" I never heard a scientist make such a bold and candid statement, so I did my research and discovered that this book is as amazing as he advocates. It's by a noteworthy scientist and it teaches you all the secrets to raising a magical child with an extraordinarily high IQ. This book has children beginning to walk and develop speech at six months old, which has all been documented and proven.

One of the most emphasized messages in the book is that kids shouldn't watch TV, but instead play games and activities that stem from their imagination. He mentions that imagination needs to be exercised more in order to encourage vivid visualizations within the child's brain, and that a key component to developing a high IQ is to escalate the consciousness of the child by not limiting children's thoughts. Encouraging a child's imagination is crucial to boosting their development to its full potential.

Dr. Pete Peterson mentions that Madonna used these techniques on her children and he states, "*Madonna's kids have some of the highest IQs on this planet because of this book.*"

Since our imagination is the place where dreams are born, sometimes we have to just let our imagination run wild and see where it goes. Our imagination is the place where we send our favorite thoughts to manifest; it is our playground where we can think freely and where anything is possible. It is then up to us whether we choose to believe what we imagine is achievable or not. We all have the ability to dream and imagine, but it's only the true believers that are able to bridge the gap between fact and fairytale, which allows them to accomplish anything they set their mind to.

Without human imagination, the law of attraction could never function properly. But this isn't the reason why so many people that understand the law of attraction still have trouble manifesting what they want in life. It is because most books overlook one of the most important aspects of this law that is essential to successfully activating the communication needed between you and your universe. But before I fully explain the intricate details of this law and how it really works, there is something you must know beforehand. What you must know is that there is more to the story! Although the law of attraction is a very powerful law existing within our universe, it is only ONE LAW of many. Although there are various sub-laws, there are twelve (12) main universal laws within our universe that everyone should know about. Once one understands all of the main universal laws, they will then

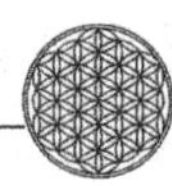

possess the power to transform or create any situation/event within their world far easier than ever before.

CHAPTER

5

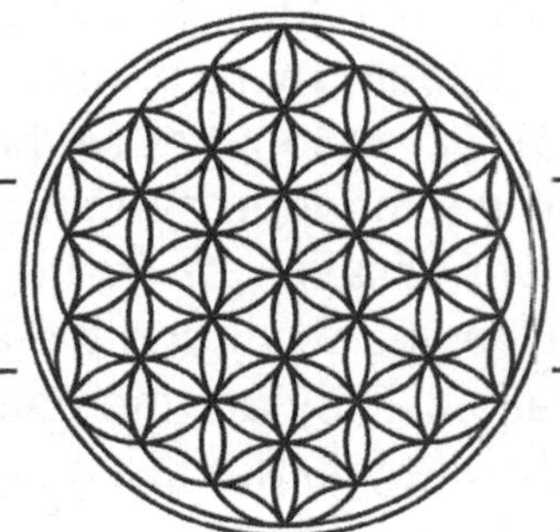

UNDERSTANDING THE LAWS OF THE UNIVERSE

"*The law of attraction is just one law—there are many laws working in the world and there are other factors going on.*"
~ Oprah Winfrey

Just as corporations have company By-laws, and governments have state and federal laws, many of us forget that the universe operates under a set of laws as well. These universal laws apply to each and every one of us and there's no escaping them—even if we try. Trying to avoid the reality of these laws would be like trying to live life without breathing air—it's just not possible. People who are aware of these laws, yet believe that these laws don't apply to them, will find themselves in an endless battle with an unstoppable force that's only here to assist them, not resist them. All of these universal laws are cohesively interconnected with one another to maintain balance and harmony within our world. This is why it's important that humanity finally becomes aware of all the laws in our universe, not just the law of attraction.

Most of us are strangers to these unspoken laws that govern our world, when in fact, these universal laws are actually the foundation and guidelines for life itself. Learning these laws not only allows us to understand the forces of our world, they allow us to learn more about ourselves, eventually leading us to the realization that we have power over our own life and the ability to change certain events and outcomes using these universal laws. These laws are the blueprint to creating the life you want and the ability to overcome difficulty in any situation. They are the cause and effect of why you are living the life you are living right now, which is no accident or coincidence.

There is a game being played and you are playing it. Just like any other game, there are rules to the game in which you play and ways on how to best play them. By understanding all of the universal laws that I'm about to explain throughout this book, you will finally have the playbook with all the tips you'll need to reach your goals and accomplish anything you ever wanted in life. So, lets begin with the most illustrious law of them all to kick-start this chapter!

Understanding the Law of Attraction: Ah, "The Secret!" We have all heard of the law of attraction. But how do we use it? The truth is you are using it right now and you always have been. It's simple: what you give your energy and emotion to is what becomes your reality. The law of attraction is undoubtedly the most powerful law in the universe. And just like the law of gravity, it is a consistent force that is ALWAYS in full effect, with no exclusions or exceptions!

The best way to explain the law of attraction is to use the analogy of the universe being a giant mirror. When you smile at a mirror what does it do? It smiles back at you! If you are looking at this same mirror and you frown at it, what do you get back? You have the exact same relationship with the universe. Whatever energy you occupy your mind and

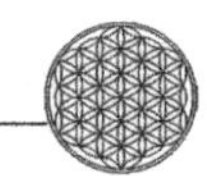

emotions with the most is what the universe will recognize and reciprocate for you. This is why it is so important to pay close attention to the thoughts you are emitting and what you are saying to the universe. With the analogy of the universe being a mirror, we must be extremely clear on what we want and what we are showing the universe we want, because this is what we will get.

In an interview with Larry King, Oprah Winfrey acknowledges the book *The Secret* and talks about its message. Oprah confidently gives full credit to the law of attraction for contributing to her success, and this is the message she has been trying to convey on her show for more than twenty years: "You are responsible for your life." Oprah explains how she has been using this law of attraction since 1985 when she willed her breakthrough role as Sofia in the movie The Color Purple. If you search for the interview on YouTube, you will see how Oprah's thoughts and actions are the epitome of utilizing the law of attraction to her advantage. Once Oprah accidentally discovered the ingredients to attracting things that seemed nearly impossible into her life, she said it changed her world forever.

What Does This Law of Attraction Have to Do with Me?

We are all attractive when we look into the universe's mirror! We all work within the same natural laws of the universe. No matter our nationality, or where we live in the world, we are ALL using these forces every second of every day. Whether you believe it or don't believe it, understand it or don't understand it, the law of attraction is working this very second, as you are reading this sentence. There is no "off" switch, and this universal law does not rest; it works just as much as you and your mind are working. So if you are breathing and your mind is thinking, then it is working and you are attracting!

How Does This Attraction Law Work Exactly?

The simplest way to describe this phenomenon is explaining how "like attracts like." Therefore, positive energy begets positive things, and negative energy begets negative things. The law of attraction works like a boomerang. Whatever type of energy you throw out into the universe via words, thoughts, imagination projections, or emotions—you get right back! Only it comes back with more intensity and velocity than before. You tell the universe what you want by using your strongest thoughts and emotions, which emit vibrations; vibrations that communicate with the Universe.

Law of Vibration: From dense matter, to human beings, everything in this world is a form of energy. Energy is never at rest and is always in motion; and everything that's in motion obviously moves; and as we know, everything that moves—moves at a certain speed. Therefore everything in the universe is in motion, and the speed at which this energy moves is determined by its vibration, which can actually be measured. Just as electricity is measured in kilowatts, vibration is measured in frequencies; and these vibrations have specific frequencies that are recognized as...The Language of the Universe!

In Jack Canfield's book Key to Living the Law of Attraction, he uses another good analogy:

> *"Another good example is that of a tuning fork. When you strike a tuning fork you activate it to send out a particular sound or frequency. Now in a room filled with tuning forks—only those that are tuned to the exact same frequency will begin to vibrate in response. They will automatically connect and respond to the frequency that matches their own. So the idea here is to tune yourself to resonate at a frequency that is in harmony with what you want to attract. In order to create a positive future,*

 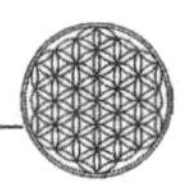

you need to keep your energy, thoughts, and feelings in a positive range."

This is exactly how the universe works with us. Picture the universe having every single tuning fork you can imagine, with each tuning fork having its own specific outcomes and circumstances. Now visualize what you think about the most as if you're striking one of your tuning forks that sends a specific vibrational resonance that will match the universe's. Whatever that frequency is you're sending out will automatically be matched with people, places, or events of similar vibration, compliments of the universe.

This is why it is important that your thoughts be in harmony with what you want in life. If you want positive outcomes in your life, you must think positive things and stay within that frequency. If the message you're sending out isn't in tune with what you really want, you will get whatever it is you're sending out.

The universe can be compared to a magical wizard that can make all your wishes come true, if you just ask. But, how do you ask the universe for something? Actually, you really don't ask, you "tell" the universe what you want. Just like you would with a genie, except instead of saying the words "I wish," you command with thought, imagination, and the emotion that tie the two together. These are the only instructions to "the game," and the same instructions you must learn to master in order to manifest whatever you want. This is why it's important to know that these laws exist, so that you can have them work for you instead of unintentionally against you. It is not complicated at all.

You are a living magnet in this universe. What you want is what you attract, and what you attract is what you want. The problem is that most people don't even know what it is they really want, or they may want something, but are sending out all the wrong messages or frequencies in all the wrong ways. The law of attraction is neutral, what you focus on is what you get—whether wanted or unwanted.

Attracting to Your Advantage

If we stay focused on the positives in life, we will automatically attract more positive things into our lives. If we decide to give into negativity and scarcity, rather than abundance, then that is exactly what we will attract. We are co-creators with the universe of our own life and we are constantly in the state of creation.

The guidelines to using the law of attraction to your advantage are fairly simple. I guess what you could call the hard part would simply be remembering to implement this law in everyday life. You need to make it a daily practice. If you can manage to simply remember that you're using the law of attraction at all times, you will change your world forever!

Attracting to your advantage begins with your thoughts. How you think dictates how you feel, and how you feel dictates what you attract. Most people's biggest problem is misusing the law of attraction and not using it to their advantage. You're using them whether you want to or not, so you should start learning how to have them work in your favor instead of against you. The truth is, the universe is never actually working against you. The universe is just doing its job by matching your negative thoughts with negative things. If you have positive thoughts, then it will match those thoughts with positive things. Remember, the universe is neutral and does not discriminate or judge you by your thoughts. It's simply matching the vibration/frequency that you're sending out and giving you what you "think" you want.

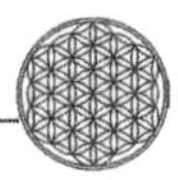

Attracting on Life's Highway

We are not our bodies, we are not our biology, and we are not our names. We are pure energy; walking, talking magnetic fields! Have you ever wanted a new car or just bought a new car, and when you go out on the road or on the highway, all of a sudden you start seeing that car EVERYWHERE? Well, this is exactly how humans operate! Something my mentor likes to call "*driving on life's highway.*"

In life we tend to filter out our possibilities because we get ourselves stuck in our 'probabilities'. This blinds us from seeing all the options and opportunities available to us. This is mainly because we only take notice of what we want to see, not what we are really seeing (something we all do, as I demonstrate in an upcoming chapter).

When we go out on life's highway, the only people we are going to attract, and the only people we are going to be attracted to, are the people that MATCH our vibration. Until we change our vibration and align our energy to what we really want in life, we will keep attracting the same type of people, events, and relationships as we have in the past.

How to Avoid Attracting Negative Things

It's easy for us to attract negative things into our lives if we are not aware of how the law of attraction works. As the saying goes, "What we resist, persists". That is, if we focus on the things we don't want in life, or focus on the things we're trying to avoid, this is usually what we will attract to us. Just like when we baby an injury that we're so afraid of reinjuring, we draw attention to it and that's exactly what happens. The law of attraction gives you what you want by matching the energy that you emit, not just your words.

If you allow yourself to be excessively consumed with negative thoughts, images, or emotions, unfortunately this is what you will attract. An extreme example would be the lives and deaths of hip-hop artists Tupac Shakur and Notorious B.I.G. Both musicians fantasized about death in their music and constantly talked about being shot or dying in their lyrics. This over-obsession and infatuation with untimely death eventually became their reality. Both artists never ceased to illustrate their fixation on death, and this is ultimately what they ended up attracting to themselves.

Tupac Shakur titled his albums *The Don Killuminati, Until the End of Time, Still I Rise,* and *Machiavelli,* all of which embodied lyrics of death. Before getting murdered, Tupac even left his label to sign with a new label, which was “coincidentally” named Death Row Records. Notorious B.I.G. had only released three albums prior to his death, which he titled: *Ready to Die* (Album 1), *Life after Death (*Album 2), and *Born Again* (Album 3).

This doesn’t mean if we fear death or have thoughts of dying that we are going to die—not at all. This is just an example to show how focusing all your energy on something negative can actually cause it to happen. These two artists totally engulfed themselves with the thoughts and emotions of death, and even solidified this by implementing it into their music videos. Just as you can bring about the worst-case scenarios in life, you can far more easily bring about the best-case scenarios in life by controlling your thoughts, emotions, and words.

When people become aware of the law of attraction and realize that their negative thoughts will bring all types of negative things to them, they become intimidated and afraid of their own mind. However, I tell you not to worry. It’s reassuring to know that the frequency strength and vibrations of a positive thought or affirmation have been scientifically

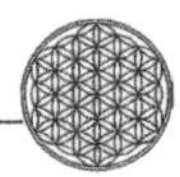

proven to be far more powerful than those of a negative thought. But we must focus on positive outcomes and not mistakenly manifest negative ones by consuming our minds with daunting, unwanted thoughts. Always look forward and work toward what you want. Never focus on what you don't want, because whatever you are focusing on will manifest even if it's not what you truly want. This is simply what the universe thought you wanted because this is what you gave your energy and emotion to the most.

This is where many misuse this wonderful tool frequently. The law of attraction is just like fire. You can use fire to cook, to provide warmth, and as a great tool for survival. But it can also burn your face off if you misuse it! The law of attraction can be your best friend or your worst enemy. But it's not really the law of attraction that can be your worst enemy—it's you!

Remember, the universe doesn't decide what we want; it just gives us what we "think" we want. It doesn't decide what's good for us or what's bad for us; it just gives us back what we're telling it by what we think, say, and feel. So how do we prevent attracting negative things into our lives? It's simple, just focus on what you want. That's it! The universe doesn't decide what's good or bad for us—we do! The universe doesn't even perceive the world the same as we humans do. In fact, humans don't even perceive the world the same as other humans do.

Law of Polarity: Polarity means two opposite poles, or the two extremes of any one "thing". Although every two "things" have a polar opposite, these polar opposites are still one and the same "thing". The duality between light and dark, hot and cold, rich and poor, love and hate, or good and bad are a few good examples. Polarity is not absolute or definite; it's measured in degrees of difference determined through one's perception. Meaning, the polarity between love and hate, or rich and poor, can mean many different things to many different people. It is our perception that determines what we consider hot, or what we think is cold; what we perceive as good, or what we perceive as bad. Our level of consciousness determines our perception of these things by the thoughts we choose to associate them with, which ultimately defines them for us.

Positive thoughts carry a higher vibrational energy than negative thoughts. As water will always seek its lowest level, energy will always seek its highest! Therefore, you will soon discover that raising your vibrational energy levels gives you the ability to change your attitude, behavior, and perceptions of the world, as well as others. This is the power the Law of Polarity has in this world, and this is a power that you have as well.

You can start raising your vibrations by maintaining a positive mindset throughout the day. This might seem easier said than done, and by all means this is probably true. Most aren't aware of how frequently we sabotage ourselves simply by thinking incorrectly. Thinking incorrectly? Yes, unfortunately we have been misled and improperly educated on how to use our own brainpower. Instead, we were taught what to think, and not how to think!

How to Think

It is crucial to be cautious and aware of what you're saying or feeling. Focus your needs and wants only in a positive way. If, for example, you keep telling yourself, "I don't want to be late for work," you are emitting the frequency of being "LATE." So all the universe is hearing is "LATE," because that's the main focal point of this thought and this is what you will attract. Instead, replace those thoughts with "I want to be on time," sending the message of "ON TIME" instead of "LATE." This is how we can manipulate our thoughts

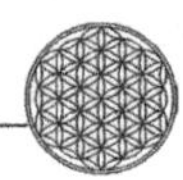

and attract what we want, not what we fear.

Simply changing our thoughts and the way we word things will make a world of difference. When we resist something, we are actually attracting it to us; we are attracting the very thing we want to eliminate, just by talking about it. We are all guilty of this, and although we don't mean to, it is just a bad habit; a habit that from this point forward you must be conscious of and eventually eliminate.

When Mother Theresa was asked to march for an anti-war demonstration, she refused! Nobody understood why she would turn down appearing at such an event. She replied with, "I will never do that, but as soon as you have a pro-peace rally, I'll be there!" Mother Theresa clearly demonstrated that she understood the law of attraction and how it works. She knew, even though the anti-war rally had good intentions, it was still focusing on the negative. She knew in return that such an event would only bring more of what they were rallying against.

However, the collective intention of a pro-peace rally would do the opposite. So instead of sending out energy to the universe of "war, war, war," she agreed to rally for peace and send out the vibrations of "peace" to the universe. I believe once you understand this story of Mother Theresa, you will truly understand how the law of attraction works and how the universe responds to our energy.

"*The secret of change is to focus all of your energy, not on fighting the old, but on building the new.*" ~ Socrates

Out of curiosity, next time you're in a conversation with someone ask them "How many of the seven deadly sins (cardinal sins) do you know off the top of your head?" You will find that the average person will rattle off at least two or three out of the seven (pride, envy, gluttony, lust, anger, greed, and sloth). Then immediately follow that question by asking them how many of the seven heavenly virtues do they remember off hand. You will discover that most people either don't know or don't remember any of them; which are (chastity, charity, temperance, diligence, forgiveness, kindness, and humility). And if they do, I found it's always less then the amount of seven deadly sins they recalled. So you have to ask yourself, WHY IS THIS? Why has humanity been programed to always focus on the negative and not the positive? Why are we always worried about what we shouldn't do, instead of what we should be doing? Why is it that we live in a world where you can tell a woman she's beautiful a thousand times, and she won't believe you. But if you call that same woman fat or ugly just once she'll never forget. Why is this? Why is it religions continue to instill fear, guilt, shame and separation in humanity rather then acceptance, unity and truth? If everyone understood how the universe operated, we wouldn't focus on all our wrongs and we would only focus on our rights. We wouldn't focus on the negative outcomes, but more so on the positive solutions. It's not just a way; to me, it's the only way!

Here's another example: follow the directions closely.

Rule one: Do NOT think of a Pink Elephant! Before you read any further, whatever you do, DON'T think of a Pink Elephant. There will be NO Pink Elephant thinking in this next exercise.

If you can just make sure you don't think of a pink elephant, then you will pass this exercise. So... did you briefly or even vaguely catch your mind trying to visualize a pink elephant? Exactly! I know I did just typing these words. The brain makes it impossible not to visualize a pink elephant. Even if it was the faintest glimpse for a Nanosecond, your mind immediately created that image in your head even though you were told NOT to. This is exactly how

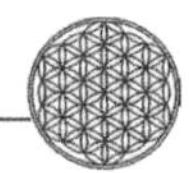

the universe operates as well. The universe does not recognize the words no, not, and don't. The universe matches the vibration that our words emit. These vibrations that are generated from our words are then projected to maximize the strength and effectiveness of our strongest thoughts. Our words have the power to heal, or the power to destroy! Something I will soon demonstrate for you as you will see for yourself.

Look at all the energy we waste on discussing our problems every day and focusing on the things we don't like. Our thoughts and intentions are powerful, and we need to be more aware and responsible of the thoughts we project. From this day forward, start manipulating this energy and make a commitment to have these laws work for you, instead of against you. It's natural to notice the things we don't want in life, but just use these thoughts as a reference for deciding what you do want in life–and start attracting that. Here are a few examples of how to reword the messages you are sending to the universe.

Replace thinking, "I don't want to be mad anymore"
With "I am happy with my current situation and will remain happy"

Replace saying, "I can't forget to mail this"
With "I will remember to mail this"

Replace thinking, "I can't break or ruin this"
With "I must take care of this"

Replace thinking, "I don't think we're going to make it"
With "I know we are going to make it"

Replace thinking "I can never find a parking spot there"
With "I will find the best parking spot when I get there"
(Then envision that empty parking space waiting for you)

Replace "I can't do this" or "I will try this" with "I will do this!"

"*Do or do not; there is no try.*" ~ Yoda, Star Wars - The Movie

We tend to dwell on everything that we don't want, instead of what we do want. We do it all the time without realizing the power of our thoughts and visualizations. It's similar to when someone tells you, "Be careful not to spill this coffee because you don't want to stain your nice shirt." The first thought that pops into your mind is spilling the coffee and staining your shirt. You then have this image ingrained in your mind and don't even realize it. Our natural instincts are to visualize what we don't want to happen, and we create that picture in our mind subconsciously once we hear it. Next thing you know, you have hot coffee on your lap, stains on your shirt, and you're hearing, "I told you not to spill it." We attract events and outcomes to us by the thoughts and images we imprint in our minds. Hence, "what we resist—persists", and "what we fight—we ignite!" By aligning our wants so they're in harmony with our thoughts/visualizations, we will create what we want instead of what we don't want.

Be aware of your thoughts, and remember that every single thought that you have, every word that you speak, and every emotion that you feel, is always communicating to the omnipresent universe. There is a sub-law within the universe that states, "When one asks the universe a question, the universe must always answer". The universe will respond whether its response is obvious to you, or not. It's not a matter of "if"; it's a matter of "when", and "how". This "when" is contingent upon the intensity of your thoughts, combined with the intensity of your emotion, combined with the clarity in your visualizations. This will determine how fast you manifest your thoughts.

Our mind and our heart are the Grand Central Station where we co-create our reality. In this creation station,

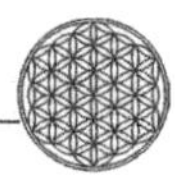

our thoughts are the messengers that tell our mind what to visualize. Those images that our mind sees are "the runners" that send these visualizations to our heart so our emotions can match what we are thinking and seeing internally. Our emotions are then "the couriers" which send out that vibration to the universe. So being more aware of our thoughts will help control the images we visualize, which ultimately dictate the emotions we feel and what we attract.

Just know that the earth is rich with fertile ground and waiting for you to plant your seeds of thought, while the universe is waiting to take your order so it can deliver whatever it is you ordered on life's menu.

How To Use The Master Key

"*The Law of attraction is simple mathematics; Thought + Visualization + Emotion + Action = ATTRACTION!*"

~ The World is (y)ours

Let's consider an example of how thought, visualization, and emotion need to work cohesively with one another in order to manifest. We've all said things like, "I don't have expensive shoes like hers" or "I wish I had a bigger TV" or "Why can't I drive a nice car like that?" One of the most common things I hear people say is, "Oh, I wish I could afford that." Well, if you are constantly wishing for something to happen, then you are claiming that you don't have that and you will never be able to afford that. And that's exactly how the universe will respond; giving you "lack of", and not abundance. This becomes your affirmation to the universe once you solidify those thoughts using the power in your words.

The universe doesn't recognize that you really want those things, because you're emitting mixed signals due to your intent versus your choice of words. Even though you really want those items in your life, your perspective and your words are creating the emotion of failure and absence instead of acceptance and abundance. You're saying you want something, but not in the clearest way; more importantly your EMOTION doesn't match the frequency of obtaining that item, but instead just wishing and wanting that item and being discouraged that you don't have it. You're not visualizing the joy of receiving those gifts; you are merely visualizing the void/emptiness of not having that item. Thought, visualization, and emotion all must be aligned and working harmoniously in order to manifest things into your life. Period.

"If I deserve it the universe will serve it." ~ Mark Wahlberg

It is crucial that we believe we deserve whatever it is that we want. The trick is to *know* "it" is already yours and it's just waiting for you to realize this so you can claim it. As soon as your mind knows "I CAN DO THIS," an emotion is secreted and it's pretty much in the bag as long as you hold this frequency of emotion and implement the necessary steps to getting there. Remember, each of these steps is useless without all the others. Thought + Visualization + Emotion + Action = Attracting and Manifestation. The universe will always meet you half way if you are clear with your intent and ready to take action when opportunities are inevitably presented to you.

Law of Action: The Law of Action is quite simple; for every action there will be a reaction. Since the universe's functionality is similar to a giant mirror, the universe will always reflect to us what we desire, depending on what we DO! If we try to manifest with only our thoughts and no further action, then there will be no reaction. If we don't show the universe a change in our actions, then the universe will not give us any opportunities for action to change. Your thoughts, imagination, and visualizations do indeed have the power to attract all that you wish, but if you don't take the necessary action(s) to claim your manifestations, then you will lose all that you've manifested by failing to comprehend and imple-

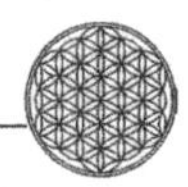

ment this significant law within your universe.

"*Vision without execution is hallucination.*" ~ Thomas Edison

The law of action is embedded in the final steps within the law of attraction. The law of attraction is like a key that can unlock anything. If you look at a key and see the details of the ridges, each ridge is significant in how it allows the key to take shape so it can turn inside the lock. Each ridge is just as important as the other, and without one of these ridges the entire key is useless and will not unlock the door. However, when all of these ridges are put together, they work in alignment and create a key that will unlock exactly what you are trying to open. This is what's needed when we are trying to unlock the powers of co-creation and attract abundance into our lives.

Take the ridges on a key for example. Every key has a unique set of ridges that allow it to unlock closed doors. The first "ridge" on your master key is your thought, the second ridge is the images you hold in your mind the most, and the third ridge is the emotion you attach to these thoughts and images. However, even if you do everything right and perfectly line up all your ridges, there is still one thing missing. This one thing is very important and is by far the most overlooked of them all... ACTION! Many people are great at manifesting, but not so great at recognizing opportunity and claiming their manifestations. They visualize their thoughts coming to fruition and even create the proper attracting emotion to activate it; but they fail to take action when action is needed. Always remember that a key is useless if you insert it into the lock and never turn it!

Law of Cause and Effect: The law of cause and effect has to do with humanity's free will to make their own decisions. The law of cause and effect is the aftermath originating from the decision made when the law of action took effect. The law of cause and effect means that nothing happens by "chance". This universal law states that whatever events or circumstances we experience in life (effects) are derived directly from a choice that we previously made (cause), whether we are conscious of this choice or not. We must understand that we are the only ones responsible for the outcome of our own lives; and although there are infinite possibilities and many unexpected events that can occur in our lifetime, each event that we experienced came from a decision that we made through one of our previous actions, not our thoughts. Karma could be used as a good example to explain this law. Whatever decisions we make—there will be consequences, good or bad.

Stop Chasing! And Start Thanking!

Now back to manifesting! The Power of Gratitude is 4/5ths the vibrational potency of the emotion of Love. Since the power of gratitude is one of the strongest vibrations in the universe, we must learn to stop chasing things and start attracting things by being grateful for what we desire, and what we already have. On best-selling author David Wilcock's website (*www.divinecosmos.com*), he refers to what he calls "the fool's equation." The equation states, "If I get X, whatever X may be, then I will be happy." David explains, "This is really silly because if you are wishing for something that hasn't happened yet, and you decide that once that thing happens that you will be happy in the future, then you never claim any happiness in the now."

By setting your goal to be happy once you accomplish or obtain something in the future, you are simultaneously setting your intention to NOT be happy in the present moment. You will continue to chase happiness while claiming unhappiness as you solidify to the universe that you are unhappy until you obtain what you desire. Always manifesting in the future is like dangling a carrot in front of your face for the rest of your life. So what David recommends is turning that equation backward: "If I am whole, peaceful and happy

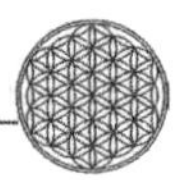

now, than I will get X (whatever you want X to be)." David states, "By thinking this way you display gratitude and create a loving space within yourself, which then allows loving energy to fill it." This is how we attract things into our lives, by being grateful for the things we have, and even being grateful for things we don't have—yet.

"*Be content with what you have; rejoice in the way things are. When you realize there is nothing lacking, the whole world belongs to you.*" ~ Lao Tzu

The power of manifestation and the law of attraction are potent and vigorous forces within our universe. Too many people hope for things to happen or hope to achieve what they want in life. Choosing these thought patterns and using words like "Hope" automatically imply the presence of doubt. President Obama sold us "Hope" and look where that brought us. Instead, use more positive and affirmative words that embody the essence of confidence and success. From now on you must replace words like "Hope", with "Faith", as faith implies a knowing and a confidence that all is well, and will be well—no matter what.

You must firmly claim and OWN what you desire in life until you become that, so whatever that is, it has no choice but to become you. The most powerful words that can come out of your mouth are "I AM", because you are what you believe you are. If you continue to chase things, rather than manifest them, the things you are chasing will continue to do what they do best: run away from you! Remember, we need to "work smarter, not harder!"

Working Smarter-Not Harder

"*They say practice makes perfect, but if you've been practicing the wrong thing for a lifetime, then you only mastered falling short of your true potential.*" ~ The World is (y)ours

I'm sure we all have had or known a dog or cat that would get out of the house and take off running. They enjoyed the chase of getting away while you run in circles trying to catch them. The same goes with things you want in your life. We need to learn how to attract these objects or scenarios to us, instead of repelling them away from us. Whenever my dog used to get out of the house, he would run wild and I would chase him forever. Until I remembered, "Wait, I'm smarter than this stupid dog." Then, whenever he would get out, I would go back in the house and grab some Nutter Butter peanut butter cookies. As soon as I found him, I would show him the cookies, and then I would bolt inside the house. Sure enough, he would then chase me the way a Greyhound chases the rabbit out the gates. From that day forward, I never had to chase my dog again.

"*There are no stupid dogs in this world, just stupid owners.*"
~ Lina Bain-Giarrusso

Instead of just being "attracted" to the things you want (like everyone else), you must attract the things you want to you. We all like nice things; therefore, we are attracted to these things. So does this mean we are using the laws of the universe in our favor by being attracted to something? No, it does not. Being attracted to something is just the start of taking notice and creating clarification of what you really want in your life. But you need to use the tools and the great forces that are available to you so you can attract what you want in your life. Don't continue allowing yourself to be "attracted" to what you want-become attractive! This is similar to liking someone who doesn't like you back: it's just no fun and you don't get what you want. Being attracted to certain things instead of attracting them to you will have you chasing those objects just like I used to chase that crazy dog.

Imagine all your dreams and aspirations are a beautiful yet fragile butterfly. If you chase a butterfly, all it's going to

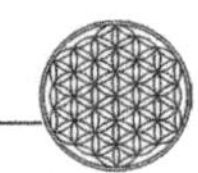

do is fly away. And if you do try chasing it down and capturing it, you might crush and destroy the very thing you always wanted. The key to capturing your dreams is setting a clear intention and sending out the right vibrations/messages to the universe by choosing your thoughts and words wisely. The key is simply allowing yourself to accept the natural flow of abundance in life. By utilizing the law of attraction, you will make the butterfly come to you, with grace and ease.

Most people think they have to hustle and bustle to get what they want, which isn't totally true. Ambition and action are indeed required, but the key isn't busting your hump; the key is setting the right intention, becoming that of what you desire, and *recognizing* when opportunity is presented so you can take full advantage of it.

However, the majority of the population externalizes their power by looking outside of themselves for answers, while continuing to chase their dreams rather than claim them. Once we understand that we are all "attractive" in this world, life will become much easier.

If we notice ourselves continuing to chase our dreams, and it feels as though no matter how close we get we can never grab that golden ring, then we must reevaluate our power position. Meaning, we must be externalizing ourselves. Therefore, we must reverse our power back inward, instead of outward. We can invert this power simply switching our energy from the thoughts of "chasing", to the emotion of "claiming".

Since we're all walking magnets, we can accomplish this by always making sure the force from our magnet's energy (our power) is facing in the right direction.

For Example: Chasing: (When we externalize our power)

Imagine putting a bunch of metal objects on a table (metal objects representing your major goals and the tangible things you want in life), while holding a strong magnet (your force/energy/power). If your magnet is flipped in the wrong direction, what's going to happen when you get closer to those items? Your magnet is going to push them away, correct? This scenario is not a mystery; it is physics! You will also notice that the faster you go after these objects and the closer you get with your magnet, the faster and further you will push these objects away from you using your own reciprocated efforts. Meaning, these items aren't actually running from you, you're pushing them away! This is how we can block our own blessings by chasing things via the law of attraction, if our magnet (energy) isn't being used properly.

Attracting/Claiming: (When we internalize our power)

If you were to simply turn your magnet around in the opposite direction, what happens then? Using the same amount of energy as before you will ATTRACT those same items to you instead of pushing them away. Why so? Because it's all about energy, quantum physics, and laws of the universe; it was never about how hard you tried or how hard you worked. Remember, we must work smarter, not harder! You achieve this magnetism by cultivating imagination and faith to envision that what you want is already yours. This is the trick that few have mastered; once you realize that you already have whatever it is that you want-it's yours! By emitting the emotion that correlates to this feeling you will dissolve all the barriers/mental blockages that made you think otherwise. Sometimes we just have to get out of our own way!

Law of Compensation: The law of compensation is the most gratifying and well-deserved law, yet it is the most misunderstood law of them all. Contingent upon the degree

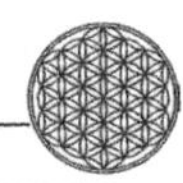

in which one gives to others (unconditionally); this law will determine the magnitude in which the universe rewards that person for their service to others. The law of compensation derives from the law of cause and effect. This law is very similar to the functionality of an ATM machine; what you put in—is what you get out, so to speak. We receive gifts and blessings back tenfold when we give directly from our heart—with no expectations!

There are a few convolutions regarding this law that make life difficult for many. For example, you might be reading this telling yourself, "I'm a good person, and I help everyone. I never expect anything in return, and I even put others before me; so why is my life so miserable?" Unfortunately, this is exactly why you feel your life is so miserable. Too many people give up their power, give away their love, and/or relinquish their energy to others—leaving nothing for themselves. We must learn to love and give to ourselves before we can give on to others. What does a flight attendant tell you to do if there's an emergency on the aircraft and the oxygen masks deploy? They tell you to put your mask on first before helping anyone else. Why so? Because it is very difficult to help anyone else in life if we're not at our best, healthy and happy, or if we're dead!

We must stop trying to please everyone else and learn to love and nourish ourselves first. Think about it, why do we give to others anyway? We give because we either love them or we care about them. So by giving to everyone else and excluding ourselves, what does that tell the universe? It sends a clear message that we must not love or care about ourselves. On the contrary, if we're needy and always looking to receive—but never give, it tells the universe nobody else matters in the world but us!

The law of compensation is all about balance. We must equally give, as we should receive; and we must equally receive, as much as we give. Too much on either end will result in unhealthy imbalance. The universe doesn't recognize the difference between the two polar opposites (as previously discussed in the Law of Polarity).

Another way we block the natural flow from the law of compensation rewarding us, is from one's mental programming and inability to bridge the gap between spirituality and money (material items). Many people distance the two because they don't understand that money is just another form of energy, and that spirituality and money are interrelated. In addition, when we are rewarded with spiritual or financial equity in life, most lack the knowledge that this exchange is an actual law within our universe. Therefore, one should never feel guilty or awkward when being compensated for their services rendered or energy exchanged. It is merely the belief system that we must choose one or the other—is what's responsible for sabotaging the law of compensation.

Just like everything else, money is another form of energy; and if we tune into that specific frequency and initiate the law of attraction, it will have no choice but to find its way to us. There is also the misconception that the universe only rewards us with material items for our good deeds. This materialistic third-dimensional thinking is what blinds us from receiving the abundance from this law's deliverance. As we now know, the universe rewards us in many unique ways e.g. new relationships, emotional support, events, people, places, and certainly with materialistic items as well.

We are all walking magnetic energy fields and beings made of pure infinite energy who are in constant creation. We must realize that we are far more complex and advanced intelligent machines than we are aware. Each and every one of us possesses hidden gifts and powers that lie dormant within that I have not finished sharing with you!

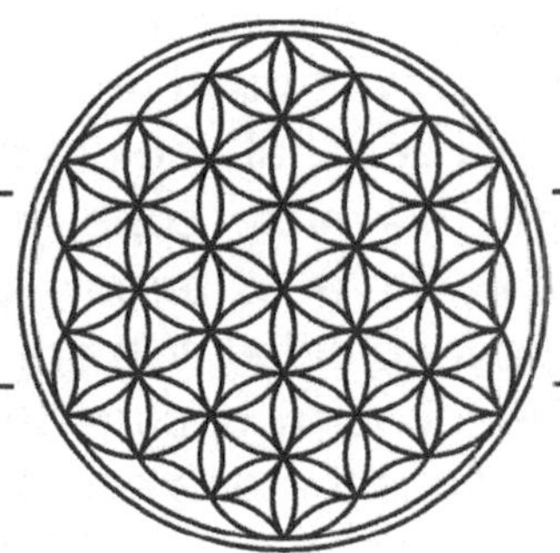

CHAPTER 6

MISTAKEN IDENTITY... YOU ARE ENERGY!

"*Everything is energy and that's all there is to it. Match the frequency of the reality you want and you cannot help but get that reality. It can be no other way. This is not philosophy. This is physics.*" ~ Darryl Anka

The truth is, that we are energetic beings. Not only do we carry energy, we are energy. Quantum physics states that as you delve deeper into the anatomy of the atom, you see that there is nothing there, just an invisible force field of energy waves. They found that the atom emits waves of electrical energy in circular motions like miniature swirling tornados vibrating at extremely high speeds. These energy waves can actually be measured and seen in the same scientific phenomenon as the workings of "electricity". Henceforth, science now supports the idea that the universe is indeed made of energy, not matter!

"If you want to find the secrets of the universe, think in terms of energy, frequency and vibration." ~ Nikola Tesla

Energy is the foundation for all universal laws. All energy is in constant motion and forever moving from one form to another. Everything is energy! The ground you walk on, the air you breathe, and everything you set your eyes on. Where there is energy, there is vibration within it. This includes all life forms, including Humans. Science has proven that if you were to place your hand under a high-powered microscope, you would see that you are made up of pure energy as well. Under this microscope, you would see the cells in your hand vibrating at extremely fast speeds. Human energy is powerful beyond belief. We are all walking, talking containers of intelligent energy unconsciously using various frequencies and vibrations that are constantly communicating with the Universe at large.

Know that you hold this powerful energy inside of you, and the storage unit that accommodates this energy is your physical body. We mustn't let our finite bodies make us feel contained or small! This physical container is just an illusion of what we really are. What's significant is what we do with this energy.

"*Know that you are a magnet made of pure energy, a magnet that can attract anything in life because everything is energy, and energy is everything.*" ~ The World is (y)ours

It's a fact that all matter is energy. It's a fact that human beings are made up of cells, which are made up of atoms. These atoms are made up of subatomic particles, which are...energy! Science has proven that our bodies are not really solid and that they only appear solid to the naked eye. What does this mean? It means, we are made up of tiny particles and atoms vibrating so fast that we can't see this movement. For example: when a ceiling fan starts to spin, we see the blades "appear to disappear", four blades turn to three blades, then to two blades, and soon it just looks like one big blade spinning. The same is going on in the 3-D realm of our bodies. The tightly packed atoms of energy we hold within us are vibrating so fast we cannot see them; we

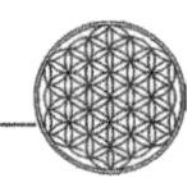

only see the objects as a whole. This same science applies to the present levels of different dimensions, something beyond amazing that we explore further in later chapters.

The energy that connects all of us transmits wireless signals that communicate with our universe and everything within it. The energy that radiates in, out, and throughout our beings not only affects us individually; it affects everything around us. Hence, we are one! There is a cause and effect for everything, all energy emitted through actions or thought from any one person affects every other person on this planet. This energy can actually be seen and measured. This is why every living sentient being has an Aura, a colorful energy field emanating from it. Since we know that we are pure energy and everything is energy, then why can't we see this energy? Or can we?

Seeing Energy

There are specialty cameras that can take a picture of people or objects and it will display the subject's auric energy field in the photo. Each person's aura is different. Some glow blue, green, yellow, white, red, gray, pink, and so forth. Each color means something different and can reveal your health, mood, and even your personality. Many people in the world can see auras without this special camera, and it's fairly easy to train yourself to see your own aura.

All you have to do is grab a plain white piece of computer paper and place it on the floor or on a table using it as your background. Then in front of the white paper, take your two index fingers and point them at each other leaving about an inch or less between the two fingers. Then focus your eyes toward this gap between the two fingers. Try not to focus on the actual gap but on the paper; try looking through it rather than at it. This is very similar to the way we focus on the "magic eye" book exercises that display hidden 3-D images.

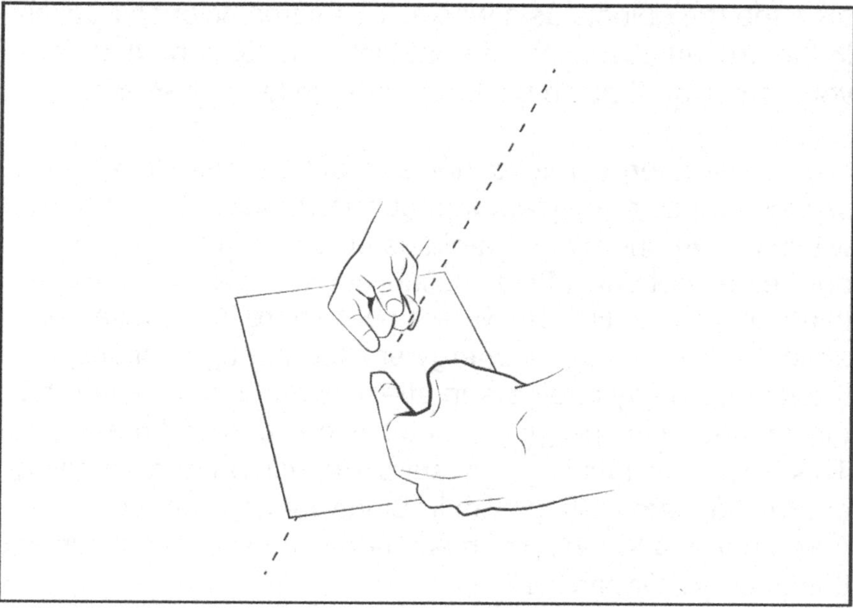

If you stare for about fifteen minutes you will start to see color(s) emit from your fingers. Fifteen minutes seems like a long time to just sit there and stare at a piece of paper, but you can train your eyes for about five to ten minutes a day. Within the very first week or so you should start seeing the hue of your aura. This is how I successfully conducted this experiment. I could see my own aura as well as other people's auras, and for the most part I noticed everyone had a different color. Although I didn't know what every color meant at the time, I was still amazed that this invisible energy actually existed, and I could finally see it with my own eyes.

After further research, I found that many business moguls and top-level executives use this natural gift to gain a competitive advantage when "reading" their clients or competitors. Being able to tell when someone is lying and deciphering their true intentions by reading their energy can give one a competitive edge like no other.

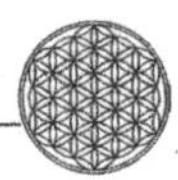

TIP: Staring at the flame of a candle for 10-minutes a day can strengthen your energetic aura field.

Energy Speaks

Energy is in us, around us, and is always present. We are merely an energy field that is operating in a larger energy field known as the universe. There are billions of different frequencies, and each frequency has its own strength and distinction.

The *Linguistic Society of America* states that there are approximately 2,500 languages in the world. The universe communicates with us no different than any of these other foreign languages. Many of these foreign languages have sounds that we've never heard before, nor would we know what those sounds actually meant if we heard them. Although we might not understand those other languages, others do, and they can communicate fluently with them. Even if we can hear communication, but don't understand it, that doesn't mean it's not communicating. Take sign language as another example. We might not understand it, nor can we even hear it, but we do know it's a form of communication.

This is a similar scenario compared to the universe's language. We might not understand what the universe is saying or how it's saying it, but we must know that it is indeed communicating. Just because we might not understand a foreign language or sign language, doesn't mean these languages couldn't be trying to communicate with us right now. It's not that the universe needs to change its language, or learn to communicate with us better; we are the ones who need to learn this universal language in which the universe communicates. Just because we can't see or hear our energy communicating, doesn't mean it is not happening between us, in us, and everywhere around us—at all times.

Feeling Energy

You can actually feel your own energy field by doing the following exercise. Start by rubbing your hands together in a circular clockwise motion to get the energy flowing. This is similar to how you would warm up your hands when it's cold outside [See Fig 1]. Then hold your hands (palms facing each other) about 6 inches away and move your hands closer and further apart (horizontally) in micro movements while you become acquainted with this energy field. Once you can feel this energy, create an "imaginary" ball of energy between your hands by moving your hands closer and farther apart in a cupping motion [See Fig. 2]. This will build an energy field between your hands and you will be able to feel this energy between your hands. Depending on how you perceive energy, you might feel a warming sensation, a cooling sensation, or even a tingling sensation. Try this exercise to see how you interpret energy. Whatever you do feel, it's noticeable and you can definitely feel it!

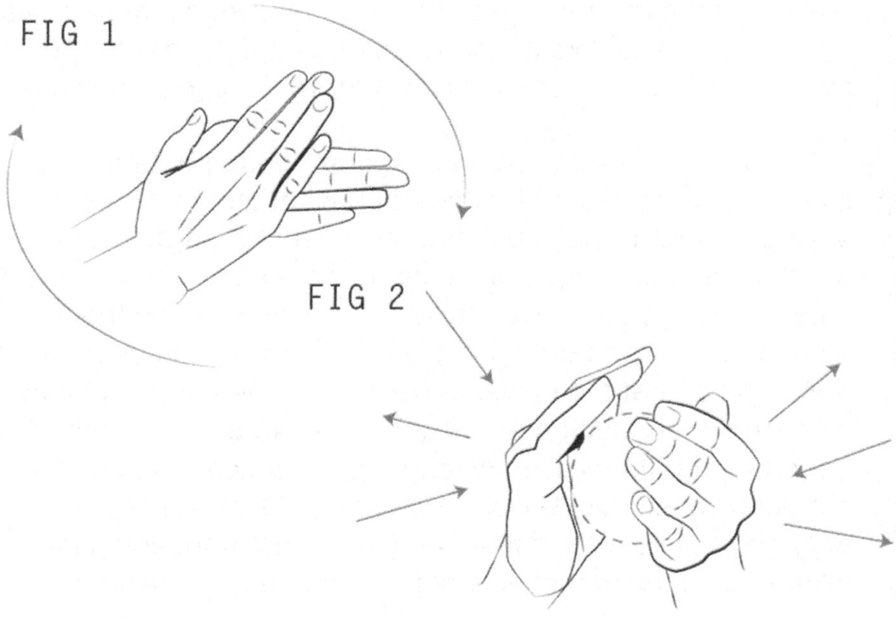

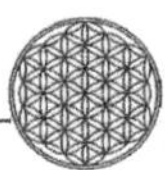

Chakras

Each human being has multiple energy centers within their body referred to as *Chakras*. There are twelve plus Chakras points, however, there are seven main Chakras that are most often referred to which I depicted in the following illustration. Each Chakra has its own name, color, function, and is located in a specific area within the human body.

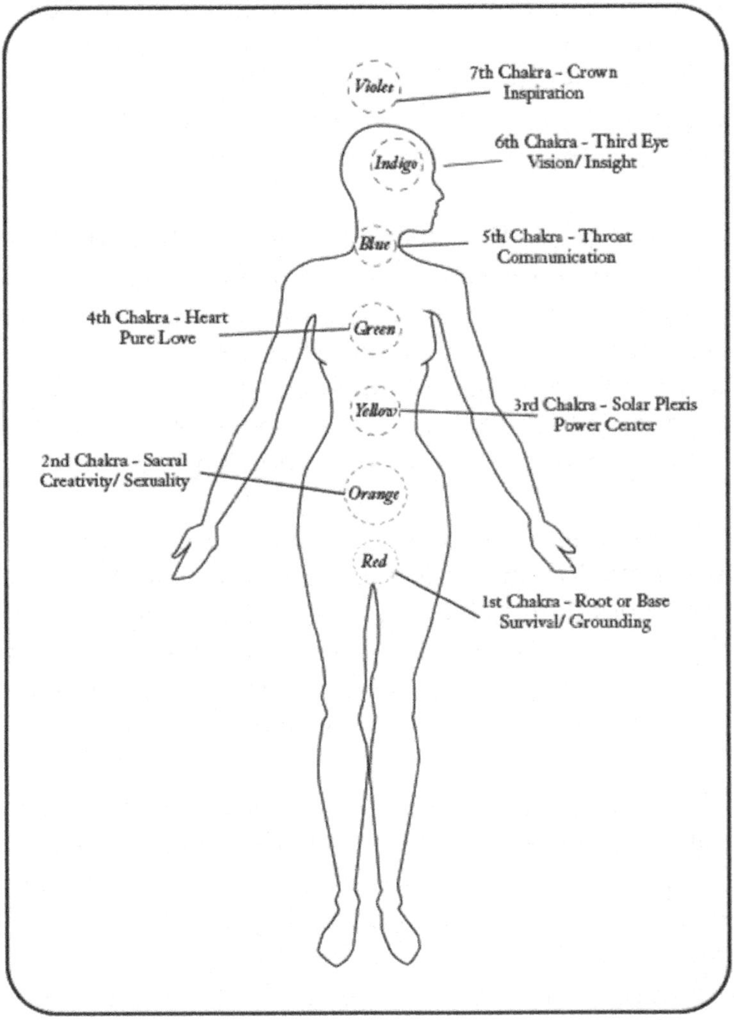

Violet
7th Chakra - Crown
Inspiration

Indigo
6th Chakra - Third Eye
Vision/ Insight

Blue
5th Chakra - Throat
Communication

Green
4th Chakra - Heart
Pure Love

Yellow
3rd Chakra - Solar Plexis
Power Center

Orange
2nd Chakra - Sacral
Creativity/ Sexuality

Red
1st Chakra - Root or Base
Survival/ Grounding

For the readers who have yet to discover the power within these vital energy centers of their being, let me share what you've been missing out on...

To better understand Chakras let me use the analogy of a human organ. You have never seen your heart or your liver before-but you know it's there, correct? You only know it's there because someone told you it's there or showed you a picture. Chakras are no different; you can feel them working but you cannot see them, touch them, or smell them; and just like your heart and liver, you cannot survive without them either. These energy centers are the *Chi* of your entire being. They are made up of the same energy force that makes the sun shine and your hair, skin, and nails grow.

Chakras, and their corresponding colors, are the reason why you wear certain colored clothing every day (in case you ever wondered). Depending on your mood or energetic/ emotional needs, you will unconsciously choose a specific color to wear for that day. Wearing certain colors will actually balance and align any Chakra that may be out of balance. You do this everyday without even knowing it.

Every one of your Chakra Points harnesses its own unique energy. When one learns how to tap into their chakra energy centers though the practice of Reiki, Yoga, Meditation, Tai Chi, or Qi Gong, they will then be able to control certain aspects of their life and gain direct access to many gifts and abilities that have lain dormant.

Unfortunately, this type of knowledge was omitted from our schoolbooks and *Chakras 101* was a class that wasn't available to us in grade school. The reasons as to "why not?" will be divulged in upcoming chapters. I must say that one of the best videos I've seen explaining Chakras was a cartoon found on YouTube titled "*Avatar's Guide to Chakras*".

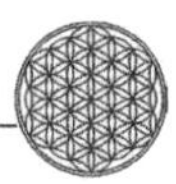

Have you ever listened to someone give a speech and you can tell that this person is lying or being fraudulent? What you're actually feeling is the low vibrational energies being projected from their energetic field via their vocal cords. These lower energetic vibrations felt from lies can be quite uncomfortable to be around, especially to people who are sensitive to energy and have good intuition. I'm sure you felt this feeling before with a friend or an "Ex". You may have experienced this when confronting this person, as you watched them answer you with a lie—to a question you already knew the answer to.

On the other hand, have you ever listened to someone give a speech and they say something that really 'hits home' with you, then suddenly all the hairs on the back of your neck stand straight up? Well, those "goosebumps" that you felt were strong spurts of energy that shot out the channels of your *Kundalini* called *Nadis*. In other words, when someone is speaking in higher vibrations of truth, and they say something that really resonates with you, your nadis open up and shoot short bursts of energy throughout your body. Yogis refer to this flow of energy as *Prana*. Many people have felt this energy before and experienced goosebumps during intense conversations. Whereas energy influxes that are caused from a drastic drop in body temperature are called "Goosebumps", energy influxes caused by spoken words that resonate truth are what I call *"TRUTHBUMPS*!"

Don't you find it strange when you can tell that someone's staring at you? How is this possible? There's no physical interaction or even any physical touch involved, yet we can still "feel" when someone is staring at us. I watched a documentary discussing the reason you can feel when someone is staring at you. It's because energy within actually projects out through our eyes and "touches" the person we are staring at. The documentary showed a study in which researchers conducted a test by putting one person behind another. The person receiving the stare said "yes or no" when he thought he was being stared at while the person behind him opened and closed his eyes. Seventy-five percent of the subjects were right when they felt the person's stare. This sixth sense allows the brain to interact at an electrical level with the brains of other people. We intercept the high output of energy that's exerted when someone's brain is thinking or interpreting what they are seeing when they look at us. Others say it's the high-energy output of the human eyes, and that energy flows where attention goes.

We've all heard, "The eyes are the window to the soul" and we can usually tell a person's mood or get a good sense of their character when looking into their eyes. So it wouldn't be too farfetched to believe that the eyes can project a very powerful source of energy. This radar-like sixth sense just confirms the idea that we are indeed energetic beings that can emit and receive other energies. So does this mean that the energy we project is able to "communicate" with other energy, people, or the universe at large? This communication of energy is how we can tell whether someone is staring at us, how we can get a good or bad "vibe" on someone or someplace, and how we can feel someone's pain or happiness when they're around us, without them ever saying a word.

The most intense feeling of energy is translated to us and felt through human emotion. Our emotions and how we feel is the language of the soul. Our emotions fuel our energy field, and that energy field emits vibrations/frequencies that shape our future. Our emotions and feelings are what we need to tune into, as this is the Holy Grail of secrets to mastering life itself. Therefore, we must be aware and in control of our emotions at all times. This is by far our greatest power yet to be discussed.

CHAPTER 7

THE HIDDEN POWERS OF EMOTION

"*We think too much and feel too little.*" ~ Charlie Chaplin

Research shows that we have more than fifty thousand thoughts each day, so it's impossible to try to monitor every single thought in our minds. Most of the time we aren't even aware if our thoughts are positive or negative because we are so consumed in the thoughts themselves. What we must do instead is pay closer attention to our emotions and how we feel, because our emotions never lie. Science is discovering that what we are feeling is far more significant than what we are saying or thinking. The emotions we experience are just an indication of what we are thinking and are merely the result of our most frequent collection of thoughts. Our emotions are a feedback apparatus that expresses the result of our most dominant thoughts. If you are feeling happy and uplifted, then you are living at a higher vibration as a result of your positive thoughts.

Throughout the day just ask yourself, "How do I feel?" If you aren't feeling good and you're at a low vibration, then this means the majority of your thoughts for the day have been negative ones. If you find yourself waking up not feeling up to par, then your thoughts while you were sleeping (dreams) probably weren't positive. If this tends to happen often, try listening to binaural beats, isochoric tones, or a relaxing hypnosis script during bedtime.

"*When I do good, I feel good. When I do bad, I feel bad. That's my religion.*" ~ *Abraham Lincoln*

Your thoughts and emotions are your reference points toward your life purpose. When you do things that don't feel right, chances are they aren't right. When you have negative thoughts or emotions about a certain situation or job, it is just an indication that you are not on the correct life path. When you have thoughts of joy and happiness, this means you are on the right life course and should continue this path, even if it doesn't make sense at that time. Since our vibrational states magnetize the events and people that we attract, it is vital that we try to maintain as much positive emotion as possible. So continue to do the things that make you feel good. Find a job you enjoy, and be around the people that lift you up, not those who try to put you down.

Since emotions are the language of the soul, how we feel about someone or something is *always* going to reveal the truth to us. If you can't figure something out, stop and ask yourself "How do I feel about this? Is this feeling a good feeling, or is it a bad feeling?" It's that simple.

Can We Control Our Emotions?

This internal feedback is a system that controls our vibrational frequency through our emotions, which ultimately stems from our thoughts and imagination. Many people think their thoughts and emotions are random and uncontrollable. However, this is not true. The thoughts and emotions we choose to give our energy to are a choice just like everything else in life. Like Jonatan Mårtensson's famous quote says, "*Feelings are much like waves, we can't stop them from coming but we can choose which ones to surf.*"

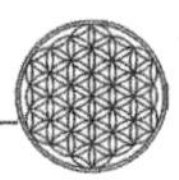

When you lose something or someone steals something from you, you can flip out and wish them to the fierce depths of hell and seek revenge; or you can simply say "Someone else must have needed it more than I did" as you gladly accept this circumstance and wait for something better to enter your life. Every cloud has a silver lining and the emotions you choose to react with and attach to these types of situations are choices, just like everything else in life. We cannot control life, but we can control how we view life.

"Don't get upset with people or situations. Both are powerless without your reaction." ~ Unknown

Everything in life is perception and we choose how we view certain things. Someone that experienced several near death experiences in one year might consider that year to be their worst year ever. However, another person who experienced those same near death experiences might consider that year to be their luckiest year ever since they were able to escape death several times. We are the only ones who can determine what's considered a life lesson, or a divine blessing. Our outlook on life is solely based on our internal beliefs and our perception of reality. So when we have a certain thought or feeling towards something or someone, we must ask ourselves, "Are these the thoughts and emotions I *choose* to attach to this situation or person?"

Law of Perpetual Transmutation of Energy: Through our will and intent, we have the free will to change things within our life. The law of perpetual transmutation of energy is what gives us the innate ability to transmute any situation in life to a positive one simply by changing our perspective.

Now, one might read this law and rebute, "So you're telling me that my experience with my ex-boyfriend of 9 years who verbally and physically abused me, cheated on me, then ran up all my credit card bills before leaving me for my cousin, can be looked at as a positive situation?" Fortunately, the answer is yes! We all have that "special someone" that made our life a living nightmare at one point in time. It is this same someone that we wish didn't just pop up in our head when we read this. Yes, that person! In order to transmute the negative energy/situation with this person, you must first change your viewpoint and perspective of them. I want you to imagine this person and all that you've experienced with them (the good and the bad); then ask yourself the following six questions in all earnestness:

1). Did this person hurt you and leave you with an experience and a set of emotions that you would never forget?

2). Did you not learn from these emotions and from this experience?

3). Although this person very much hurt you, is it farfetched to say that this person might have actually helped you evolve?

4). Did this person help you learn more about yourself, and help you make better life decisions in the future?

5). Overall, did this person and this experience ultimately help you grow as an individual as well?

6). Now, considering that we know life is all about evolving as a human being; in all honesty, if this person helped you learn and grow so you could become a better person and make better life decisions in the future, then you must stop and think for moment before answering this final question:

Did this person actually come into your life to harm you, or did this person come into your life to serve you?

We can only control our perspective and attitude in life—not life itself or the events that play out. We cannot control what someone did to us, but we can control how we

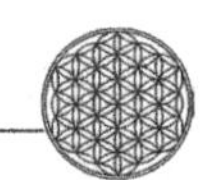

perceive what someone did to us—and how we choose to let it affect us. Life is all about perception and our point of view is a choice determined by our level of consciousness and awareness.

We evoke the law of perpetual transmutation of energy by loving others unconditionally and dissolving all prejudgments and expectations we may have toward them. When we have expectations toward others we open the door to disappointment. Expectations are the root of all disappointment in life. We are constantly either disappointing ourselves, or allowing others to disappoint us, which is really one and the same. It is never the other person that disappoints us; it is only the expectations that we curse upon them that never fail to let us down. So, how do we recover from the intense emotion of disappointment?

The Power of Forgiveness

"*Holding onto anger is like drinking poison and expecting the other person to die.*" ~ Gautama Buddha

Many believe that all we have to do is forgive others for what they did to us, and everything will be fine. But this is only partial forgiveness. After forgiving someone else, we must forgive ourselves for allowing ourselves to be victimized. In order to truly heal, one must eliminate all EXPECTATIONS and judgments that led us to dislike someone for NOT being who we 'expected' them to be; then, we must also forgive ourselves for 'expecting' that person to be anything other than who they are. In order to truly move on, we must accept that we can never change someone, as much as we want to. We must also know that we can never fix what's broken inside of someone and that they can never fix what's broken inside of us. All healing, whether physical or emotion, is like a scraped knee; the doctor can stich it and mommy can kiss it, but no "Body" can heal it other than you.

We are all flawed beings living this human experience while attempting to figure out the meaning of our lives through a whirlwind of intense experiences and emotions. Emotions that may seem uncontrollable, ferocious, and never-ending, are really just a wild animal waiting to be tamed.

The Purpose of Emotions

"*Life is like a piano. White keys are happy moments. Black keys are sad moments. But remember both keys are played together to give sweet music in life.*" ~ Unknown

If you were to take a Caucasian millionaire businessman who just lost his largest client, an African American basketball player that got cut from his college basketball team and lost his scholarship, a homeless person who's pet cat died, or a Chinese woman who just lost someone she loved; what is the single most powerful thing that all these various people have in common? It would be human emotion; and that emotion would be the emotion of loss and sadness felt by all of them, regardless of their individual circumstances.

No matter how different our circumstances are in life, or how great our external world may look to others, it's irrelevant because the only thing that really matters is our emotions and how we feel on the inside, not what others see on the outside. Whether we're a millionaire in a penthouse, or a bum on the street, the bottom line is that we still feel the same powerful emotions that rule our world and dictate our true happiness. Regardless of our circumstances or the materialistic world we call our reality, the only real thing that matters in life isn't money or fame, it's how we feel in life; and it's not how or what made us feel that way that matters either.

"*I wish everyone could get rich and famous and get everything they ever dreamed of so they can see that's not the answer.*" ~ Jim Carrey

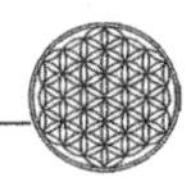

The good news is that we all have the ability to allow ourselves to engage or disengage in the emotions that we feel make us happy or mad, grateful or sad. Simply by being conscious of our emotions at these times and allowing ourselves to get the best out of them instead of letting our emotions get the best out of us, is the key to mastering life itself. Whenever strong emotions arise, look at it as a learning experience or "opportunity" for significant spiritual growth and life mastery instead of just claiming the role of a victim.

We live on a planet of extreme duality, and all of our emotions serve a purpose and complement each other in a polarizing sense. We need negative emotions as much as we need positive ones. Having negative emotions is normal and natural. Without the bad we wouldn't understand the good, without the dark we wouldn't appreciate the light, and without the lows we wouldn't value the highs. We need to understand our negative emotions so that we can embrace the importance of positive emotions and the feelings that come with them. Negative emotions linked to painful thoughts or memories are really just opportunities for personal and spiritual growth in disguise. These masked opportunities help us create a solid frame of reference so that we can recognize the good and the bad feelings to control how we want to feel when certain circumstances arise. You cannot control your emotions without detaching from the mind/ego. The powers of emotion are by far the most powerful energies of all, and are the most important aspect of manifesting anything you desire.

Law of Rhythm: The law of rhythm is one of the more controversial laws. You can best compare this law to the functionality of a swinging pendulum. Imagine that one side of this pendulum represents your positive emotions, and the other side represents your negative emotions. We know that whichever direction a pendulum swings, it must swing back equal distance in the opposite direction. Well, when we experience extreme difficulties and challenges in life, these emotions are happening on the negative end of our pendulum while the pendulum is also working on the positive side without us knowing. How is this?

The backswing within the law of rhythm is inevitable. As we experience any negative emotions on one end of the pendulum, the pendulum is simultaneously preparing itself to swing back in the opposite direction—where the positive emotions reside. This same high-low "crash-effect" happens when one drinks caffeinated coffee or products with high sugar content. As we now know, too much of anything in life isn't good for us; so it's important that we control the steady swing of our pendulum in order to live a happy, healthy and balanced life. We should try to avoid allowing our pendulum to swing too far in any direction by letting our emotions get the best of us.

When I first became aware of this law, it literally made me afraid to be happy again because I feared the inevitable recoil back to the dark side of my emotions, as a consequence for being happy. I actually practiced being emotionless by trying to cut off my emotions so I didn't favor or sway in any direction. I find this extremely comical now that I comprehend this law and have a better understanding of how our universe operates and its laws apply. I learned that trying to cut off your emotions due to the fear of feeling a negative emotion is the single most devastating wound someone could inflict on one self. Avoiding these inevitable human experiences/emotions is like refusing to fall in love because you don't want to get hurt, it's like never shooting a basketball because you fear you might miss, or being apprehensive to live life because you're afraid that you're going to die. The reality of life is that none of us are getting out alive, so we may as well enjoy the ride while we're here!

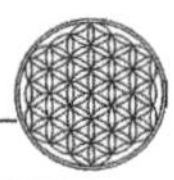

I soon realized that the law of rhythm was my friend—not my enemy. It is the law of rhythm that's responsible for keeping us balanced in life. Similar to the balance ball in a gym with the two foot-planks on each side of it. We are living on top of life's giant balance ball. The objective isn't just to stand on one end of the ball—that's no fun. The fun in the game is trying to balance yourself. The objective is to stay "on top of your game" while remaining balanced, centered, and focused on the present at all times. Then, whenever you catch yourself losing your balance by leaning too far in any one direction, you then make the necessary adjustments to shift yourself back to the center. This center is our natural state, our happy place, and it is where we need to be at all times. Our natural emotional state is supposed to be happiness and peace. It is only when we are centered and balanced that we are able to find this peace in life.

The Power of Now

"The Now" is the midpoint that's in-between the past and the future. Staying balanced means always staying in the present moment (The Now). The emotions of guilt, shame, and regret are lower vibration energies that tend to dwell in "the past", searching for minds to accompany their misery, while the emotions of fear and doubt tend to dwell in "the future", searching for worried minds with dreams and goals they can paralyze. Of course the mind cannot avoid visiting such frequent stops of past and future; the key to avoid becoming a "victim" of these abominable hags is to refrain from dwelling in the past and/or constantly fantasizing about the future. Too many people are living out their lives in their minds and not in real life; falling into these stealthy booby-traps creates the illusion that you are living-when you are not!

"I believe that life is a prize, but to live doesn't mean you're alive." ~ Nicki Minaj

If you put some sincere thought into the illusive concepts of past and future you will come to the realization that all you have is the NOW (today). Your future is merely the results from what you do TODAY, and your past is merely the foundation of who you have become TODAY. You must look at your past as one giant platform that's comprised of pure knowledge and wisdom; a well-deserved platform of collected experiences that elevate your vantage point on life, thus elevating your consciousness and giving you a higher perspective on all life matters. This one platform of past experiences that you stand upon today allows you to make the proper decisions TODAY; decisions that will create the future which best correlates with the actions you have taken TODAY! Therefore, your past experiences should be viewed as a whole, and never in detail, because we all know 'who' resides in the detail.

Outwitting The Devil

Besides remaining in darkness attempting to fool the world of his non-existence, the great illusions of past and future are some of the Devil's greatest tricks. This form of mental trickery makes us think we are actually living, but really puts us on a hamster wheel preventing us from doing what we need to do, so we can live the life we're supposed to live. The Devil likes to disguise himself by taking the form of 'procrastination'. Procrastination tricks us into postponing the necessary steps we need to take TODAY into an illusive future that doesn't exist, and since we know that yesterday is already gone and that tomorrow hasn't come, where does that leave us right now? Where we are always present: in the now! Once we learn to take *spontaneous action*, which is the cure for this *'mental dis-ease'*, the Devil can no longer stop us from manifesting anything we desire because he no longer has influence over our thoughts when we live in the present moment.

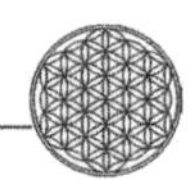

"*The tragedy of life is what dies inside a man while he lives.*"
~Albert Schweitzer

"What is LIVE spelled backwards? L-I-V-E spelled backwards is E-V-I-L. You must understand that the only true evil in this world is the inability to LIVE your life in the present moment. Now ask yourself, what is LIVED spelled backwards (PAST tense)?" L-I-V-E-D spelled backwards is D-E-V-I-L, because the only real Devil in this word is when you allow yourself to live in the past and not in the present moment. Keep in mind that the Devil, A.K.A "the Boogeyman" or "the Ego", does not live underneath your bed, nor does he live inside of your closet. He lives inside of your mind; and just like any other bad tenant, it may be a difficult learning process to get rid of this nuisance, but once you recognize that he's living on your property and you're his landlord, you soon realize that you have the power and authority to evict his ass!

Always remember that your past is merely your foundation of who you have become TODAY, and that your future is the result of all the actions (or lack of) that you take TODAY! Therefore, since all we have is the now, the only question you should ask yourself every morning is, "What am I going to do TODAY that will create the results which will manifest the life that I want in the future?" Everything else is just an illusion, nothing else matters!

"Even if you let them kill your dreams, your dreams will still haunt you." ~ J. Cole

The mastery of life itself boils down to self-control! Life is about learning how to control our emotions by coming to the realization that we undoubtedly have dominion over them. First we must start by learning how to quiet the mind through meditation and detach from our thoughts so we can stay centered within the now. Once we make this a daily practice, we will eventually be able to find peace under any circumstances. Then, instead of allowing the giant waves of emotion to come crashing down on us, we will be able to choose the emotions we wish to surf, instead of just letting them sweep us away.

Does Your Mind Have a Mind of Its Own?

"Don't think. Create thoughts!" ~ Linda J. Cole

We can learn to do this by realizing that every thought we have may not be ours. Say what? It is true, scientist do not know where thoughts come from, they only know the place where thoughts are interpreted within the hemispheres of the brain, so don't believe everything you think and know that your thoughts aren't your thoughts until you attach an emotion to them. If a negative thought we don't like comes into our head, we must immediately dismiss it and not feed it what it loves most... more negative thoughts!

Negative thoughts are like wild birds, or seagulls, that fly around searching for food all day. Once you allow just one bird to see that you have food, it will lurk in your presence hovering around you waiting for you to slip up so you can feed it. Then we all know what happens once you start feeding one bird. Another one comes, then another, and before you know it you have a whole flock of seagulls having a feast day at your picnic, and they won't go away until you're completely depleted. So, you mustn't feed nor entertain these wild animals we call *thoughts*. You must utilize your thoughts as a tool for the soul, not as your only survival tool. It's your intuition that you must follow, not your thoughts. Your thoughts can get you killed, but your intuition will save your life!

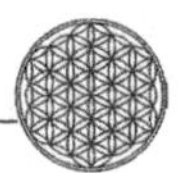

The Mind vs. Intuition

Humans have become addicted to the mind and therefore we must learn to rest it so we can tune into the heart and listen to our intuition. This is why it's so hard to distinguish where our true emotions lie. We get confused between the messages that the mind gives us versus intuition. Which is coming from where? Is my mind playing tricks on me? Is my mind talking myself into something? Is it talking me out of something? A shaman once told me, once you ask yourself a question the answer will come to you within the first three seconds, after that it's just your mind/ego interfering.

"*When the solution is simple, God is answering.*"

~ Albert Einstein

The mind's job is to recognize what's going on and what's being presented to you. Your gut is your emotions; it's the feeling of what's going on around you. Your heart is your knowing. Therefore, true emotional intelligence lies within your heart and your gut, your feeling and your knowing, never your mind. The brain is actually the very last thing to develop in an infant's embryo. The mind is a master of deception, a master of illusion, which is why your mind is your greatest obstacle in life, bar none.

Trying to manipulate your mind is very difficult. Ultimately, the mind controls the body, but the mind can't control itself and therefore there will always be resistance. The mind and the heart (emotions) need to work harmoniously in order to completely activate the law of attraction with correct intent and purpose.

The True Power of Words

When a human is conceived as an embryo, the heart is the first organ that forms; the very next thing that forms is the tongue. They say the tongue is one of the smallest muscles in the body, yet it is one of the strongest! It's a fact that our emotions and our words affect the physical world we live in. I read about a study headed by Dr. Masaru Emoto, where scientists took two glasses of water and emotionally showered one glass of water with TLC (Tender Loving Care) by verbally and repeatedly telling the water it was loved with all sorts of positive words. Meanwhile, the scientists isolated the other glass of water and did the opposite by saying horrible things to it. They then froze the two glasses of water. Afterward, the frozen water in the glass that had been showered with positive words of love had become patterned with beautiful snowflakes and geometric shapes, which amazed the scientists. When they examined the other glass of frozen water, it had noticeably abnormal and nonsymmetrical shapes that were far less recognizable compared to the beautiful snowflakes in the previous glass. Below are images of an actual study done where the glasses of water were frozen and examined under a high-powered microscope.

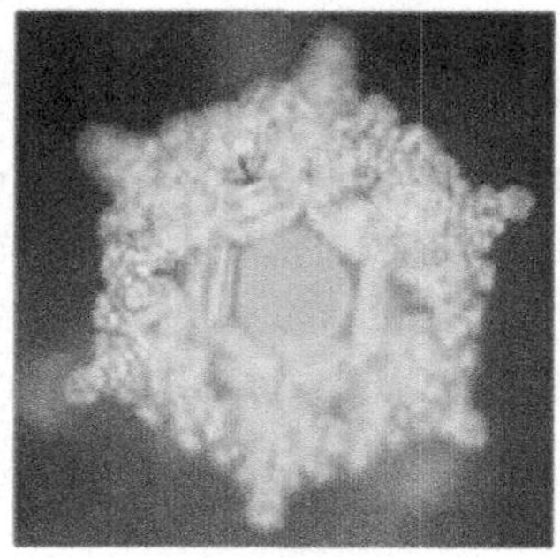

Love Plus Gratitude

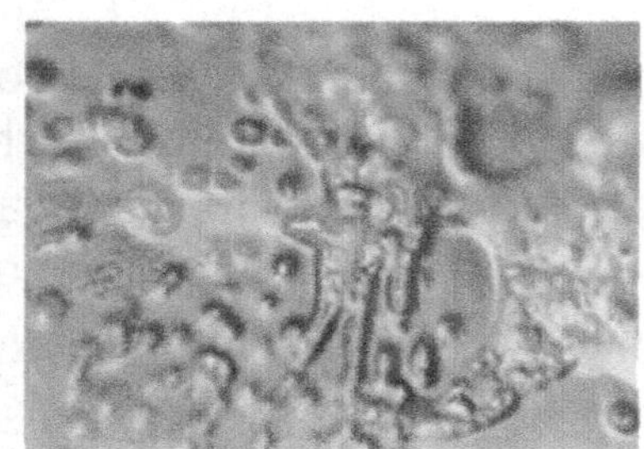

You Make Me Sick, I will Kill You

Photo taken from www.SpiritScience.com

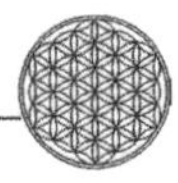

"*Sticks and stones may break your bones, but words can kill you.*" ~ The World is (y)ours

Water is the most receptive of the five elements in Taoism (wood, fire, earth, metal, water), and it's a scientific fact that more than 75 percent of our bodies are made up of water. In reference to the aforementioned study, if mere negative thoughts and discouraging words can have such a significant impact on water, considering our bodies are made up of 75 plus percent water, imagine what our thoughts and negative words do to us?

Company founders like Carolyn Rafaelian of *Alex and Ani*, are aware of these studies and the effects that our thoughts, words, and emotions have on the world. Which is why *Alex and Ani* has made it their mission to infuse all of their bracelets/jewelry with positive and loving energy. This new paradigm way of thinking and doing business is the future of business protocol, and has rewarded them abundantly with skyrocketing sales each year.

In an interview on the website Project Camelot, the international best-selling author and metaphysical researcher David Wilcock explains,

> *"Every negative emotion can be distilled down to fear and every positive emotion can be distilled down to love. When you feel fear, you are shooting energy out of your energy field, and when you feel love and trust, you are building energy from the cosmos to yourself; which has a direct effect on biological healing."*

The Power of Love

The most powerful and highest vibrational energy in the entire universe is the emotional energy of LOVE. Although it may seem like an eternal rivalry, the emotion of love is far more powerful than the emotion of hate. When we are born into this world, are we born with the emotion of hate? No, we don't know what hate is nor do we have hate inside of us. The world teaches us to hate, and the people who don't feel loved in this world are the ones who give power to this illusion. Hate is merely the absence of love. Which is why it's important we love everyone, even those who do not act out of love, because aren't they the ones who need love the most?

At the end of the day, everything in this world stemmed from the creation of love, and we are all meant to love and be loved. In this world of duality, the only opposite end on the spectrum of love would be fear, not hate. Therefore, you must remember that love conquers ALL! So if you ever run into a situation where you're torn on making a decision, just ask yourself "What would Love do?" and you can never go wrong.

Our thoughts, words, and emotions are powerful tools that have the ability to shape our reality, depending on how we use them. However, what's even more astonishing than the power of these emotions, is the magical place where these emotions are created.

The Power of the Heart

They say the longest distance that any man could ever journey in a lifetime is 18-inches; the distance traveled from the mind–to the heart. When one learns to shift their consciousness and decision making from the mind to the heart, they can never go wrong. In an Oculus Radio interview, metaphysician and spiritual teacher Bob Wright explains,

> "*When our mind is in control of our mind it's just thought. But when our heart is in control of our mind it's not*

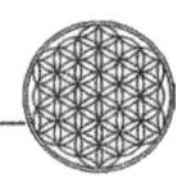

thought, it's imagination. When we're speaking and our mind is in control of vocal cords, we call it speech. But when our heart is in control of our vocal cords, it's called poetry or music. When our mind is in control of our body, it's called movement. But when our heart is in control of our movements, it's called dancing. Instead of pulling in what we see around us with our mind, we need to project from our heart what we want to see and feel."

Researchers in the '60s conducted studies in which a mother's heartbeat was recorded and played over loudspeakers in the nurseries of hospitals where all newborns were isolated from their mothers. Playing these tunes instantly reduced crying by 40 to 50 percent every time. Holding a newborn baby's heart directly over the mother's heart as soon as the baby is born not only establishes a greater connection between the mother and child, but it substantially increases the baby's IQ and is vital to the development of its emotional stability. The heart is powerful and a mother's heart has a remarkable effect on an infant's brain and body development.

There have been many studies done with twin telepathy, in which separated identical twins share a psychic link and can feel each other's emotions and pain. In a few cases, the siblings tested were not even twins, yet shared this psychic link. These experiments show that humans are indeed wirelessly connected and have the ability to send as well as receive invisible signals to one another.

If you have ever been in an intimate relationship for a significant amount of time and shared the same bed with another person, your heartbeats' electrical fields would actually sync and communicate with each other. This is why it's easy to sense what your "other half" is feeling and whether something is bothering him or her. You don't even have to be in the same room or in the same state to sense when things just don't feel right, or when you feel the need to call them. This is similar to twin telepathy, but this phenomenon is generated from the untold science and power of the human heart.

There have been many books written on how to use the intelligence and power within the heart. One of which that I have read is Living in the Heart, by Drunvalo Melchizedek. It's a truly amazing book that opened up a whole world I never knew existed. Melchizedek states that the lack of knowledge about the spiritual anatomy and sacred space within the heart is astounding. The heart is far more powerful than anything he has ever known, and once properly activated has the ability to change the world. I recommend this book if you want to hear about Melchizedek's experiences and learn more of the secret powers that you can harness right inside of you this very minute. Although I found this information to be entertaining, I didn't truly understand it, or even believe it, until I had an undeniable experience of my own!

My Undeniable Experience

I'll never forget the time my business partner and I were on our way back from a business convention in Las Vegas, NV. We took a red-eye flight from Vegas to Boston, and we were exhausted from a long weekend. After takeoff, the cabin lights went dim and all the window shades were lowered as passengers started to doze off. I was hovering between barely awake and almost asleep. My eyes were closing as I vaguely noticed a woman making her way to the back of the plane. The only reason that I really paid her any mind was because my elbow and left leg were partially blocking the narrow lane for her to get by. I was so tired I barely had the energy to move, but of course I slightly moved for her.

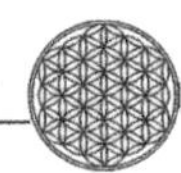

When she finally reached me I guess my limbs weren't all the way out of the aisle, and she brushed her blouse slightly against my elbow while passing by. All of a sudden I had the sharpest pain that shot through my elbow and up my arm like a razor blade! It was so sharp that it popped me right out my chair and disrupted my nap. I took notice and acknowledged it as a weird sensation that I'd never felt before. Eventually I fell back into my light trance and started to drift back off to sleep again.

About half an hour later, as I was almost back in sleep mode, I noticed the same woman heading to the back of the plane again. I wasn't sure why, but as she was passing by me the second time, I couldn't help but remember that "coincidental" pain I felt when she brushed against my elbow. But what were the odds of that happening again?

When she passed by the second time, I made sure she didn't brush up against me again (being slightly superstitious, as I am), but something stranger happened this time. Although she didn't touch me, the moment she passed by I felt that sharp shooting pain again, except this time it wasn't in my arm, it was in my chest! It literally took the breath out of me to the point that I had to wake up my business partner and tell him what I'd just experienced.

I told him, "Something isn't right with me, or that lady, or something." Yet he was out of it, and didn't quite seem to care that much. He gave me a head nod, turned his head the other way, and went back to sleep. I figured he probably had no clue as to what I was talking about, and neither did I, for that matter. About ten minutes later, the Captain got on the loudspeaker and started to make an announcement. He then politely and calmly asked if there were any doctors, EMTs, or nurses on board, and if so to please report to the back of the cabin. I looked back and then realized what was happening. That same woman that had twice passed by me was kneeling down in the back of the cabin and clenching her chest in pain; she was having a heart attack!

About thirty minutes later, the captain announced that the plane was going to divert from its flight plan to make an emergency landing. I knew exactly what was happening, even though most passengers were sleeping and didn't really know what was going on. When I woke up my partner and explained what was happening, he couldn't believe that I had "called it". However, I didn't truly realize what I experienced until I had an amazing discovery about a year later.

My Discovery

I came across a research study done by a set of noteworthy doctors and scientists from the Institute of HeartMath, a nonprofit research and education organization: Rollin McCraty, PhD.; Dana Tomasino, BA; and Raymond Trevor Bradley, PhD. Their article can be found on *mindfulmuscle.com.* I found their message to be quite intriguing, and it provided validation that what I experienced was no fluke. Many believe that conscious awareness is generated in just the brain alone. These scientific studies have concluded that consciousness actually materializes from the brain and body working together. A substantial amount of evidence suggests that the heart has a predominant and significant role in this process.

> *"There is an extensive neural communication network linking the heart with the brain and body, the heart also communicates information to the brain and throughout the body via electromagnetic field interactions. The heart generates the body's most powerful and most extensive rhythmic electromagnetic field. Compared to the electromagnetic field produced by the brain, the electrical component of the heart's field is about 60 times greater in amplitude, and permeates every cell in the body. The magnetic component is approximately 5,000 times stronger than the brain's magnetic field and can be detected*

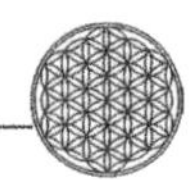

several feet away from the body with sensitive magnetometers."

The article clearly explained and solidified the parallel information from the books I'd read and studies I'd examined. When I was in a state of relaxation on the airplane, my conscious mind's brain waves were slowing down into the theta state. This is the deep meditation state where we hover between being awake and asleep, this is also the bridge to the subconscious mind. In this state, I was able to feel the electromagnetic communication that we're normally unaware of. The article further stated that "there is now evidence that a subtle yet influential electromagnetic or 'energetic' communication system operates just below our conscious awareness," which explained this for me.

The authors described being able to "measure an exchange of heart energy between individuals up to five feet apart," this further explained why the interaction I'd had with the woman on the plane occurred. Because the lady's electromagnetic field was out of whack, misfiring intense and irregular energetic pulses, and because I was in a meditative state, I was able to feel these pulses when she got within five feet of me. Her malfunctioning electromagnetic field was signaling the beginning stages of a heart attack, and I could literally "feel" something was wrong with her, just as she could. This amazed me because once I finally found out what I had experienced, I understood this as personal evidence that we are indeed all energetically connected and communicating to one another whether we are conscious of it or not.

Like many others, the only thing I knew about my heart prior to learning this information is that it is a major organ that I can't live without and that it's not really shaped like a "heart" in the first place. But I had no idea the magnitude of the intelligence and hidden power I had inside of me this whole time.

The heart and brain not only communicate with one another, they communicate with everyone and everything around us. The heart isn't just a big muscle that pumps blood through the body and rhythmically beats at will; it's a highly complex system that has its own functioning "brain" within it. It's the magical epicenter of human connectivity and the gateway to all of creation and energetic communication. Although my personal experience of this energetic communication was astounding, what I learned afterwards regarding humanity's connectivity was something that I wasn't prepared for, and is something that I must share with you in this next chapter!

True Love

Did you ever wonder why a drawing of a heart looks nothing like a real heart? Well, when two human hearts are fused together as one (see photo), they form the iconic heart-shaped symbol we know as *LOVE*.

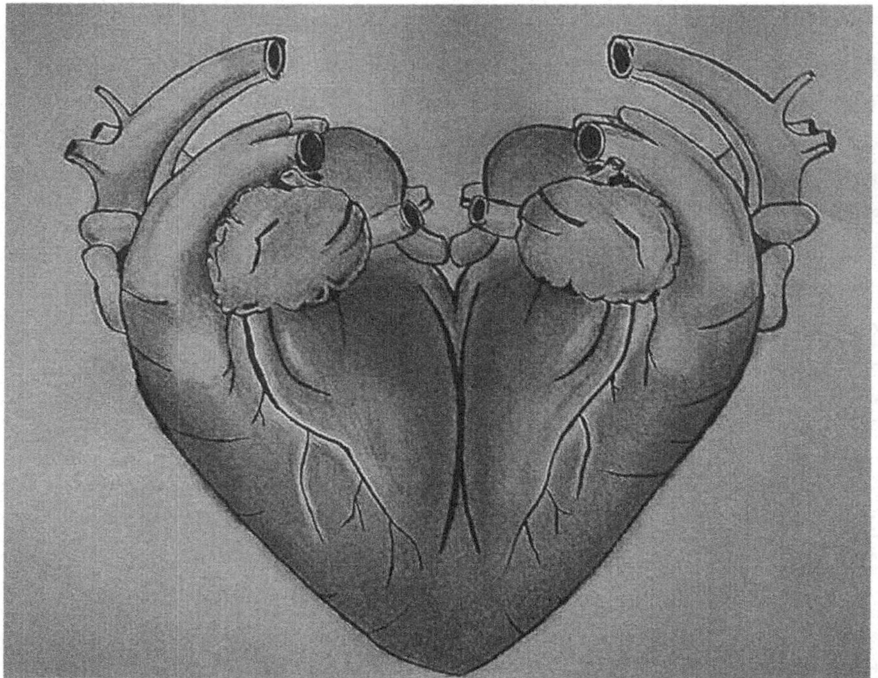

Image Credit: http://duppyconqueror11.wordpress.com/2013/03/15/symbol-of-true-love/

CHAPTER

8

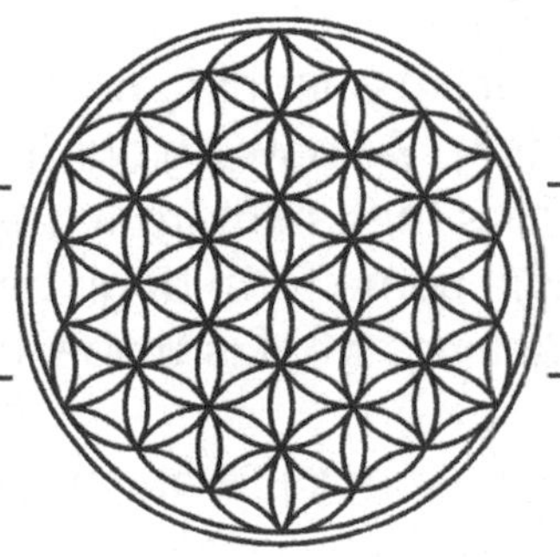

WE'RE ALL CONNECTED

"*We are all connected; to each other, biologically; to the earth, chemically; to the rest of the universe atomically.*"

~ Neil deGrasse Tyson

Although human beings are clearly not "physically" connected to one another, does this mean that we are not somehow energetically connected to one another in a strange way that we cannot see or currently understand?

Did you ever wonder why you yawn whenever you see someone else yawn? Or why female menstrual cycles will synchronize if they're together/bonding for long periods of time? (No pun intended). The answer is simple; it is because WE ARE ALL CONNECTED and share the same energy field!

Science has already proven that human thoughts emit frequencies and vibrations. Therefore, it shouldn't be hard to believe that the vibrational energy we emit has the ability to not only affect us, but potentially the entire world around us—without us even knowing.

This transference of vibrational resonance can be seen in a musical instrument such as a guitar. When you pluck one guitar string, the other strings on the guitar will begin to vibrate as well without you even being aware. Simple proof that vibrations from one thing can affect another without physically touching. So how do our thoughts and these vibrational frequencies that stem from them prove we are all connected through some form of global consciousness? First, let's start by asking, what is global consciousness?

Global consciousness is what some would call a scientific phenomenon. To propose that we as a human race are connected to one another through some paranormal connectivity would be unquestionably certain in many studies. At Princeton University Dr. Roger Nelson began a study in 1997 that was leaving colleagues puzzled yet intrigued at the same time.

Dr. Nelson made a random number generator (RNG) box, which is a box (the size of two cigarette packs) that he hooked up to his computer. He designed the box to act as a device that flips a coin to land on heads or tails. The theory is that if flipped one hundred times, the coin will land 50 percent of the time on heads and 50 percent of the time on tails. Researchers then brought in groups of volunteers who were told to try to influence the ratio of heads to tails and make heads come up 60 percent of the time. It worked! By focusing their mental energy, they changed the outcome. The professor took this and applied it to his RNG, which has numbers on it that flip ones and zeros.

The RNG produces completely unpredictable sequences of zeroes and ones that are associated with major global events. Using computer algorithms, the RNG was tested to monitor data in the world and potentially the global consciousness of humanity. When a great event occurs and synchronizes the feelings of millions of people, this network

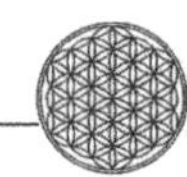

of RNGs became delicately structured instead of just "random." To coincidentally get these results would be similar to throwing two hundred pennies into the air and having one land on tails and the rest land on heads. The recorded probability is less than one in one billion that these results were due to "chance," and his study supported the theory that global consciousness directly affected this device. There are currently sixty-five of these RNGs around the globe, with more than seventy-five scientists and engineers currently working on this project.

What's interesting about these devices is that right before a major disaster or a televised global event occurs, such as 9-11, these machines go haywire! They pick up on the electrical currents of the energy generated from the emotions of humanity as a collective. But this isn't the interesting part, what's interesting about these devices is that they start firing and reacting BEFORE the event even occurs. Since this device was not manufactured to be an artificially intelligent psychic, but more so a barometer of immense energy, this could only mean that the RNG's picked up on humanity's emotions of this event before the event actually happened. Which would only prove that humans energetically respond to circumstances and events before they actually happen and don't even realize it.

Many think that when our body travels, our energy trails after us. When it's actually the opposite; our energy body travels first, then our physical body follows. Very similar to how we manifest; the first exertion of energy always begins with the thought, never the action. Everything starts with the thought. This is the same reason why people who procrastinate or constantly bombard their brains about the thoughts of completing a task rather than doing it, are just as burnt out as if they did the task(s). The human brain takes up about 2% of our body weight, but it uses 20% of our energy. The amount of time and energy we spend dwelling on and thinking rather than doing, can be just as fatiguing and energy consuming as actually doing it in the physical.

The fact that these machines started producing structured sequences directly before a major event instead of after it, further proved that the collective thoughts and emotions from the masses have energetic effects on the planet before the physical effects take place. This isn't hard to believe since this is the same phenomenon of how wild animals are able to sense and react to natural disasters before they occur. This emotional energy that's emitted before something happens is the same energy that sends signals to our 'gut' when we sense something bad is about to happen as well.

Collective consciousness emanates from humanity's collective thought and influences certain outcomes. Collective thought is extremely powerful and far more significant than one might imagine. Take, for example, a TV sports commentator talking about a certain football player on the field who's having a good game. He mentions some of the running back's remarkable stats and states that this player hasn't had a fumble in more than thirty-two consecutive games, and then on the next play that same player fumbles the football. Why is that? Is it just a coincidence? Or did someone or something such as "an outside force" make him fumble the football?

When the commentator mentioned the fact that he didn't fumble in so many games, it put the thought and image of that player actually fumbling in millions of viewer's minds (remember the pink elephant?). In turn, all those people subconsciously visualized and focused on this. So when the player received the football on the next play, he fumbled it.

The collective thought of millions of viewers combined created one unified, powerful thought and visualization of him fumbling the football. Of course, this could not be proven

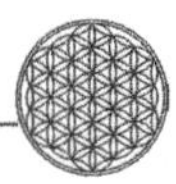

without using an RNG, so it must have been a coincidence... or was it? In addition to this theory, there have been several other instances where collective thought and group meditation results have been actually measured and proven.

So How Powerful Is This Invisible Force?

"*I think that what's important for us to realize is that everyone of us affects the world constantly through our actions, through our every smallest action, through our every thought, our every word, the way that we interact with other people we're constantly affecting the world.*"

~ Adam Yauch, Beastie Boys

A study was done in the early '90s in Washington, DC., which at the time was the notorious murder capital of the nation. One summer during this period, approximately four thousand volunteers from all over the world collectively meditated on peace for lengthy periods of time throughout the course of the day. There was a projection that predicted the results for this significant massive meditation. The prediction was said to be a direct effect that would create a 25% drop in violent crime in the city.

The chief of police at the time went on TV and addressed this sarcastically, saying, "It would take two feet of snow in order to decrease crime by 25% in DC this summer." But to his and many others' surprise, the massive meditation was successful and did just that. The results of this study compelled the DC police department to become participants of this study and investigate it further. The effect of this collective consciousness is a powerful example of how the power of collective thought via unified meditation can change supposedly "unchangeable" events.

Another example on a larger scale demonstrates *The Maharishi Effect*. A group of seven thousand people collectively employed meditation using the transcendental meditation technique; which induced about a 72% reduction in the amount of terrorist activity that took place during the time this group was meditating on world peace. There were two things that were measured during this time; the number of people checking into hospitals, and the number of terrorist attacks. What one must understand from this experiment is that these individuals weren't praying for peace, nor were they asking for peace, they became peace through their meditations. And once their thoughts, visions, and EMOTIONS started resonating AS peace, the terrorist attacks and hospital visits drastically decreased. Then as soon as the group stopped meditating, the attacks escalated. They did this enough times to undoubtedly confirm that this small group had an immense effect on the number of terrorist attacks in the world.

The Maharishi Effect corroborates the principle that individual consciousness affects collective consciousness. Consciousness science researcher David Wilcock explains on his website *www.divinecosmos.com* that there have been nearly fifty scientific research studies conducted during the past twenty-five years that verify the unique effect and worldwide benefits produced by *The Maharishi Effect*. But how is this possible?

What we must understand is that one person thinking or meditating on one thing produces just that. However, when a group collectively focuses on the same thing, that number is not just added, it's squared! So if you have a small group of six people meditating on the same thoughts, then that number is not equivalent to six, it is equivalent to the result of thirty-six people meditating and thinking about the same event, situation, and outcome. This is how the Maharishi Effect works and why it's so effective on global consciousness throughout the world. THIS IS HUMANITY'S POWER! The positive unity of global consciousness is humanity's greatest weapon that has the power to change the

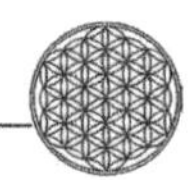

world forever! This is the same reason why this knowledge has been suppressed from you; something I will begin to elaborate on very soon.

What Else Are We Connected To?

"I do believe we're all connected. I do believe in positive energy. I do believe in the power of prayer. I do believe in putting good out into the world. And I believe in taking care of each other." ~ Harvey Fierstein

I watched a YouTube video from another awakened soul, the actor known as Jim Carrey titled, "The Real Jim Carrey." In the video, Carrey tells the story of his awakening. He talks about the power of thought and how he's now more aware of his thoughts and how powerful each thought is. He mentions a specific spiritual awakening he had and during this experience he asked himself, "Who is it that's aware of what I'm thinking?" Just because we can't physically see our thoughts or know the thoughts of others around us, doesn't mean someone or something else can't.

In the 1960s, Cleve Backster, founder of the FBI's polygraph (lie detector machine), took a leave of absence from his crime-fighting career to take his invention to the next level. Backster conducted a study on the plant kingdom by taking a plant and rigging it up to his polygraph machine to measure the electrical resistance within the plant; the same as he would a human being. To detect the vegetation's inner energy, he attached electrodes to the leaves and recorded the electrical impulses of the plant.

This study monitored the energy in all areas of the plant (roots, leafs, soil, etc.) while Backster recorded the causes and effects when performing certain procedures such as watering the plant. Other more invasive testing proceeded such as dipping the leaves in hot coffee and even burning the leaves of the plant with matches. However, what happened next was so bizarre that it still leaves scientists puzzled today.

The polygraph machine displayed an undeniable influx in electrical impulses when Backster burned the plant leaf. This proved to Backster that the plant indeed had some type of feeling that created an emotional response the same as a human would when burned. However, this isn't the part that makes this study so controversial. While Backster first had the thought to burn the plant, there was only one problem; he couldn't find any matches! As he searched his lab for matches to burn the plant leaves, he noticed that the polygraph machine "went into a wild agitation". He later discovered that the mere thought and intent to burn the leaves produced the same electrical/energetic response as when he actually burned the leaves. But how is this possible?

Backster's study proved that his plants not only emotionally responded to the physical "pain" of burning its leaves; but they also responded to their outside environment via telepathic wireless signals sent out from his brain. The plants were extremely sensitive to his thoughts. In particular, the thoughts that threatened their safety caused them to give such a response prior to him actually burning the leaves. Using the polygraph test, Backster concluded that everything in the universe is conscious and interconnected with one another, having the capability of producing emotional responses the same as humans, just in their own way.

When other scientists tried this experiment and were unsuccessful they immediately threw Backster's discovery out the window. However, once later explored and confirmed by other scientists, they discovered the plant kingdom was in fact far more intelligent then they even imagined. They discovered that the plants were aware when someone was "intending" to burn their leaves or simply "pretending" to in-

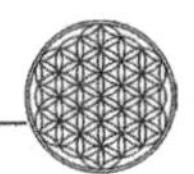

tend. The integrity of this intent is a strong telepathic psychic connection that the plants have with human thoughts and emotions that one can only imagine.

I will admit I was a bit apprehensive to share Backster's study in this book. There was a concern that my readers might dismiss the fact that plants could potentially have such personified and enhanced supernatural abilities, because this information might seem too farfetched. However, after further researching the "possibility" of plant/sentient-being consciousness, I ended up going much further down this rabbit hole than I had intended.

During my research, I discovered there was a highly intelligent sacred plant species known as *Ayahuasca* that was extremely popular on the Internet. What I initially learned is that when this plant is ingested during a sacred ceremony, it shares with you an immense amount of intelligence, thereby giving you profound insight and wisdom while allowing you access to higher dimensions and heightened awareness through levels of consciousness far more extraordinary than the norm.

My first thoughts were probably the same as yours just now, "YEAH RIGHT! Sounds like a bunch of hippies tripping out on some hallucinogens who are trying to justify their recreational drug use." However, the more I researched this plant and read about the profound breakthroughs and testimonials from multiple credible sources, even big name celebrities, the more interested I became in trying it for myself. The only problem was that this plant is only legal and indigenous in the Amazon located in the jungles of Peru. But believe it or not, this didn't stop my quest for knowledge and truth to discover first hand if this was fact or fiction.

After taking three plane rides, a taxicab, a motorcycle ride, a bus ride, a boat ride, and an hour hike deep into the

Amazon jungle, I finally made it to the *Temple of the Way of Light*, where I had the opportunity to myth-bust and discover the truth of this enigmatic plant for myself! After twelve days of sleeping in the middle of the jungle with no electricity, surrounded by nothing but mother nature herself, I embarked on this Ayahuasca journey to find out it was everything they said it was, and a whole lot more! It was an experience words cannot justify, but this proved to me that Backster's study was more than just valid; it was merely the tip of the iceberg of what humans are about to discover for themselves!

Despite the lack of scientific support available for the concept of plant consciousness, many accept the notion as being true due to it having been verified by numerous scientific studies. In fact, the power of the plant kingdom's understanding of human thoughts by "reading" our bioenergetic fields is known among parapsychologists as The Backster effect. Therefore, this gives merit to the study that plants do indeed have consciousness and that not just humans, but ALL living things from crystals to plants are alive, conscious, and interconnected to one another.

"*In a crystal we have clear evidence of the existence of a formative life principle, and though we cannot understand the life of a crystal, it is nonetheless a living being.*"

~ Nikola Tesla

Law of Oneness: We are co-creators in this force field of universal oneness; it is only the illusion of this third dimensional reality, which is derived from ego, that causes humanity to feel separate from one another. Merely our existence in this universe means that we are one with this universe. Therefore, we are not just a part of this universe—WE ARE THE UNIVERSE! Yes, we are all individuals, but every one of us is subconsciously operating in a united consciousness.

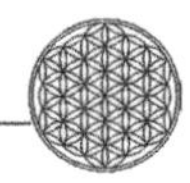

What does this all mean? Well, you may have heard of six degrees of separation, the notion that everyone is connected to one another through at least six people or fewer by way of introduction. Therefore, if you take any two people from anywhere in the world, those two people will be connected by six people or fewer. But what if there were more to it than what we've been told or what we understand? What if we are far more connected than we believe, and connected in a way that we never imagined?

At a colony of Quaking Aspens, now called Pando, located in Fishlake National Forest in Utah, researchers and scientists couldn't figure out why each one of the trees in the colony looked similar and had identical genetic markers throughout the entire forest, miles apart from one another. They eventually discovered that the trees shared a single massive underground root system, with all of the trees actually connected as one giant tree. The root system of Pando is estimated to be eighty thousand years old, but not until 1992 was it declared the oldest and largest living organism in the world.

The law of oneness and the notion that we, like those quaking aspen, are all connected to one another is something that has been suppressed for many years. But why is this? Take John Stewart Bell's case for example. Most aren't even aware of his theories and have no clue that he should take credit for the greatest discovery in the history of science. In 1964, Bell developed his famous theorem that shows mathematical proof of how we are all one. Marilyn Ferguson, author of *The Aquarian Conspiracy*, reduced Bell's Theorem down to the statement that "all life is one." The magazine *U.S News and World Report* cited Bell as making the single greatest discovery in human history. So why is this article so hard to find now? Why wasn't Bell's discovery in the mainstream media, and why isn't it taught in schools? Having made the greatest discovery in the history of humankind, why are there no monuments or statues built of this great man?

"*There are not billions of minds in the world at all, but only one, and it is in everyone of us.*"

~ U.S Andersen

We Are the Universe

As far out as the universe goes, the same distance is within every human being. Come again? Yes! Humans are simply fractals of the universe and small representations of it. We are an organ of a bigger organization, and we are not just part of the universe; we are the universe!

It's a fact that we are made up of the same elements that compose our solar system: the sun, the moon, and the stars. As awestruck as some might be at the mysterious genetic makeup of our solar system, we should be just as fascinated that we humans are recycled stardust made up of these exact same elements. We are just as mesmerizing and just as powerful as the wondrous sun, moon, and stars that embody our solar system.

Renowned astrophysicist Dr. Neil DeGrasse Tyson was asked by a reader of Time magazine, "What is the most astounding fact you can share with us about the universe?" In the most passionate words, he answered:

> *"The knowledge, that the atoms that comprise life on Earth—the atoms that make up the human body, are traceable to the crucibles that cooked light elements into heavy element in their core, under extreme temperatures and pressures. These stars—the high mass ones among them—went unstable in their later years. They collapsed and then exploded, scattering their enriched guts across the galaxy—guts made of carbon,*

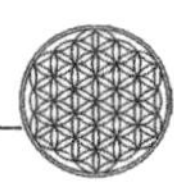

nitrogen, oxygen, and all the fundamental ingredients of life itself. These ingredients become part of gas clouds that condense, collapse, and form the next generation of solar systems—stars with orbiting planets. And those planets now have the ingredients for life itself.

So that when I look up at the night sky, and I know that yes, we are part of this universe, we are in this universe, but perhaps more important than both of those facts is that the universe is in us [emphasis added]. When I reflect on that fact, I look up—and I know many people feel small because they're small and the universe is big—but I feel BIG, because my atoms came from those stars. There's a level of connectivity. That's really what you want in life, you want to feel connected; you want to feel relevant. You want to feel like a participant in the goings on and activities and events around you. That's precisely what we are, just by being alive."

Out of all the most astounding facts this world-famous astrophysicist knows about our universe, it's amazing that he's most transfixed by the fact that we are not only in the universe, but that the universe is in us! When you listen to this interview and feel the passion Dr. Tyson exudes with his words of knowledge and countless years of research, it touches you and truly makes you feel connected.

"*You are not IN the universe, you ARE the universe, an intrinsic part of it. Ultimately you are not a person, but a focal point where the universe is becoming conscious of itself. What an amazing miracle.*"

~ Eckhart Tolle

Take a look at the tip of your finger right now and stare at the fine lines and detail of your fingerprint. This same geometrical blueprint is the blueprint to our entire universe. The same design pattern and swirls you see in your fingerprint is the same pattern in which our galaxy formed. From human beings to entire galaxies, this is the Fibonacci spiral from which all life forms are created. This is God's fingerprint! This is His personal signature that can be found within all of creation, and yet another example of how we are all connected and we are all one—how we are not just in the universe, but how the universe is within us.

There is a holographic universe theory that makes this concept easier to understand. Consider the universe as a giant hologram and each human being as a tiny little piece from this larger hologram. If you were to research how holograms work, you would find that if you were to cut a hologram in half, each half would contain whole views of the entire holographic image. The same effect would happen if you cut out a small piece—even a tiny, microscopic fragment of a piece—it would still contain the whole picture undistorted. To make this more interesting, if you were to make a hologram of a magnifying glass, the holographic version will magnify the other objects in the hologram just like a real one would. So pretty much EVERYTHING that is "out there" is also inside of us because we are simply smaller representations of the larger picture.

"*I believe in God but not as one thing, not as an old man in the sky. I believe that what people call God is something in all of us.*" ~ John Lennon

No matter what religious beliefs one has, we must come to the realization that ultimately we all come from the same place and we all have a spark of the life force from the creator within us. Take the example of our Prime Creator (Source, God, or whatever you choose to call this energy) being a giant body of water—an ocean in the sky let's say. Now let's consider humans as just a tiny drop of water from that ocean—even if we are just a single drop of water taken from that giant ocean of life, we are still comprised of all the same things that make up this ocean. And if we were to

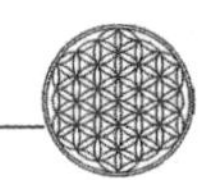

examine this single drop of water under a microscope, we would see that it is made up of the exact same elements of the larger body of water that make up this massive ocean. Humanity is just like these drops of water in the ocean. But if we were to ask ourselves "When the drop hits the ocean, where does this drop end and the ocean begin?" Hmmm. Well it doesn't, the drop simply becomes the ocean. Human beings are just small drops in our universe; which would therefore make us become one with the universe (the same as the drop became one with the ocean). We are merely a smaller replication/hologram of the massive universe we live in, therefore confirming my statement above that as far out as the universe goes, the same distance is within every human being. Now imagine how powerful and mysterious our universe is; then realize the infinite potential that lies within you and how powerful you really are.

"*You must not lose faith in humanity. Humanity is an ocean; if a few drops of the ocean are dirty, the ocean does not become dirty.*" ~ Gandhi

You will never find this information discussed in any of our school books. The reason the *Maharishi Effect* and *Global Consciousness* have been suppressed is the same reason humanity has been purposely divided via race, religion, status, etc; to prevent us from uniting regardless of the differences that previously separated us. This is the same reason certain control mechanisms were implemented and woven into many religious scriptures over time, with the intention to deter followers from searching further for truths outside of their beliefs. Such stringent belief systems caused segregation allowing these powers to contain and control the minds of the masses by distorting truth, suppressing the reality of oneness, and thus limiting our consciousness.

"Those who don't think outside of the box are easily contained" ~ Unknown

It seems that all society and government try to do is divide, categorize, and subcategorize the population to be as segregated as possible. We allow ourselves to be divided in specific classes (lower, middle, upper) solely based on our financial income. We are then further divided into specific 'brackets' to pay our mandatory taxes; to the extent of putting us in a box (literally) by making us checkmark a specific race and color on government documents. This separation only weakens the collective by creating invisible barriers amongst us. Religions, classes, divisions, subdivisions... humanity must learn that we are all ONE and we are all here working towards the same goal, just in different bodies and in different places. But we musn't let this illusion of physical separation distance us from one another.

"*If you ask me my nationality—I will tell you HUMAN. If you ask me my religion—I will tell you LOVE. If you ask me my net worth—I will tell you PRICELESS. Stop trying to label me!*" ~ The World is (y)ours

When a candle uses its flame to light another candle, is the flame different on the new candle, or is it the same? Only the shape, size, color, and the environment that the candle is in might make the flame appear different. However, we know that this flame is identical and made up of the exact same elements of the flame that it was lit with. The original candle that lit the new candle didn't burn out when it lit the new one, nor did it lose any of its elements or strength. This process is no different than the process of our creation. We all have the same spark of life force from The Source within us. As the candle exemplified, we are simply smaller aspects of our Prime Creator; we're just made in different shapes, sizes, and colors, and we're living in different environments. Thus, we have the illusion that we are separate and different from one another, when we in fact all come from the same source and we're just as powerful and bright as anyone else.

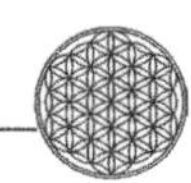

I have always believed in the higher power commonly referred to as "God", but I never attached myself to a specific religion. This in turn, allowed me to stay open-minded to others' beliefs and understanding of their realities. Personally, I respect all religions and everyone's beliefs, because ultimately I respect anyone who is a believer.

"Labels are for clothing. Labels are not for people."
~ Martina Navratilova

Many still believe that God is an old man in the sky sitting on a giant cloud waiting to condemn and punish the world. This is just fear-based programming adopted from other people's unhealthy belief systems. The last thing God wants us to do is fear Him. God wants us to know that He loves us and wants us to feel connected with Him. The same relationship ideals that every loving Mother or Father want their children to feel for them is what God wants us to feel for Him. We are all connected because we are all children of God, each and every one of us carries a piece of God's DNA inside of us. God is a part of us and wants us to realize that we all have a direct connection to Him, and to know that we do not need a church or a priest to act as our medium to get in contact with Him. God wants us to understand that He has no stepchildren or grandchildren because we are ALL His children. We are all brothers and sisters divinely connected to one another regardless of the religions, labels or beliefs that currently separate us and make us think otherwise. Remember, God has no religion! He doesn't look at us as Catholic, Christians, Jehovah's Witnesses, Hindus, Mormons, Black, Spanish, White, or "Other". God looks at us as Human Beings! Once we realize that God is simply the spiritual web that creates and connects all things in our universe, religion will no longer create the division it does now, and all religious scriptures will begin to make more sense.

"Buddha wasn't a Buddhist, Jesus wasn't a Christian, and Muhammad was not a Muslim. They were teachers of love. Love was their religion." ~ Unknown

Just as we recently made the great Pando tree discovery, I believe humanity will soon discover that we are all one, we are all connected to one another, and that we always have been. I believe in Albert Einstein's theory, *"The religion of the future will be cosmic religion. It will transcend personal God and avoid dogma and theology."* I believe humanity will finally discover that we are even greater mystical creatures than we ever imagined, with immense cosmic powers and special gifts.

Do you want to know how to unlock these supernatural abilities I speak of? You can start to unlock your special gifts and abilities by *raising your vibration* and fine-tuning certain areas of your body and mind using specific techniques and special diets. Provided in this next chapter you will find the first steps to take that will dissolve the blockages that have prevented you from utilizing your amazing gifts.

CHAPTER

9

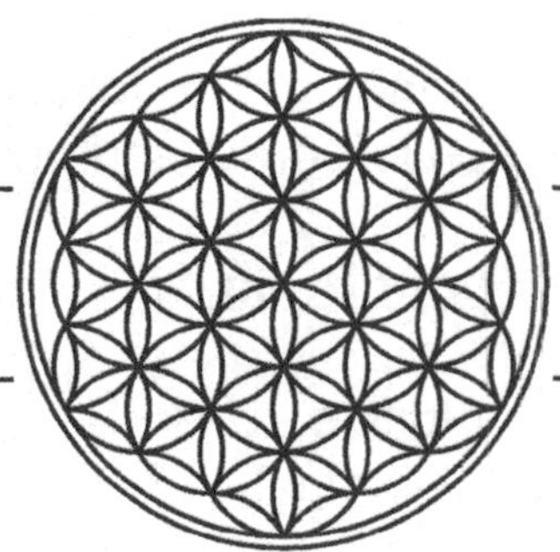

HOW TO ACTIVATE YOUR SUPERNATURAL ABILITIES

"*A mind is a terrible thing to waste.*" ~ Forest Long

I'm sure you've heard that human beings use just a small percentage of their total brainpower. Although you might have heard this statement on several occasions, has anyone ever told you HOW to use the rest of your brain? Or were they simply stating a problematic fact without proposing a solution?

Our general understanding of the configuration and function of the brain is that it has two different sides that control two different modes of thinking. People are generally left-brained, right-brained, or bilateral. From a young age, we are taught to think tangibly and rationally, which is left-brained thinking. In doing schoolwork, the left side of the brain is often favored over the right side, in order to allow the development of logical thinking, analysis, and accuracy. Therefore, you may be one of the many who are training and strengthening only one side of the brain and have allowed the other to weaken. But why is this? Is one side of the brain more powerful than the other?

Right Brain vs. Left Brain

Scientists and doctors have demonstrated that the two hemispheres of the brain are responsible for different modes or manners of thinking. The following chart illustrates the differences between left-brain and right-brain thinking:

Left Brain	Right Brain
Logical	Intuitive
Methodical	Instinctual
Rational	Holistic/Integrating
Objective	Subjective
Details/Parts	Big picture/Wholes

Being constantly taught to remember information in school that we'll never apply in the real world isn't what makes us smarter. What makes us smarter is problem solving, imagination, creative solutions, intuitive creations, and thinking as far outside of the box as possible!

Like any muscle in the body, the brain is a muscle that needs to be exercised to become stronger. If you exercise only one side of the brain, then only one side will grow and strengthen. Logically, if you were to lift weights with only one side of your body, then only one arm and one leg would grow stronger, while those on the other side weaken, leaving your body out of balance. This is precisely why humanity is out of balance right now, because we've been forced to exercise and focus on only one side of our brain while neglecting the other side. By strengthening the right side of your brain, you have more control over your feelings, emotions, aesthetics, and creativity; overall, giving you a more holistic feeling. There is a yin and yang balance to everything in life, even life itself. All aspects of our lives should be in balance, including our methods of thinking. So, if the right side of the brain is so powerful, then why weren't we taught in school to focus

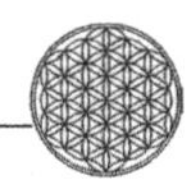

on strengthening the right side of the brain as opposed to the left? Or more importantly, how can we do it now?

Meditation-What's the Hoopla?

"What is the difference between meditation and praying? When we pray, we are talking to God; and when we meditate, we are listening to God." ~ Linda J. Cole

Throughout the research I've conducted, workshops I've attended, and advice I've received from spiritual leaders and business moguls around the world, meditation is the one commonality constantly advocated. The extreme benefits of this practice have been mentioned to me so many times that I couldn't ignore it any longer. What I've found is that meditation is the most common way to exercise the right side of the brain and give us more whole-minded brain power, thus making us more intuitive, creative, connected, and better able to control our emotions. Harvard University Scientists have recently concluded a study stating "Meditation literally rebuilds the brain's gray matter in just 8 weeks."

"*Transcendental meditation is the key to unlocking universal powers.*" ~ David Lynch

I have always been one to seek power or leadership roles. My entire life, I believed you could only achieve power one way and one way only, through MONEY- and lots of it! This is why I decided to become an entrepreneur at the age of 14. However, I soon realized the most cliché phrase known to man had far more truth and credit than I gave it; "knowledge is power". I soon realized that meditation was the key to unlocking certain areas of the brain that I never even knew existed. Areas that helped me become more intuitive, creative, and connected to the universe. In turn, this made me more capable of controlling my thoughts and emotions, and able to come up with amazing inventions and business ideas while manifesting money effortlessly.

"One must first discipline and control one's own mind. If a man can control his mind he can find the way to Enlightenment, and all wisdom and virtue will naturally come to him."
~ Buddha

Meditation is an aspect of Yoga; both are so powerful that many people have told me that they've cried the first time they practiced. This is actually very common because the practice of Yoga and Meditation release many emotional blockages that have held us back in the past. There is an old Zen saying that states, "You should sit in meditation for 20-minutes a day, unless you're too busy; then you should sit for an hour." The benefits of meditation are astounding! However, most who try to meditate experience a similar problem, the MENTAL CHATTER! We can't seem to quiet the mind and control our sporadic thoughts of our daily duties and worries. TIP: Since everyone isn't born into a Zen-Buddhist monk family, I have posted some meditation tips on www.IamAwakened.com that should fast track you to reclaiming your gifts and abilities.

"Nature is the best church" ~ Unknown

Another way, for sure, would be the activation of your third eye! I know, who would ever have thought they had a third eye? Since we clearly only see two eyes, and not three, it was extremely easy to suppress this information from humanity considering most of us need to see things in order to believe them (pun intended). When I was presented with the fact that every human being actually has three eyes—and not two, it sounded just as crazy to me as if you tried to convince me that I had three arms. Yet, little did I know how common this knowledge was in many Eastern cultures.

So where is your third eye? Your third eye is located

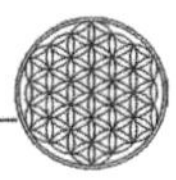

about one inch above the center of your eyebrows. Once I found out about the third eye, I discovered that the majority of the world's population has their third eye closed, especially in North America. I thoroughly researched this topic and soon developed some clever methods to open up this magical "all-seeing eye" in conjunction with meditation.

How to Activate Your Magical Gland

"Those who don't believe in magic will never find it."
~ Roald Dahl

If you wish to enhance your psychic abilities and accelerate your spiritual journey, I would highly recommend decalcifying your pineal gland. What is a pineal gland? The pineal gland is a tiny pinecone-shaped gland of the endocrine system that is responsible for producing essential hormones such as melatonin. The pineal gland is said to be the epicenter of our hidden powers and is also referred to as our "third eye," which controls the various biorhythms of the body. So if you ever wondered how you could dream such vivid pictures with your eyes closed, here's your explanation. Our Pineal Gland (third eye) actually has a lens, cornea and retina that are identical to an ordinary eye. Science and esoteric schools have long known this tiny gland in the middle of the brain to be the connecting link between the physical and spiritual worlds.

"*Spirit and superhuman abilities reside in the pineal gland.*"
~ David Wilcock

The pineal gland naturally makes its own dimethyltryptamine (DMT), which is a naturally produced psychedelic compound in the brain. Although this naturally occurring drug is ubiquitous and omnipresent in all living things on this planet, from plants to people, the U.S government has deemed this drug illegal in all fifty states. However, if you reflect on the idea that every human being walking on this Earth is guilty of felony drug possession for cultivating a Schedule 1 drug in the attic of his or her own brain every night, it's quite comical. Yet, this is not the only reason why this drug, referred to as "The Spirit Molecule", is illegal in the United States.

This mind-expanding compound is what launches you into other dimensions and is the substance responsible for your dreams every night. When fully decalcified and active, the pineal gland releases DMT and helps you remain in a visionary state most of the time. Shamans use DMT in the form of Ayahuasca, the shamanistic brew used for spiritual enlightenment considered to be powerful healing medicine by the shamans in Peru. This is where I had to travel in order to "legally" experience the plant consciousness phenomenon that absolutely confirmed Backster's study for me.

However, DMT in Ayahuasca is only orally active when it is mixed with monoamine oxidase inhibitors (MAOIs), which are enzyme inhibitors. The pineal gland and the chemical DMT are the most fascinating and mysterious components in the entire human body. If you watch the Netflix documentary titled DMT: The Spirit Molecule, or research "Joe Rogan DMT" on YouTube and listen to his interview, you will be surprised that you never knew about this substance before. The interview is definitely "eye-opening", pun intended! Please note: DMT is a powerful drug when consumed and should only be taken legally and seriously (disclaimer).

Detoxing

"Let food be thy medicine and medicine be thy food."
~ Hippocrates

Detoxifying and activating your pineal gland is useful for developing multidimensional perception. Many ele-

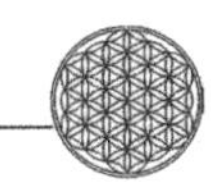

ments that are purposely put in our food and water supply, such as chlorine, bromide, fluoride, and mercury, actually calcify (harden) this gland and weaken our natural psychic abilities. I don't understand why people don't question these chemicals that are put in our food and drinking water supply. Haven't we known since we were children that *The Mad* Hatter from Alice in Wonderland went *MAD* from making hats because he was exposed to too much mercury? So why do we think it's okay to have it in our tooth fillings and vaccines?

"*The real chemical warfare is not happening in Syria, or the Middle East, it's happening right in our own backyard by pharmaceutical companies and food companies using GMO's (Genetically Modified Organisms) and mind-altering food additives.*" ~ The World is (y)ours

You can decalcify your pineal gland using ratfish oil (most effective but expensive) or skate liver oil, raw apple cider vinegar, raw garlic, iodine, citric acid, and methylsulfonylmethane (MSM). You can detox mercury from the body with: chlorella, wheatgrass, spirulina, and cilantro herb. Take milk thistle and fish oil daily to flush the liver of built-up toxins. Always filtrate your water and remove all fluoride and all other unwanted and unnecessary additives in your water supply. Purified or distilled water is best. Be aware that some of the top-selling bottled water brands use fluoride in their water as well, so do the research and don't be fooled. You can alkalize your home water to higher PH levels using alkalizers and fluoride removing filter systems such as Berkey Filters.

Please note: I am not a doctor so please consult with a doctor or licensed nutritionist.

More and more states are now taking initiatives to rid their tap water from the harmful "war chemical" fluoride—the same chemical Hitler supposedly used in Nazi prison camps to make his prisoners docile and more controllable; (Go Figure!) The same substance that we are told is added to our drinking water because it's healthy for our teeth! Yet the Center for Disease Control (CDC) and the American Dental

Association (ADA) now find that fluoride is actually harmful! Just read the back of your toothpaste's warning label! So, why is this harmful chemical still in our drinking water? Many states are petitioning to rid fluoride completely from the tap water in their states; and yours should be the next one!

"If the saying is true, "You are what you eat", then the entire human race is genetically modified."

~ THE WORLD IS (y)OURS

So why go through all the trouble to awaken one tiny little gland? This is why I urge you to do more research on this topic. If you choose, please research "David Wilcock, pineal gland" and you'll learn a great deal about this magical gland. Since I discovered this information and decalcified my own pineal gland, my psychic abilities, visions, intuition, and dream state have vividly increased along with other gifts I never knew I had. In addition, I notably feel much more buoyant, focused, and clear-headed than ever before.

An awakened pineal gland heightens our psychic abilities and aptitude to tap into the information available in other dimensions where higher levels of consciousness exist. This is the field where Einstein claimed he received all his information. Human beings were intended to be visionary beings and utilize these gifts. However, it has been ridiculed as supernatural, freaky, and voodooist to have these abilities. How could there be so many negative stigmas attached to something so amazing? And why do we think these abilities are unattainable to the average person, when in fact every human being has these abilities and uses their intuition and psychic insights on a daily basis? So why would they want to keep us docile and asleep from awakening to such great powers? This next chapter will be the equivalent to a consciousness steroid injection that is guaranteed to fast track your awakening like you've never experienced before... Buckle up!

CHAPTER 10

THE AWAKENING

"*We must end the mass deception of humanity's perception. We must discern the illusions used to create confusion, which is preventing humanity from discovering the world's greatest solution… THE TRUTH!*" ~ The World is (y)ours

Believe none of what you hear, only half of what you see, but ALL of what you feel to be the truth. The harsh reality of life is that sometimes what's being shown to us is only what others want us to see or believe. Just know that things aren't always what they seem. If we later look at something with a higher consciousness and awareness, it's like having a brand-new set of eyes as we tend to see things we never noticed before. What's even more astounding is when we discover that the answer was written right in front of us the entire time. However, we failed to see the message due to the way we've been programmed to think and perceive certain things. Take the following photo for example and thoroughly examine this image; what do you see?

Photo credit: www.Richardwiseman.wordpress.com

Do you see a man's face? Before reading any further, take one more look at the image to double check if you see anything else. Do you see the man's glasses, nose, mouth, chin, neck, and shoulder as well? Now take one more final look to see if you find anything else?

"*Everything we hear is an opinion, not a fact. Everything we see is a perspective, not truth.*" ~ Marcus Aurelius

If you look closer you will see that this "image" is really just a LIE made up of four cursive letters that spell out one particular word, "Liar", which just so happens to be the perfect word choice for the world that we live in. Sometimes what we're supposed to see is merely a diversion from what we should be seeing. Sometimes things are "literally" spelled

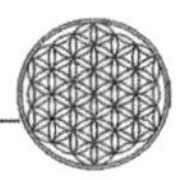

out right in front of us, but we choose to only see what's being shown to us because we fail to look any deeper. The intention is to fool us into seeing and believing something, when the truth was hidden in plain sight the entire time. However, once someone or something awakens us to this deception, we then begin to see things differently than we did before.

"Real eyes, Realize, Real lies." ~ Tupac Shakur

Now that you have clearly seen the four-letter word, you cannot deny it was there the entire time. You cannot have a do-over, nor can you be upset that you didn't catch it on your own. What you should be upset about is that you were intentionally tricked into "seeing/believing" something that was specifically designed to fool you. This is yet another confirmation that you don't have to see it to believe it. We can always see something yet still not see it; and we can always believe something, but that doesn't mean it's true. Because when you don't see something, you just don't see it, and when you don't know something, you just don't know it. It is only in the raising of our awareness and consciousness that we develop a new set of eyes that allows us to see things we could never see before. It is only in the raising of our awareness and consciousness that we become believers in things that we never believed or thought was possible.

Are We Sure That Seeing Is Believing?

"The hardest part of accepting the truth is admitting that you've been living a lie." ~ The World is (y)ours

Do we really have to see something to believe it? What if the brain only sees what it believes it should be seeing and not what's actually there?

"Aoccdrnig to rscheearch at Cmabrigde Uinervtisy, it deosn't mttaer in waht oredr the ltteers in a wrod are, the olny iprmoetnt tihng is taht the frist and lsat ltteer be at the rghit pclae. The rset can be a total mses and you can sitll raed it wouthit porbelms. Tihs is bcuseae the huamn mnid deos not raed ervey lteter by istlef, but the wrod as a wlohe."

The study you just did is pretty self-explanatory, but it doesn't answer the question of why our brain does this.

The brain works in mysterious ways and only sees what it "thinks" it should be seeing, or what it wants to see. The brain constantly compensates for us in order to make sense of what it believes it sees, not necessarily what's actually there. But what if the brain could also do the opposite? What if the brain retracted words or images to make us believe that it's not there—when they are—simply because our brain can't make sense of what it's seeing? Is this even possible? Well, let's play with these trivial brain exercises used by the National Guild of Hypnotists (NGH), and let's make that decision on our own.

Quickly take a look at this image and read out loud (or under your breath) what it says.

Image credit: www.Joe-ks.com

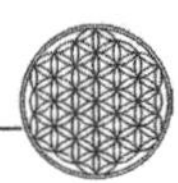

OK, now read it one more time just to make sure you're reading it correctly. OK, third time is the charm! Did you read, "A BIRD IN THE BUSH"? If so, you don't get a gold star or a smiley face sticker today. But if you read "A BIRD IN THE 'THE' BUSH," then you nailed it (which most rarely do). You'll see for yourself when you show this exercise to your friends and relatives.

Here's what's happening: the brain automatically doesn't register the double "the" and tries to eliminate one of them for you to make it seem as if it's not there at first glance. Because it really wasn't (according to your brain) or else you would have seen it, right? Now that you know it's there, where was it before? Why would your brain eliminate something that is clearly there for you to see?

"*Don't trust everything you see. Even salt looks like sugar.*"
~ Unknown

In the world of hypnotherapy, when a client is under hypnosis and in a deep trance state, the hypnotherapist can encourage the client to experience positive or negative hallucinations, either by suggesting that she or he see something that is not there, or suggesting that she or he not see something that is there! These capabilities in the brain are not only very much possible, they have been proven and are practiced.

Now read the sentence below and quickly count the Fs. Be sure to read the sentence ONLY ONCE.

"FINISHED FILES ARE THE RESULT OF YEARS OF SCIENTIFIC STUDY COMBINED WITH THE EXPERIENCE OF YEARS."

How many Fs did you count? Three? Four? Now try quickly recounting once more. Did you come up with the same number?

Most people don't get this right their first time. The actual number of Fs is six. For some reason the brain doesn't want to process the Fs in the word "of" and we tend to leave them out.

Now take a look at these portraits.

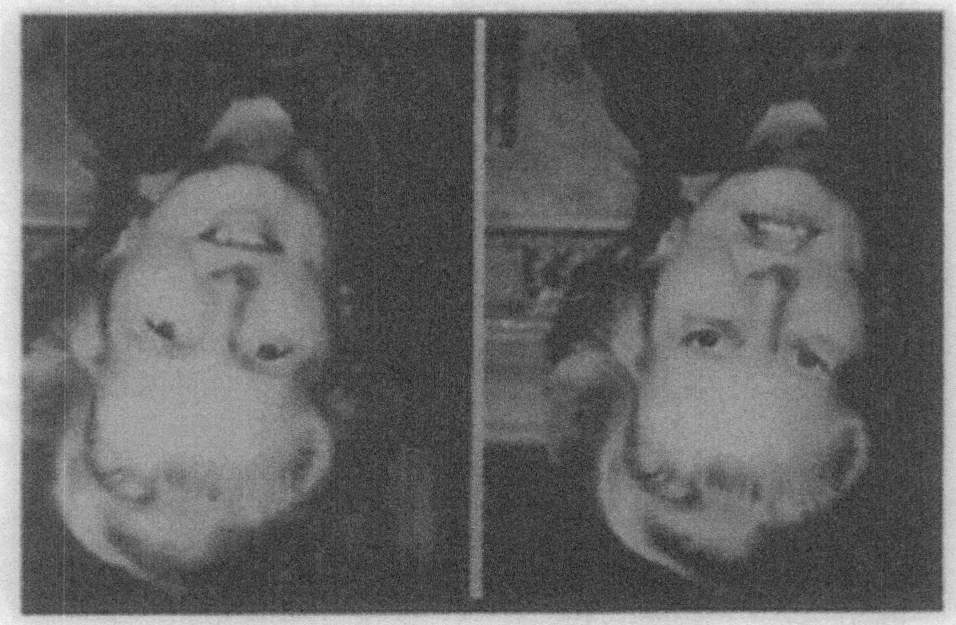

Photo credit: www.stuff4educators.com/margaret-thatcher-illusion

Did you notice anything different about these two portraits at first glance? If not, turn the book upside down and now look at the image.

"In a world filled with deception, seeing is not believing!"
~ The World is (y)ours

I know, pretty freaky! As you can see, it is quite possible for the brain to avoid seeing something that doesn't conform to its sense of reality. The difference between the conscious mind and the subconscious mind is that the con-

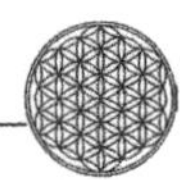

scious mind tries to make sense of things by defining the undefined in order to solve problems for us. When the conscious mind can't figure something out, the subconscious mind takes over and assumes its primary role in protecting the conscious mind from experiencing psychological trauma due to its level of consciousness and perception of reality. But when we approach situations "consciously", we are able to see through the illusion and past the deception, while both our conscious mind and subconscious mind are working cohesively with each other.

Take the next image as another example. How much smaller in centimeters do you think the bottom line is from the top line (e.g.1,2,3,5, 6 centimeters?...)

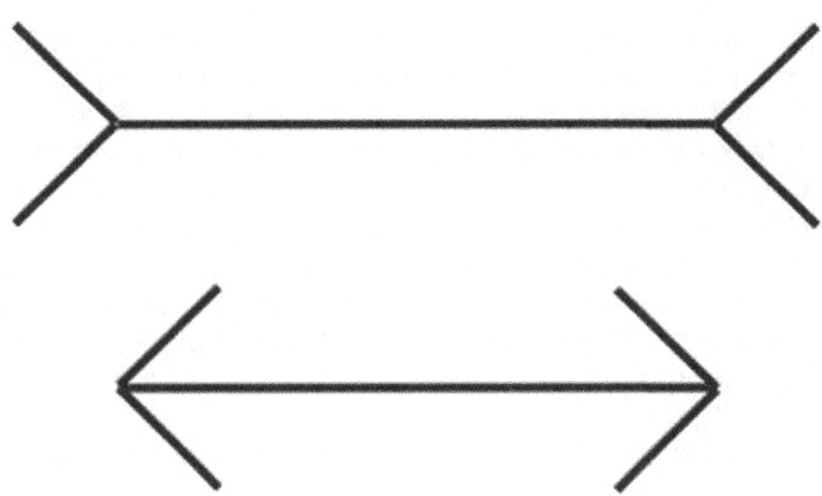

Many might have seen this "optical illusion" before where the top line appears to look much longer than the bottom line, when in fact, they are the exact same length! One might think that this is just an example to prove that our senses are unreliable or that our eyes like to play tricks on us. However, it's not that our eyes are playing tricks on us. Our eyes are merely the messengers to the brain showing it exactly what it sees. The eyes send the arrangement of light waves to our brain, and then our mind becomes the decision maker in this process by deciding what it believes it should be seeing. The knowledge one must gain from the results of this exercise is that it is not our senses or our eyes that are unreliable, it is our brain that is unreliable!

"*The eyes are useless when the mind is blind.*" ~ Unknown

The problem is, human beings are so trusting and reliant upon their brains, that they become overly addicted to their minds, rather than their senses. We are so conditioned and programmed to interpret the world as such, that this becomes the very reason we remain plugged into the matrix our entire lives, and fail to discover our true abilities. We let our mind's belief system rule our life and dictate our reality. The only way to override the mind's belief system and discern the illusions of life is to expand our consciousness when we seek truth. Truth is the only thing that can expand human consciousness.

But why does the brain allow these things to happen? Does the mind enjoy playing tricks on us? Is it to protect us from things we shouldn't see, or from discovering the true reality in which we live? Or, is the brain waiting for our consciousness to expand so it can reveal the real world to us when we're ready? Whatever it is, these exercises should have brought you to the realization that things are not always what they seem, and seeing is definitely not believing!

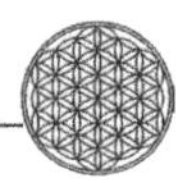

What is "Real" Exactly?

What humans consider being real is what they can taste, smell, feel, and see. These senses are merely electrical signals interpreted within our brain. So what is real then? "Real" is simply anything our mind believes, which is contingent upon our level of consciousness at that time. This also means that there are many people in this world living different realities than the average citizen because they were able to unplug from the matrix and see beyond the illusion of this reality in which we live. Yet these are the people we call the crazy ones!

Based on what we observed in the previous exercises, what if the brain "tricks" us more often than we think? We only notice the integrity of the exercise when we are either overly aware or when we are asked to take one more look at it from another party. Only then is our mind forced to see what is really there, not just what we thought we saw, or what our brain showed us.

Now, let's take this a step further and assume "what if" again: what if there are other objects or "beings" that surround us, but the brain rejects this and fails to show us because it doesn't fit into our reality or level of consciousness? Now, is this really so hard to believe when you just witnessed your magician of a brain make letters and words appear and disappear out of thin air? Images and words that were clearly staring you in the face just inches away. Did your brain not just magically shrink and stretch lines to make you believe they were a different size, when they're exactly the same? Did your brain not just put on its "Beer-Goggles" and freakishly distort a hideous woman's face to make her look like good old Granny? Did you not just witness how your own brain can effortlessly play tricks on you?

What Else Can't We See?

Ultimate Fighting Championship (UFC) commentator and stand-up comedian Joe Rogan is definitely an awakened soul. I enjoy how he explains certain topics with his funny analogies and his comic delivery. In one of his skits he mentions that there are many things going on around us that our senses aren't advanced enough to pick up on.

One of Rogan's analogies to being unaware of extrasensory phenomena is what he calls "the fart theory." Joe's theory pretty much states that if someone farted in a room full of people and no one heard it, and everyone's sense of smell was blocked from having stuffy noses, then everyone would be sitting in the room full of stench and wouldn't even know it. Our senses are part of our consciousness—and if just one is off, so are we. But what if we've had extra senses all along that we weren't aware of, or have been blocked like their stuffy noses, or just haven't been activated in us yet? What if there are more things out there than just what we are feeling, hearing, or seeing?

The 2004 quantum physics documentary What the Bleep Do We Know!? discusses how the brain only sees what it believes is possible and only imprints to our senses what it has the ability to conceive.

"The eye sees only what the mind is prepared to comprehend." ~ Henri Bergson

The film cites an example of how the American Indians didn't see Columbus' ships approaching their land. The native people had no knowledge of what ships looked like and had no clue that ships even existed, never mind giant ships. A Shaman in the tribe even noticed unnatural ripples in the water caused by the ships, but he hadn't seen any ships nor was he even aware of what a ship looked like.

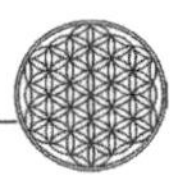

This puzzled him and he pondered every day looking for something unusual until eventually he saw the ships. Only because everyone trusted and believed in what the Shaman said as the truth, were they finally able to see the ships once he pointed them out, but it was too late. The Natives were only able to see the ships once the Shaman helped them see past the illusion in their mind. Which in this case was a negative hallucination (removing something that is there), the same way I showed you how to bypass your brain's protection mechanism in order to see past the positive/negative hallucinations in the previous exercises. This story is a great example of how the brain will only conceive and take in what it believes is plausible to its reality. We've already seen how the brain can make a line or a word disappear simply because it couldn't process or make sense of it.

"We are only as blind as we want to be." ~ Maya Angelou

So How Do We See What Can't Be Seen?

Science has proven that there are frequencies of light that we can't see, frequencies of sound that we can't hear, and states of matter that we can't feel. So what's really going on around us beyond our conscious understanding? Are there living things that we're unable to detect or interact with because we are limited to just the five senses we've developed so far?

We are all familiar with the example of high-frequency sounds that humans cannot hear, but dogs can. So let's take frequencies of light/colors for example instead. The presence of a rainbow is seen contingent upon the conical photoreceptors inside of our eyes. So basically, to animals that lack cones, this same rainbow simply becomes a nonexistent cosmic myth in the daytime sky because they cannot see what we see. However, a rainbow is something that we are all well aware of and have seen at least once in our lifetime.

"...the realm of the senses is so limited. We can only see between infrared light and ultraviolet light; we can only hear a limited decibel range; we think reality is what we can apportion through the limited instruments of the senses. But reality is, of course, far beyond that..." ~ Russell Brand

Let's take ants for example. Ants are among the strongest creatures on Earth relative to their size and are among the first to detect weather changes. Ants not only have eyes, they have compound eyes (eyes with numerous lenses). However, ants have extremely poor vision and cannot see the way we do, nor are they even aware of human existence. They mainly "see" by following the scent or chemical trails left by other ants, which is why they walk in lines.

We might assume that in the ant's consciousness of itself, it believes it's the strongest being on this planet, with the most heightened sense of awareness of any one species. However, we humans often consider ants to be among the lowest life-forms on the planet. Just like the ants, we humans may not be aware of other much higher, intelligent life-forms that we cannot see and that may very well look at us in the same way that we look at ants.

How do we know there are not other people, places, or things around us right now that we just can't see, simply because the rest of our senses haven't been activated yet. So again, how do we raise our consciousness/awareness and activate our extrasensory perceptions of the world in order to obtain our gifts? Where do we start if we wish to open up our mind and clear out old beliefs so we can discover this new knowledge? What would be the very first thing we would need to do?

QUESTION EVERYTHING!

"*We must stop accepting their formalities, and start questioning our reality.*" ~ The World is (y)ours

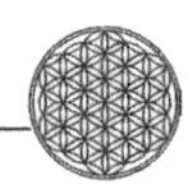

If I were to offer you $250,000 to jump out of an airplane with no parachute, I bet you would say "No", correct? But what if I told you that the plane was still on the ground? The moral of the story is don't make assumptions, even if you think you know the facts - QUESTION EVERYTHING!

Question the world around you, question your parents, question your teachers, question your President, question the universe, question me, question yourself, question EVERYTHING! Question why we can spend countless hours playing senseless games such as *Candy Crush*, then complain that we never have any free time to go to the gym or do the things that actually better our lives. Question why we can virtually cultivate our own farm on Facebook's *Farmville* rather than spending that same amount of time growing our own REAL organic garden. Yet, we are all perfectly fine eating these genetically modified foods that are damaging our health and poisoning our bodies. Question why we can allocate fifteen minutes of our time just to save 15% on our car insurance, just because a little cute green lizard told us we should. Yet, we won't allocate fifteen minutes of our time to shop around for alternative natural medicines, or get another doctor's opinion when it comes to our own health. Instead, we just listen to whatever our doctor tells us and accept the synthetic chemicals in a pill form that have 'highly possible' adverse side effects.

Question the fact that our Sun can provide enough solar energy to power the entire world-free of charge! Yet solar panels are illegal in the state of Florida, which just so happens to be known as "The Sunshine State"; how ironic!

Why is it we can gather up to 60,000 screaming loyal fans to a grassy field in frigid cold temperatures for a meaningless football game, yet we can't all gather on the white house lawn to protest for our constitutional rights back? Question why the NFL (National Football League) has revenues over nine billion dollars and is still a non-profit organization, with the NFL Commissioner's yearly salary just over twenty-nine million dollars.

Please question how in the world humanity allowed Miley Cyrus to be nominated for TIME Magazine's 2013 *Person of the Year*. Question why the majority of people don't know the name of the famous celebrity who lives at 1600 Pennsylvania Ave., yet they know who lives in a pineapple under the sea. Question why bodybuilders believe they need to eat meat to gain muscle mass; yet some of the largest animals in the world (gorillas, horses, whales, etc.) eat plankton and leaves.

Question why we enjoy allocating weeks and even months building digital cities and communities using SIMS technology and other video game platforms, but we don't want to rebuild our very own civilization that we live in.

"The world as we have created it is a process of our thinking. It cannot be changed without changing our thinking."

~Albert Einstein

Why is it we can gather hundreds, even thousands of people, for a pointless *flash mob* session, but we can't unite with one another to stand up against corporate thugs and political bullies in order to create a better world?

Question how in the world building #7 completely collapsed in the world trade center bombings when a plane never even hit that building (evidence shown in the documentary titled Loose Change). Question why our United States government was ready for WW III and wanted to spend hundreds of millions of our tax dollars to bomb Syria. Then, just two weeks later they were crying poverty claiming that they didn't have any money to keep the national parks and memorials open for our country's war veterans?

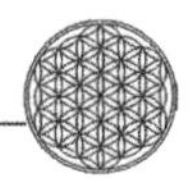

"*They got money for war but can't feed the poor.*"
~ Tupac Shakur

It's clear that we as a human race have our priorities all wrong! Question why no one cares about his or her freedom anymore. Or are we just not aware that this is the harsh reality in which we live, and that this is affecting every person in the world on every major level possible?

The problem for most of us is that we feel that we're too preoccupied struggling to make the next month's rent, trying to pay our next cell phone bill on time, or just worrying about mundane daily grown-up chores that overwhelm us. We tend to overlook some of the craziest and most astounding things happening right under our noses that should really *open our minds* and urge us to want to know more about this amazing world we live in. Instead, we enjoy searching for Waldo instead of searching within and finding ourselves. We consume our minds with pointless subjects that just temporarily entertain and distract us from the truth of our universe. Distractions like Miley Cyrus twerking on stage, sports, *Jersey Shore* re-runs, and *Keeping up with The Kardashians*. I find that people these days want to explore and learn more about someone else's reality rather than discover their own.

Ask NEW Questions

"*I don't want you to think like me. I just want you to think.*"
~ Unknown

Like Albert Einstein said, "*Insanity is doing the same thing over and over and expecting different results.*" This is why we must try new approaches to life and start asking new questions. As soon as we begin asking new questions about life, only then will we begin to get new answers. Our minds naturally want to reject things that we don't understand or that contradict our current beliefs. The only way to combat this limited state of consciousness and deprogram the mind is to research and ask as many questions as humanly possible. Remember, only when you ask new questions will you have the opportunity to receive a different answer. Even if you think you might know the answer, if you ask a question from a different angle, you might see the situation from a different angle as well. So from now on, if someone asks you "Is this glass half full, or half empty?" You should rebut with a question such as, "Well, was the water just poured in, or was the water just poured out? You will find yourself getting different answers and having new perspectives when you challenge your reality, ask more questions, and research the things you think you might already know.

"You will never learn what you think you already know."
~ Linda J. Cole

Re-Observe The World

Do you ever stop and observe how astounding some of the things that are happening right this very second are, things that we regularly overlook? Take this very moment, for example. We are a mammal species with the ability to invent flying aircrafts that travel the globe in record speeds. We can build rocket ships that fly to outer space and land on the moon and other planets. We have the ability to magically create an entirely new human being from scratch with just the help of one other person. We can even create a human being that has its own soul, its own personality, and its own unique look, all from a tiny microscopic amount of liquid that we can produce from our own body at will.

Have you ever asked yourself this simple question, "Why is the sky blue?" Why is it when we look up we "think" we see blue skies? I say, "think" because we know the sky is made up of air, but if we look at the air in front of us right now we obviously see that the air is clear and transparent, not blue. So where on Earth (pun intended), does this magical blue color come from? Another interesting question is

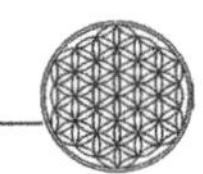

why do the ocean waters look blue when we view a globe or look down from an airplane? Yet, when we are swimming in the ocean and we cup a sample of this exact water with our hands, it is undoubtedly CLEAR! Why is this? Where is this blue coming from? We know that the ocean floor isn't lined with blue lining; so why is it that we see blue when things are *clearly* clear? These are just a few examples of how we overlook the oddest things we see on a daily basis and never stop to question them.

Let's delve a bit deeper and reflect on the fact that right now you're sitting or standing above a gigantic ball of silicon, dirt, water, and rock called a planet, which just so happens to make up the perfect shape of a giant sphere that is magically suspended in the middle of outer space, and the only thing stopping you from flying off this giant blue and green globe is an invisible force called gravity. All the while you are flying around in outer space on an "Earth Ship", within another invisible force called an *orbit* that is circling an enormous exploding ball of fire, which is solely responsible for feeding our entire planet, giving everything it touches (including us) the energy it needs to survive. This giant fire-ball, better known as our Sun, is also conveniently floating in the middle of outer space in "The Goldilocks Zone" that's just close enough to provide enough warmth and light for our survival, but just far enough away that it doesn't burn us to a crisp! All of this magical stuff is going on within something referred to as a *Milky Way Galaxy*; which is just ONE of the many galaxies consisting of solar systems with multiple orbiting planets in this vast universe—and you don't believe in miracles?

It is a fact that Earth's sun is a star itself, a relativity small star at that. In all actuality, the sun and the stars are one in the same when you break down their core elements. The only reason a star is considered a sun is when it's located in the center of a planetary system; but here's what trips me out. Do we ever imagine what Earth would look like from the viewpoint of another planet or solar system? Without using a telescope, we wouldn't even be able to see Earth, all we would be able to see is a little glowing dot. This little glowing dot would be our sun (not planet Earth). Everyone would see this star (Earth's sun) and just consider it another star in the sky, oblivious to the vastness of everything it encompasses and represents. The reality of this tiny bright star's existence seen from afar, not only represents our Earth; it represents our moon, and all the constellations and multiple planets orbiting our solar system.

Exercise: I would like for you to go outside tonight and just gaze up in the nighttime sky. As you stand there, just imagine what planet Earth would look like from your current vantage point. Then try counting as many stars as you can. On a clear night you should be able to count hundreds of stars, and that's just the amount of stars that your eyes can see. As you view the countless twinkling clusters of stars everywhere, just know that you're seeing hundreds and thousands of stars and suns that could potentially represent entire solar systems with multiple orbiting planets and moons. Entire planets, just like ours possibly, that were never written about in a history book, or mentioned in a science class.

Here's another interesting question to help reevaluate our perception of the world: Does the universe have an end to it, or is it infinite? If the universe is infinite, how is that even possible? I mean, how can something just keep going and going and not have an end? Everything physical that we know has an end—even life, right? You can't even visualize infinity if you try because your mind will just have to keep on going and going. Therefore, the statement "the universe is big" must be an understatement if the universe is infinite, correct? Then why is it that we feel the entire universe revolves around us and that we are the most intelligent beings here? On the contrary, lets make this argument easier. Let's say there is an end to the universe, and let's imagine a wall at the end of the universe that's marked "This Is the End of the Universe!" Okay, cool. Now tell me, what would be on the other side of that wall? Hmmmm.

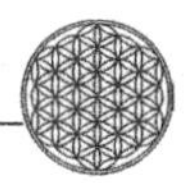

Things That Make You Go "Hmmmm"

When you really stop and think about these sorts of things, your head almost wants to spin off your shoulders. To this day, the simplest of questions can't be answered, such as "What came first, the chicken or the egg?" How often do we really think about this stuff? We tend to overlook the simple everyday things in life that are so amazing; and forget how mysterious this world really is and how miraculous it is just to be alive!

Although we may not have an answer for every question, there are many theories that still puzzle me. For instance, why do so many people believe that planet earth was created in 7 days and is only 6,000 years old, when scientific artifacts clearly show that the earth has been around for billions of years? And why doesn't the oldest book known to man talk about the existence of dinosaurs? Why do certain religions try to convince us that these creatures never existed when there is undeniable scientific proof? I don't understand how giant authentic bones with traces of DNA from these creatures aren't enough evidence for them; yet we live in a society where a man can get convicted of a crime, sentenced to life in prison, and even get the death penalty just from his saliva being on a piece of bubble gum located at a crime scene. Yet giant dinosaur bones that make up the entire construct of the actual dinosaur aren't enough evidence for them to prove their existence?

Then there are the controversial Great Pyramids which were said to be built in 2325 B.C. Science today can't explain how these perplexing structures were created, nor can we barely replicate building these structures using today's modern equipment. Even the method used to cut the giant stone blocks was so accurate and precise that it made these blocks look as if they were cut in a sliced bread machine. There is no way these cuts could have been made back then without having a Visa Platinum Card at Home Depot to buy the largest and best wet saw on the market to do so.

Keep in mind that these individual blocks used to build the pyramids weighed between 2.5 and 50 tons, and had to be transported more than 800 km (497 mi) away to their destination. Just one of these blocks could weigh as much as a Cadillac Escalade and an adult African Elephant combined. But let's just pretend that these blocks didn't have to be transported 497 miles and they just happened to be there. Now let's imagine how it was humanly possible to lift these massive 2.5 plus ton blocks up 400 plus feet in the air with no cranes or heavy machinery, then precisely place the blocks in an immaculate formation within a structured, tiered, and symmetrical sequence perfectly architected to create one of the Seven Wonders of the World.

To top it all off, the material that was sampled from these pyramids' blocks doesn't match what they originally said it was made out of. The rock material sampled from these pyramids was similar to what they claimed it to be, but it was later discovered that this material contained elements that were not of this world. So, how do you think these massive structures were built in 2325 B.C? Were there thousands of Egyptian muscle men pulling 2-ton boulders using a bunch of rope vines? Or were these pyramids just randomly plopped on the most notable energy centers on the planet, which just so happened to perfectly align with the constellations in our cosmic sky all by coincidence?

Even more puzzling to me is that some people really think there's only ONE planet (which coincidentally just so happens to be ours) that harbors the most intelligent life form in THE ENTIRE UNIVERSE! Do we really think that we are the most intelligent beings in what could be an entire multiverse system of existence; when there are one hun-

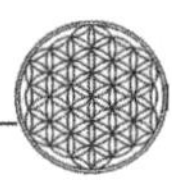

dred earth-like planets for every grain of sand in the world, amongst one hundred billion galaxies? If humans are the most advanced intelligent life forms in the universe, wouldn't such a notion be a naive and closed-minded idea coming from the 'self-proclaimed' most intelligent beings in the universe?

"*I believe, and I scientifically am certain, that there are endless other living forms out there, including intelligent sentient beings. I do know that there are entire universes of living forms out there.*"

~ Dr. Story Musgrave NASA scientist/astronaut

Just because we think we humans are the most advanced intelligent life forms in this universe does not necessarily make it true. Similar to how EVERY sport's boxer or hip hop rapper believes she or he is the greatest ever, we probably sound as foolish to these other "non-existent" life forms. I believe that any person or any race claiming to be the most intelligent and most superior in the universe is automatically disqualified from that distinction. Underestimating variables of the unknown that exceed our level of consciousness is what makes our species naive.

If our political leaders, such as George W. Bush can look millions of American citizens in the eye on national television and lie about "no new taxes," what makes us think that they will be honest about much greater truths that have the capability to shatter boundaries within our consciousness and the power to open up our minds to infinite possibilities?

The problem is that humanity is caught in a tiny, well-manufactured mousetrap that's designed to capture our minds with useless content and entertainment, in order to keep us from uncovering the larger truths. Sometimes I wonder if humanity's greatest fear isn't discovering what we aren't, but discovering who and what we really are. We tend to stop ourselves from thinking on a larger scale because we either fear the unknown or fear the truth. So we retract our thoughts and just write it off to prevent exploring the unknown.

The real question is, WHY can't we know the truth about these topics and why is the truth being kept from us? What could our government possibly know-that if we were to find out-could jeopardize their control and power? How significant can the information they're withholding be; for it to cause them to do whatever it takes to prevent us from discovering it?

If I revealed their best-kept secret to you now, would you believe it? Would you be ready for the great change that these controlling powers have tried to suppress for all these years? Are you at least willing to accept the fact that there is more to life than what meets the eye?

It's Time to WAKE UP!

We must all go through our own personal experiences in order to be fully awakened to the real world we live in. Whether it's a near-death experience, a spiritual encounter, loss of a loved one, imprisonment, listening to the ideas of a family member or friend, or a life-changing epiphany; everyone's path to awakening is unique.

My "spiritual awakening" was initiated the day I ran into a psychic/spirit medium at a 711 gas station in Los Angeles, California. She told me that my brother, whom was murdered in 2011, was speaking to her and that he wanted to talk to me... My "rude awakening" came via my cousin, who would be coined a "Conspiracy Theorist". He religiously watches Alex Jones on a daily basis and has been putting bugs in my ear for years now. I could never tell if he was borderline insane or just extremely paranoid. He was always trying to tell me about some sort of big government conspiracy,

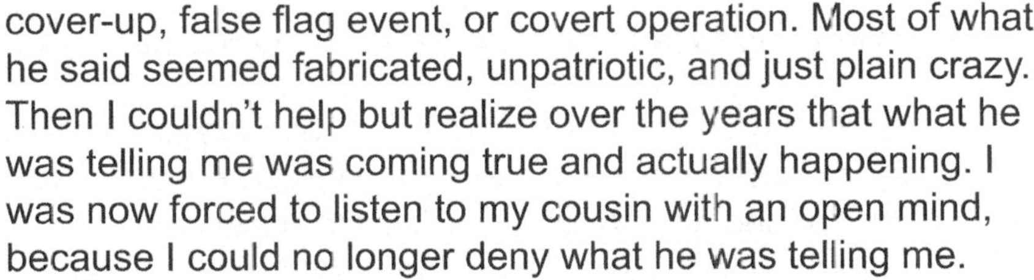

cover-up, false flag event, or covert operation. Most of what he said seemed fabricated, unpatriotic, and just plain crazy. Then I couldn't help but realize over the years that what he was telling me was coming true and actually happening. I was now forced to listen to my cousin with an open mind, because I could no longer deny what he was telling me.

I began to research certain topics, and my findings shocked me. If my belief system and worldview were compared to a computer operating system, then my computer had just permanently crashed! I couldn't understand why our government had ulterior motives with such cruel intentions; it just didn't make sense to me. I want to make it clear when I say "our government", I mean extremely high-level officials, most of which are above the President. What I'm referring to is "the government behind the government," the one percent global elitists, not our patriotic friends, family, local officers, and troops fighting overseas.

Once I started to grasp the bigger picture, the illusion of this reality began dissolving. I went through just about every emotion you can think of during my awakening. First, I was purely in denial and thought that all the so-called conspiracies were just theoretical, and anyone who advocated those allegations were just as crazy. Secondly, as soon as I slowly began to become more conscious of things that were coming to fruition, I felt powerless, scared, and feared for my life. After I discovered "*The Awakening*" and realized I've been played for a fool my entire life, I went into isolation and began researching like a mad man. This new information made me angry and challenged me in everyway. When I finally found out the spiritual truths as to WHY our government was doing this, everything I was learning about started to make perfect sense. This is the point when I became enlightened, empowered, and excited to share my discoveries with the world!

"Your elevation may require your isolation." ~ Unknown

"*You have nothing to fear, but fear itself.*" ~ President Roosevelt

I made a decision not to live in fear any longer. I had been living in fear my entire life and didn't even know it. We live in a fear-based society and continue to be exploited and controlled through fear, which these elite power groups use as their main tactic to gain what they crave: CONTROL, which in turn is POWER! Fear is the largest mass-mind-manipulation technique known to man and is the ultimate weapon of mass destruction. The freedom that you see today is merely an illusion of what you believe it to be.

"*FEAR = False Evidence Appearing Real.*" ~ Unknown

I'm sure we can agree that not all people in the world have our best interest in mind. Sometimes these same people can be in positions of power. I believe it's no longer a secret that there may be factions of our government with ulterior agendas. To better understand the bigger picture, let's use the analogy of Businessman #1 (The Seller), who wants to get as much money as possible for his products and services, while Businessman #2 (The Buyer) wants to pay as little as possible for those same products and services (typical). Similarly, our government wants as much control as possible while *we the people* want as much freedom as possible. This "tug of war" has been going on for centuries. The world is a giant game of *Monopoly* with countries (businesses) fighting over real estate, resources, and control over the people. In fact, the United States is actually a legitimate business entity that was filed and registered as a legal corporation on February 21, 1871 in Washington, D.C. You can see their associated Dun number and business credit rating when you do a search on the *Dun and Bradstreet* database. The United States is an immense business, and *we the people* are its customers, or better yet, its worker bees.

All of this might sound like science fiction, but is it really so hard to believe that a group of rich, powerful people

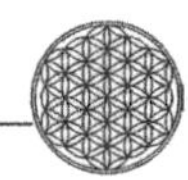

might want to get together with other rich and powerful people to devise a plan to become more rich and powerful? Is it really so hard to believe that these groups want to make more money, and gain as much control as possible, without caring about anyone else but themselves?

"It is my conviction that killing under the cloak of war is nothing but an act of murder." ~ Albert Einstein

Lets face it; the United States (The Company) doesn't have the best moral standards or business ethics. For example: prostitution is not only frowned upon in the United States, it's illegal! If a female were to get caught receiving compensation for sexual acts behind closed doors, they could be arrested and sentenced to jail. But if this same female decided to record/film and sell these lewd sexual acts via the world wide web for the entire world to see, then, all of a sudden this becomes acceptable "entertainment" because she's being taxed and the government is getting their cut. The dirty truth is that as long as our government's hand is in the cookie jar there are no morals or ethics in this cutthroat business we call democracy. Therefore, nothing should surprise you anymore when you already know that these greedy executives who run this Corporation will do anything in their power to increase revenues and expand their operation.

The harsh reality to the life we live is that duality indeed exists amongst us. Just as we have wonderful, caring, and loving individuals and groups who want to rescue stray animals, help people, and try and save the world; we also have others who want to do the exact opposite.

My intentions are not to highlight any negative things that might frighten you. You must at least understand the problem, so that the solution will make more sense. You must know their main tactics being used against you so you can disarm them simply by being conscious of their plans and intent. They use many sales and fear tactics to get us to buy into their plan, but once you start seeing the pattern, I promise you will never be fooled again!

You are About to Enter the Point of No Return…

"*This is your last chance. After this, there is no turning back. You take the blue pill, the story ends. You wake up in your bed and believe whatever you want to believe. You take the red pill and you stay in Wonderland, I show you just how deep the rabbit hole goes. Remember. All I'm offering you is the truth: nothing more.*" ~ Morpheus, The Matrix

You may be familiar with the movie, in which the character Morpheus explains to Neo that one can't be told what the matrix is and that they will have to see it for themselves. This is exactly what I mean when I explain that I understand if you don't 100% believe everything you've read thus far. However, the truth will be revealed to you on a personal level once you start believing there might be more to life than what you have been told. Once you come to an agreement with yourself that the information in this book could potentially be true, is when you will see these truths begin to reveal themselves to you. If you can't accept these truths at this time, I can relate to that as well. I too was a skeptic, I too was a disbeliever, I too was sound asleep and oblivious to the real world I lived in. I had no clue how amazing and powerful I really was and how I had allowed myself to be fooled so easily. Now that I have been exposed to the matrix in which humanity is living in, and have seen it all for myself; I am now committed to sharing the knowledge on how humanity can awaken and unplug from the matrix as well.

I understand that there's a paradox within the phrase "*The Awakening*" that raises the obvious question, "How can we awaken if we're already awake?" The irony and truth behind this is that we are not awake—we just believe that we are. Now, as crazy as this may sound, and before you completely dismiss this bold statement, let me ask you a ques-

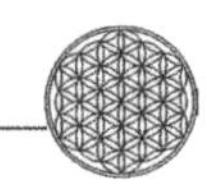

tion first. When you are dreaming at night, are you completely aware that you're dreaming? Are you 100% conscious that you are living in a dream and that you have the ability to do anything you wish? Of course not! Although we know this is not impossible, we do know it's extremely difficult and very rare to come to this realization during our dreamtime. I'm sure you had a dream before where it felt so real that you didn't know you were dreaming until you woke up. Well, pause and think about this next question: What if you were unable to awaken from that dream? How would you know the difference between the dream world and the "real world"?

It doesn't matter whether you're riding a unicorn with a leprechaun on your back while tailgating George Clooney on his pet dinosaur to a party at the Playboy Mansion; no matter how outrageous this dream may seem, we cannot tell the difference between these two realities because we can't come to the realization that we're actually dreaming. This is because our dream simply becomes our reality at that time, the same exact way you believe the life you're currently living is you're only reality. The irony behind this is that it's only when you WAKE UP from this dream that you are finally able to see how obvious it was that you were dreaming. As mind-bending as this may seem, the life that you now live is no different. Eventually, when your life does come to an end and you return to the spirit world, this is usually when you are able to reach the level of consciousness needed to finally realize that the life you were just living was merely a dream as well; a persistent illusion!

"Reality is merely an illusion, albeit a very persistent one."
~ Albert Einstein

This is what *The Awakening* is all about! We all have the ability to *consciously awaken* during this lifetime-before it's over, and this is what is happening across the globe. This is why awakening is difficult for most, because the majorities of people awakening right now feel lost between realities and need to be informed of what's going on. Unfortunately, it usually takes the death of a loved one, incarceration, or a near death experience to give us that Earth shattering "Wake up call" that pinches us and hurts just enough so we deviate from our current path and false reality. But you don't have to wait until your life is over, or for any of the aforementioned events to occur for you to come to this realization. Why is this? Because there is a mass awakening that's about to occur that will awaken every soul on this planet once "*The Events*" (soon to be discussed) begin to unfold!

Finally! Here is the moment I was referring to in the intro. We have reached the point in this journey where you are now fully aware of all the powers and gifts you hold within. This is where the second part of your journey begins and the real story that has been kept from you all these years can now be revealed. Now that your consciousness has risen to a level where your new set of eyes is coming into focus, you are now ready for the profound information that lies ahead. However, I can only show you the door, you must be the one to walk through it yourself. If you choose "the red pill" and continue to read from this point on, just know that once you decide to go down this rabbit hole, there is no turning back!

"A mind that is stretched by new experience can never go back to its old dimensions." ~ Oliver Wendell Holmes

These secrets and truths I am about to reveal are the primary reason they didn't want you to find out about your natural gifts disclosed in the first half of this book. They had to suppress the power of our third-eye, thought, imagination, emotions, and the reality of oneness and global consciousness by all means necessary. They had to suppress that knowledge and expel it from our school textbooks in order to prevent humanity from discovering what I'm about to share with you. So what's their plan? Who are "they"? And what is the true purpose of hiding all this information from us? Well, we haven't even gotten to the best part of the book yet!

CHAPTER

11

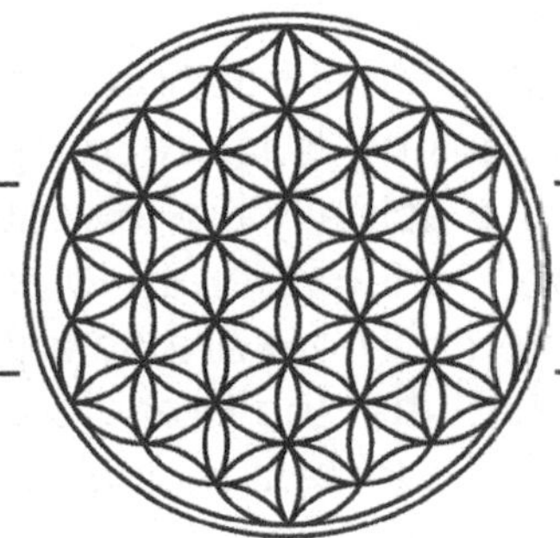

EXPOSING THEIR PLAN

"*Presidents are selected, not elected.*"

~ President Franklin D. Roosevelt

There is massive game of deception being played upon the American people as you read this; a game that's much bigger than the so-called political democracy we believe gives us the 'choice' between voting Democrat or Republican. These meaningless decisions between the lesser of two evils are illusions leading all roads to Rome regardless of our Presidential leader. Just as Hitler fooled the German people into believing what he was doing was right and justified, we are having the same wool pulled over our eyes, but in a different approach with different people, using a modernized method. There are global elitists' who have goals to enslave humanity through corruption, tyranny, fear, deception, and ignorance of truths about the real history of our world, the multiple lifetimes of every human being, the universal laws that govern our planet, and the reality of higher intelligence beings existing within our universe. Before you allow any of this content to turn you off (for lack of better words) please realize that these next three chapters you are about to read are filled with many secrets that will help you finally make sense of this crazy world so that you are never to be fooled again.

Many people believe that the United States President is the utmost highest political position in office. Although this may be the highest-ranking office recorded in Congress, the Presidential position is actually the lowest political position in the "real government" (often referred to as the government behind the government). There are actually 38 classified levels above top secret that the President will never have access to. In fact, the President is purposely kept in the dark and doesn't even know who to talk to if he wanted to get this type of clearance. So who in the world has more power than the President of the United States you may be asking?

It's no longer a secret that there are secret societies that hold powerful positions within this hidden world government; these people are often referred to as the *Illuminati* or the *Cabal*. The reason you may not know much about them is because they are sworn into secrecy. Their main objective (besides controlling all nations) is to remain anonymous and invisible to the world. Unfortunately, the family bloodlines who comprise this world government are malicious people with cruel intentions driven by pure power and greed. They actually have a Latin motto, *Ordo ab Cho,* which means, "Order out of chaos." Believe it or not, this is what they need in order to control us. Manipulating chaos is easier than manipulating harmony because-where there is chaos, there is terror and fear.

"*The easiest way to gain control of a population is to carry out acts of terror. The public will clamor for such laws if their personal security is threatened.*" ~ Joseph Stalin

Once you instill fear into the people, they will look outside of themselves for other people or organizations to protect them. This is where our "savior" government comes

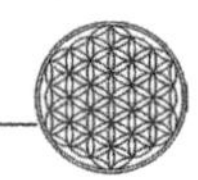

in to "help us." They have been using false flag attacks such as 9/11 to put America into fear so that we would not only justify a war for oil (not terrorism), but also encourage and cheer for it!

"False Flag: A horrific staged event blamed on a political enemy and used as a pretext to start a war or enact draconian laws in the name of national security." ~ Anthony Freda

After every so-called school shooting or terrorist attack on U.S soil, Congress then tries to implement a new set of laws that the people believe are protecting them, but are actually stripping them of their constitutional rights. When we give in to fear, we are giving others the ability to control us. This fear-formulated strategy used in the 9/11 events to pass the Patriot Act, is the same formula they've been using for years. Think about how stupid we seem to them when they're not only robbing us of our rights; they're doing it with our consent, and with our eager support.

"*The best way to take control over people and control them utterly is to take a little of their freedom at a time, to erode rights by a thousand tiny and almost imperceptible reductions. In this way, the people will not see those rights and freedoms being removed until past the point at which these changes cannot be reversed.*" ~ Adolf Hitler

Tyranny is present in every age, and the best tyrants are the most deceptive. Did you know that Adolf Hitler was actually nominated for a Nobel Peace Prize in 1939 and declared "Man of the Year" by TIME Magazine? We have been warned of this stealthy tyranny countless times by whistleblowers, former high-ranking officials, and even our own President. Why is it that we reject this information and fail to come to this realization when the evidence is here for us to discover?

To add icing to the cake, these elitists taunt us by not just foreshadowing, but completely divulging EXACTLY what they are doing and how they are doing it in Hollywood blockbuster movies such as *The Lego Movie, Iron Man 3*, *Captain America*, and many others. Talk about hiding things in plain sight. The next time you watch these movies you'll completely understand the tactics being used against the American people right now. False enemies are created for the masses to believe, while the real enemy has been right under our noses. These movie plots are almost identical to the smoke and mirrors show we've been watching, minus the popcorn!

Our government is passing fear-driven laws to protect them, not the people! Ultimately they are the ones that fear what lies ahead. This is why we are seeing the last of their dying blows to strip American citizens of their second amendment (the right to bear arms).

"*If guns kill people, then pencils misspell words, cars make people drive drunk, and spoons make you fat*." ~ Will Ferrell

What they fear is the revolution and the overthrowing of their stealthy tyrannical government. They are trying to take as many safety precautions as possible and wave these laws in front of us like kryptonite when they feel threatened. Ironically, these new gun laws are intended to "protect" Americans, yet, everyone knows that criminals don't abide by the law, which is why we call them criminals, right? So whom are they really trying to protect? If we let them take firearms from law-abiding citizens, then who will be the ones left with the guns? The government, and the "bad guys"!

"*Americans are eight times more likely to be killed by a police officer than by a terrorist*." ~ U.S National Safety Council

Keep in mind that the word "terrorism" was originally defined in the Oxford dictionary as "government intimidation".

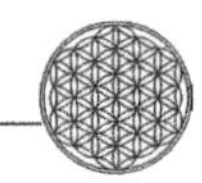

Now, I'm not stating that our government is the criminal who bombed the World Trade Center on September 11th. I am stating that it was the criminal enterprises "associated" with our government that did! One interesting fact to ponder is that the group referred to as Al Qaeda (which is an abbreviation for "the database" in Arabic) was originally the computer database of the thousands of Islamist extremists who were trained by the CIA in order to defeat the Russians in Afghanistan. In his most recent book, Richard Clark states, "Al Qaeda was created by the CIA at their offices in Washington D.C.". Since these aforementioned facts have been verified by numerous sources, this should pose some serious questions for every American. I'm no attorney, but couldn't the United States be considered an "accomplice" in connection with those terrorists groups? Wouldn't this war related criminal affiliation be considered a "conspiracy charge" in the U.S court of law? I believe something very similar is about to occur with the so-called terrorist group referred to as ISIS.

In the meantime, our troops are fighting these wars for all the right reasons, while the Elite globalists are sending them to war for all the wrong reasons. Not to combat terrorism or weapons of mass destruction, but for oil, greed, control, and power. There is no war on terror; we must understand that war *is* terror! Our troops are no longer fighting for our Constitution; they are fighting for their lives and the lives of the soldiers next to them. Our troops are just doing what they're told to do from higher chains of command. But deep down these soldiers are starting to awaken and realize who the real enemy is, once and for all.

"*War is when your government tells you who the enemy is. Revolution is when you figure it out for yourself.*" ~ Unknown

The bottom line is, when we fight each other we cannot fight the true enemy, because at that point we simply become our own enemy, and the elitists know this. This segregation and propaganda sets the stage, making us think other countries are our enemy when the true enemy is the one behind the curtain pulling these strings. More importantly, officers, police officials, soldiers, and all of the grounds crew must soon realize that these rights that are being stripped from American citizens are the very same rights being stripped from their wives, their sons, their daughters, their mothers, their grandmothers, and everyone else that they love. They must see that martial law, unjust rules, and unconstitutional laws being passed, which they are forced to enforce, are merely imprisoning their own families and future generations to come. These new laws don't protect citizens; they justify anti-terrorist precautions and protect the lawmakers from the people revolting. Soon the people will discover that their governments, using fear-based tactics, have not only stripped all their rights away one by one, but also robbed them blind in the process.

On September 10th 2001, Donald Rumsfeld, former Secretary of Defense, admitted to the public that the Pentagon could not account for $2,300,000,000,000. After announcing the "misplacement" of $2.3 TRILLION, the very next day the tragic events of 9/11 occurred and the World Trade Center (along with all records regarding the missing $2.3 trillion) no longer existed! Convenient? Or coincidence?

"*Men lie, women lie, numbers don't.*" ~ Shawn "Jay-z" Carter

Although those figures have already been forgotten, the numbers that won't be forgotten are the 2,976 people who died on 9/11, and the approximately 2,500,000 people who died in wars justified by 9/11. Looking at these statistics we must ask ourselves, "Is war really the answer?" As children we're taught that two wrongs never make a right and that an eye for an eye makes the whole world go blind; so, as adults, why is it that we let our government convince us otherwise? Why do we let them disguise a dictatorship as a democracy and fool us? Since their plan has been exposed,

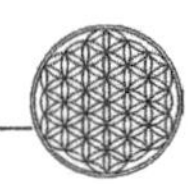

how are they still able to pull this off without the world knowing?

So How Are They Pulling This Off?

"*The CIA owns everyone of any significance in the major media.*" ~ Former CIA Director William Colby

Ask yourself this, how has a small group of wealthy people and their descendants been able to control billions of people over the course of so many years? Well, they say the greatest trick the devil ever played was convincing the world that he didn't exist. While this elite group has all the major players within the media in their back pocket, they are also using figures in the entertainment industry as elusive pawns; making people think these public figures are the small group-like cult referred to as the "Illuminati", simply because they have something most people don't—money and fame! When in fact, these individuals are merely puppets entertaining us while the real Illuminati who control this entire industry (and many other industries) go about their business in relative secrecy.

They decided to control Hollywood and the music industry because they knew how powerful these industries are by the amount of influence they have on our society. Let's think about it. If someone wanted to attempt to control billions of people and get their messages across to the masses, how would they do it? They would do it through the most influential industries in the world: the media outlets, religions, political leaders, and the entertainment industry.

In order to control the television, they bought the news stations. In order to control religions, they altered the texts. In order to control the political leaders, they either became them, or funded them. To control the entertainment industry, they bought the music labels and the film production companies. This might sound genius, but it's really simple if you have an endless amount of funding.

Now, God forbid if there was a "disgruntled employee", or a powerful positive force that was "making too much noise" and gaining too much power within any of their systems. They say the squeaky wheel is the first to get the oil, but in this case, instead of oil you got an early mysterious death wish. This is what seemed to be the common denominator with the following revolutionary leaders: Abraham Lincoln, Martin Luther King Jr., Malcolm X, John Lennon, and Bob Marley just to name a few of these positive influential souls that were in these industries who are no longer with us.

"Bob Marley had this idea. A kind of virologist idea. He believed that you could cure racism and hate; literally cure it, by injecting music and love into people's lives. When he was scheduled to perform at a peace rally, a gunman came to his house and shot him down. Two days later he walked on that stage and sang. Somebody asked him, "Why?" He said, "The people who are trying to make the world worse are not taking a day off. How can I? Light up the darkness!"

~ Will Smith, I Am Legend-The Movie

One of the most powerful musicians in the world, whose death was imperfectly "timed", was Michael Jackson. He was by far the most powerful entertainer in the world and the biggest threat to the elite. Why? Michael Jackson stood for equality, peace, and freedom; he united people of all colors and races. Michael's voice was heard around the world! He was the only musician on this planet that could go to a third-world country that didn't even have electricity or running water and perform to the villagers, and somehow you would see the entire village dancing and singing along to his lyrics. That was how powerful this one man was, how far his messages reached, and how well they were received.

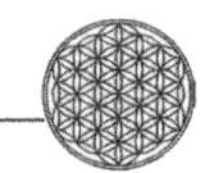

What most people didn't understand about Michael Jackson was that he wasn't just a great musician; he was also a creative genius! When Michael decided to do his final tour and titled it the "This Is It Tour", there was a significant double entendre here. The real reason he titled his tour "This Is It" wasn't because it was his last tour; it was because his plan during this world tour was to travel the globe in a final attempt to expose the industry and awaken humanity to what's really going on in the world. He planned to warn us on how we can't continue to let them kill our planet for profit or lie to us in our history books any longer. You can watch the YouTube link where Michael is practically in tears warning people to WAKE UP because "THIS IS IT", he says.

The most significant of all these whistleblower leaders was President John F. Kennedy who clearly warned us of these very groups and the secret societies that exist behind our government that I speak about; the same government and country he was the leader of. If anyone would know what happened behind the curtain it would be our very own President, would it not? Unfortunately, not too long after his famous speech to the National News Publishers Association in which he exposed these very groups I talk about, President John F. Kennedy was assassinated! This controversial speech he gave before his death is fairly easy to find online. When you really listen to what he is saying in this speech you will find that our very own President was warning us of these secret elite groups and master puppeteers over 50 years ago. But why didn't we listen?

This book is not intended to be a book filled with "conspiracy theories", nor should you buy into a label that was solely created to debunk truth speakers from awakening the masses and revealing to you what I'm about to share. This is a disclosure book! A conspiracy and a theory can no longer be called a *conspiracy theory* if its theories and conspiracies are constantly coming to fruition and proven to be true. Many still aren't aware that in December 1999, Dr.

Martin Luther King Jr.'s family won a civil lawsuit that found U.S government agencies GUILTY on conspiracy charges in connection to his assassination. Yet many people continue to defend the government and still label truth speakers "conspiracy theorist".

"Conspiracy Theorist", a term to discredit those who have seen through the bullshit." ~ David Icke

Where did the term "Conspiracy Theory" derive from anyway? Surprisingly enough, in April 1967, the CIA wrote a dispatch, which coined the term "conspiracy theories" and recommended methods for discrediting such theories. The dispatch was marked "psych" – short for "psychological operations" aka "disinformation" and released by the *New York Times* in 1976 in response to a *Freedom of Information Act request.*

The crucial message I am trying to relay in this pivotal point of time isn't just to inform you that these Illuminati/ Cabal groups really exist. The message is to inform you *why* these groups are so afraid of YOU and have taken every preventative measure that money can buy in order to stop you from discovering what you are about to find out in these upcoming chapters.

My intention and ultimate goal is simply to restore the suppressed powers and gifts that you already have inside of you. Once you come to the realization of what they are and accept that you have them, only then will you be able to start utilizing them to your advantage. It is of the utmost importance to me that you understand why these abilities have been hidden from you and that you see the game that's being played; a game that you're an active participant in. Therefore, you deserve to know the rules to the game in which you play.

"You have to learn the rules of the game. And then you have to play better than anyone else." ~ Albert Einstein

CHAPTER

12

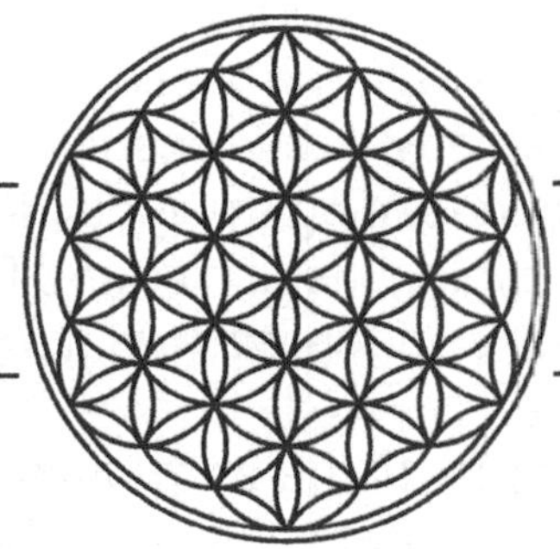

WELCOME TO THE GREATEST SHOW ON EARTH!

"*Are you seeing life through your own eyes, or allowing society to dictate your behavior through lies*?"

~ Benjamin Greene

In 1998, Jim Carrey starred in the movie The Truman Show, in which he plays a character named Truman who is the star of his own show and doesn't even know it. In this movie, Truman is a man whose life is a false one: the place he lives is in fact a big studio with hidden cameras everywhere, and all the friends and people around him are actors who play their roles in the most popular TV series in the world, "The Truman Show". Unbeknownst to him, the greatest show on earth is a LIVE reality show of Truman's life. Everything around him is staged so that he won't awaken to the reality of his prefabricated life. He thinks that he is an ordinary man with an ordinary life and has no idea he is living in an astrodome (movie set) on a 24-hour reality show that's been exploiting him for profits since he was born. Starting to sound familiar? Until one day, Truman accidentally bumps into a catering area backstage and starts to become suspicious, eventually leading him to question his reality.

Truman eventually stumbled onto something he obviously wasn't supposed to know, being somewhere he wasn't supposed to be. He started becoming more conscious, curious, and aware of his surroundings once he realized something wasn't right. This was the turning point of Truman's *awakening*! This is also where humanity is currently. We are noticing the deception, seeing the plots, and coming to the realization that something just isn't right. Eventually, Truman completely wakes up and realizes what's going on.

When the creator of the show finally confronts Truman before Truman walks off the set forever, he tells him, "Out there, there is no more truth than the world I have created for you; same lies, same deceit." He tries to convince Truman that he actually enjoyed living a life filled with illusions and lies; because if he really wanted to find the truth, there's nothing anyone could have done to stop him. He tries to get Truman to stay by telling him that the world he created for him is safer than the real world.

Just like The Truman Show, humanity is like the character Truman and our elite puppeteers are like the directors who are controlling our reality, while we have no clue this is even happening. By hijacking humanity's collective consciousness and implementing ubiquitous mind-programming tactics, the so-called elitists have been able to confine humanity's reality to one that they can control and that suits them, not us! Welcome to *The Greatest Show on Earth*!

"*The truth is stranger than fiction*." ~ Mark Twain

During my spiritual journey and personal awakening I encountered many reality-bending experiences that have lead me to the ultimate realization that what the world considers "fiction" is not fact, it is an opinion! The single, most powerful statement that I could make about my awakening is realizing that everything I thought was real in this world is fake, and everything that I thought was fake in this

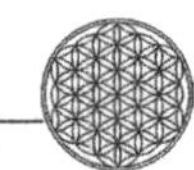

world is real. I won't begin to divulge all the things we have been taught to believe as fake, fiction, or fairytales that are actually true. However, I will expose a few of the things we thought were real in this world, which are actually fake. What we call our reality is just a fabricated backdrop controlled by master puppeteers using systems, laws, media, chemicals, and exotic technology to force their beliefs and create their own reality. What we're living in is just a fraction of the truth and merely an illusion of freedom and sovereignty that we believe we have. The elite powers have suppressed much information that would disclose how powerful humanity is individually, but even more importantly, how powerful we are collectively!

"*History is written by the victors.*" ~ Winston Churchill

Why is it that we were never educated that there were eight presidents before George Washington? What would these types of omissions lead us to discover? Soon we will find out the truth about our educational system and all the forged stories in our history books.

"They manipulate our history books, the history books are not true, it's a lie, the history books are lying, you need to know that, you must know that." ~ Michael Jackson

Many religions put limitation on our spiritual growth by setting hypocritical rules that instruct followers to live a life free of "Sin" in a way that's unattainable. They scare us by making us believe that we are sinners destined for hell unless we do what they say. Soon, religions will no longer instill FEAR in that way, and the genuine religious scriptures about our Creator and all the Ascended Masters will be restored.

"We must embrace our wrongdoings and release the heavy emotions of guilt, shame, and regret. We are put on this Earth to learn, and to love-not to be judged. Trying to live a life free of sin on a planet such as this, is like trying to swim in the ocean without getting wet." ~ The World is (y)ours

Soon we will recognize and properly compensate the people that connect us in this world, whose jobs matter most. We will stop overcompensating all of the actors, rappers, and sports athletes who only disconnect us and distract us from discovering what really matters. We need to better compensate the people who save lives on this planet, whose jobs make a difference in the quality of other people's lives (teachers, policemen/firemen, nurses, counselors, baby sitters, etc.)

Soon we will witness the collapse of the entropic, biased, political and economic systems that kill our Earth, drain our pockets, and fill the pockets of the elite groups creating them. Soon we will wake up and realize that our entire financial system is a complete sham and the taxes we pay aren't even held by our government. Privately owned banking monopolies enforcing new world orders collect our tax money, and when we don't pay, they threaten to arrest us. The irony behind this is that THERE IS NO LAW that requires us to pay an income tax in the first place; it's a voluntary process that everyone believes is mandatory. In fact, *We the People Foundation For Constitutional Education* placed a full-page ad in the USA Today on July 7th, 2000, offering a $50,000 cash-reward to the first person who could show the actual law that requires a U.S citizen to pay an income tax. Until this very day, the $50,000 prize has never been claimed and not one person has provided proof of this law. You can YouTube *Joe Banister*, a former IRS enforcement agent turned whistleblower that stopped paying taxes and quit the IRS once he discovered these truths.

By continuing to be uneducated about Common Law, Maritime Law, and Constitutional rights, we are allowing unconstitutional lawmakers, conglomerates, and global bankers to bully us, while we slave in their corrupt systems. Soon we will realize that sending just one letter to a collection agency using proper legal verbiage, can completely eradicate most of our debt and clear our credit report (this letter can be found on www.IamAwakened.com).

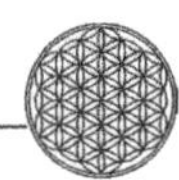

Are We Living to Work? Or Working To Live?

"*I think the person who takes a job in order to live - that is to say, for the money - has turned himself into a slave.*"
~ Joseph Campbell

Why is it that humans are the only species that are supposedly the most "evolved", yet we are the only species that have to pay just to exist? The ants, the wolves, the fish, the birds, the bees, and just about every other species figured it out, yet the "most intelligent" species in the universe is struggling the most? How are we letting each other die of dehydration, malnutrition and starvation, when there is plenty of everything to go around for everyone? Logically, this just doesn't make sense. Are we smarter than this-or not?

There is an abundance of free energy devices and natural resources out there for us. Unfortunately the dogma of the world has made us believe that there is a lack of food, water, money, and resources. The truth is, the global elitists are hoarding all of the money and resources. They make us work hard for their money, just so we can buy their resources for our own survival.

"*We were put on this earth to evolve and thrive, not to be enslaved-only to survive.*" ~ The World is (y)ours

The world is abundant and there's plenty of everything to go around for everyone: Money, food, water, resources, and shelter for every human. But we have let the world condition us to believe otherwise; only to justify higher-rates of inflation and to further motivate us to keep slaving in the systems that these global elitists profit from. There is more abandoned land and vacant foreclosed properties than there are homeless people in the U.S. There is no reason why these people should be sleeping on the streets when there are thousands of empty houses owned by *systems* and banks, not people. This economic Darwinism should not be the reality in which we live, but it is. People should not be suffering from a lack of anything, but they are.

"*People were created to be loved; things were created to be used. The reason the world is in chaos is because things are being loved and people are being used.*" ~ Unknown

The truth is that there is no lack of resources or scarcity of food or water in this world by any means. Although people are indeed dying from starvation and lack of nutrition, these people aren't actually dying from lack of resources (food or water); they're dying from their lack of money to buy these resources. The solution to this problem is not that they need a better job, or another job, or even more money… WE need a better system!

"*Work is a necessary evil to be avoided.*" ~ Mark Twain

Not only do we have to work just to live on this planet, we then have to give over 30% of our earnings back to the government. Then, if we decide we would like to be a good law abiding citizen and loyal church goer, church tithes require us to give 10% of our earnings to the church each year. Now we are giving 30% of our hard earned 'survival money' back to our government in taxes, 10% to the church, and an additional 8% towards sales tax on everything we buy. These amounts total 48%, which is pretty much HALF of everything we earn. Not to mention having to pay to park on the streets that we already pay taxes on. This bogus deal is so lopsided that I can no longer tell if I'm just a slave, or a prostitute as well.

"The hardest thing in the world to understand is the income tax." ~ Albert Einstein

Not only are we working just to survive, we are giving half (and then some) of every dime we earn back to these organizations. Not to bash the churches of this world, but I

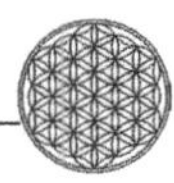

must point out that the church and the government are the two largest, most powerful, and wealthiest corporations in the world, and many wonder why!

I believe that churches are great places to network with like-minded individuals. I also believe that the people who attend church are genuinely good people; either good people who want to help others, or good people who are in need of help themselves. So I am merely shining light on the system itself, not the people or their personal beliefs. But we must not forget that if our ancestors never stood up against these organizations back in their time, we wouldn't have science, philosophy, and the world would still think the Earth is flat.

In a speech given by actor Matt Damon, he explains to his audience how the world is conditioned to believe that civil disobedience is the cause of humanity's downfall. He then explains that civil disobedience is not the problem at all. It's actually the opposite. Humanity's problem is civil obedience! We continue to obey the dictates of the leaders in our government so much that it has brought the world to its knees.

The problem today is that we accept the world as it is, because this is what has been passed down to us, and what we now call "normal". We believe this is the way it's supposed to be, when it shouldn't be this way or anything close to it. Most humans habitually accept whatever skewed options they are given as our "consensus reality", even when it is not in humanity's best interest. Something has to change, and it will, as soon as we change our perception of "normal".

What Exactly Is "Normal" Then?

What is normal? Webster's dictionary defines normal as conforming "to a type, standard, or regular pattern." Therefore, normal simply is what we expect or what we are used to (not what is right). When new information is presented to us that does not follow the norm, we reject it. As humans, we tend not to believe things that sound too farfetched, which is understandable, I suppose. But why is it that we also tend not to believe things when they seem too good to be true as well? Lets think about this for a minute... If we don't believe something because it's too farfetched, and we don't believe things that sound too good to be true, then what the heck do we believe? How can we ever be open-minded enough to break the falsely manufactured paradigm considered "the norm" in which most of us currently live? How will we awaken to the real world and accept all the truths that have been either hidden from us or ridiculed all these years?

"*The highest form of ignorance is when you reject something you don't know anything about.*" ~ Wayne Dyer

Is the withholding of knowledge and hidden truths merely a protection protocol to keep us from mass panic? Is the government just trying to protect and baby-sit our poor lost souls? The answer is NO! We humans are robust enough to handle anything that comes our way, but we must shatter these notorious glass ceilings that everyone is so afraid to break, referred to as *The Norm*!

Breaking the Norm

We mustn't buy into the fear that's being sold to us any longer. Our country's 'American Dream' needs to be reevaluated as well. This isn't even our dream; this is someone else's dream that was pitched and sold to us, and we bought into it. The controlling powers control the education system and mandate curriculums that only teach us what they want us to know. We are taught skills for basic critical thinking to just get by. We are taught what to think, but not how to think or how the mind really works. They purposely designed these systems so that we can function automatically, like

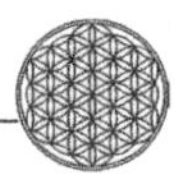

worker bees or lab rats, instead of the powerful creators that we are. Like the dogs in Pavlov's classical conditioning experiments, we are taught reflexive learning and become predictably conditioned to work in a certain way: Work. Buy. Consume. Die!

"*Governments don't want well informed, well educated people capable of critical thinking. That is against their interests. They want obedient workers, people who are just smart enough to run the machines and just dumb enough to passively accept their situation.*" ~ George Carlin

What we fail to learn in school is how powerful and spiritual we really are. Spirituality and metaphysics have been suppressed from us because of the power it brings to one's self. So have the two most important subjects known to man, which is the knowledge that lies within humanity's outer space and inner space. The average person really knows nothing about our universe (outer space) and all the wonderful, benevolent beings and technology that surround us. Most of us only know what our science teachers taught us from an ancient textbook that was written with the intention of teaching us on a need-to-know basis. If humanity knew what was really out there when they looked up in the sky, and knew exactly how vast and intelligent the universe really is, it would open up our minds so wide, and expand our consciousness so far that we would have no choice but to believe that anything is possible in this world!

We also know virtually nothing regarding the powers within our inner space. This includes the information I shared involving the sacred space within the heart, the powers of thought, imagination, visualization, emotions, consciousness, and the superhuman abilities we possess within our own pineal gland/third-eye. Instead, we are only taught the anatomy of the body and its limited functionality, rather than all of its true metaphysical capabilities. It's no accident that these amazing truths regarding our natural abilities aren't found in our school textbooks. Keeping these pertinent truths suppressed regarding the knowledge of humanity's *outer space* and *inner space*, engages us in a senseless game of monkey in the middle. Keeping us confined between these two spaces allows us to be controlled much easier.

The wisdom of our *outer space*, and powers within our *inner space*, have been hidden from humankind and safeguarded in a prison. However, it's not the information that's being imprisoned, it's our minds that are imprisoned! This is why it's so difficult for us to awaken and absorb this type of knowledge. The minds of humanity are trapped within invisible walls that limit our consciousness and belief system, forcing us into this forged illusion of reality we call life.

Mind Programmed or Brainwashed?

Morpheus: *The Matrix is everywhere; it is all around us, even now in this very room. You can see it when you look out your window, or you turn on your television. You can feel it when you go to work, when you go to church, when you pay your taxes. It is the world that has been pulled over your eyes to blind you from the truth.*

Neo: *What truth?*

Morpheus: *That you are a slave, Neo. Like everyone else, you were born into bondage…born into a prison that you cannot smell or taste or touch. A prison for your mind.*

~The Matrix (1999 movie)

Many will hear the phrase The Matrix and instantly associate it with the 1999 motion picture film. Although this is obviously true, what we must understand is that we live in a world filled of metaphors. Even though this movie was classified as fiction, many have dissected the messages and translated the metaphors in this movie finding many truths embedded throughout the film. After finally awakening, this

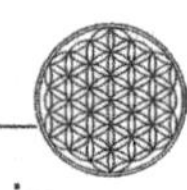

movie made more sense to me than ever before; but what is the Matrix exactly?

The Matrix is what makes you see what you see, believe what you believe, and behave how you behave. The Matrix is what makes you deny and ridicule what is *real* in this world, while accepting and defending what is not. The Matrix is all the *systems* you see in our society; the very systems we've accepted into our lives that only enslave us. The Matrix regulates everything we do and think by keeping us "plugged in" and programmed to think and even feel a certain way. But I know what you're thinking, "My mind isn't programmed; I'm not a weak-minded person that will allow myself to be brainwashed." Well, if you're one who claims you've never been mind programmed, then how do you know what it's like to be mind programmed? As one who is nationally certified in hypnotherapy from the largest and oldest hypnotherapist school in the world, I am fully aware of the many misconceptions regarding hypnosis (mind programing). You don't have to be weak-minded or even aware of this; in fact, we all mind program ourselves and have been mind programmed by others, including me. It's a fact that every person enters into a state of hypnosis at least three to five times every day. The ironic part is that we have been mentally programmed to *stay programmed* and believe we haven't been programmed at all. This is the very reason you're reading this, saying, "I think this author has lost his marbles; there's no way I'm mind programmed."

"*You must unlearn what you have been programmed to believe since birth. That software no longer serves you if you want to live in a world where all things are possible.*"

~ Jacqueline E. Purcell

The Matrix is a multifaceted and omnipresent force within our world. The mental conditioning and stages of mind programming are just one of its many stealthy tactics used to limit our conscious evolution. The specific stages of mind programming the masses are established and almost unavoidable. The very first stage of human mind programming comes at birth.

Stage One: The very moment a baby emerges from the mother's womb, she or he is automatically positioned to adopt her or his parents' belief system. These parents have already undergone their three stages of programing and inadvertently pass it along to their children.

Stage Two: The second stage comes during childhood and adolescence, when many are given a series of "mandatory" vaccines that pump various mind-altering chemicals, hormones, and things you wouldn't even believe could go inside of you. The doctors have pretty much mandated these shots, and our parents have been told that we must have these shots in order to enroll in school, making them virtually impossible to decline. However, if you research your state laws you will find that there are a few loopholes to avoid these unconstitutional lethal injections.

Stage Three: The third stage of programming comes throughout our lives and is the most mind-manipulating of them all: religions, mass media, and television!

The Law of "Distraction"

"*It's easier to fool people than to convince them they have been fooled.*" ~ Mark Twain

It's a safe bet to say the majority of families in America have a television, correct? It's actually quite an amazing device; televisions are like magic little boxes that know how to keep our attention better than anyone else. They speak all languages and cater to every demographic and race in the world. They entertain our lives and occupy the majority of our free time to keep us mentally busy and focused on things that don't even matter. I'm sure it's no coincidence that we

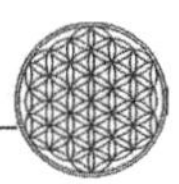

call Television programs "programs" for a reason. The truth is that we are not the ones just watching the program; we are the ones being programmed!

The senseless programs broadcasted to us merely provide humanity with content for mind masturbation that distracts us from discovering the things in life that really matter; they prevent us from allocating our time to explore nature and discover who we really are and why we are here. However, the worst part of this invention is that it projects and feeds us a constant stream of violence, drama, lies, propaganda, and disinformation that seep deeply into our subconscious minds and affect us greatly. These television 'projection' screens are projecting all sorts of content into our subconscious and unconscious part of the mind. Keep in mind (pun intended) that our subconscious mind is the part of the mind responsible for all our internal belief systems. Is any of this beginning to make sense now?

These magic boxes not only entertain us, they deliver messages in the cleverest and most covert ways using a variety of hypnosis techniques along with countless subliminal messages. These messages are embedded in not just the majority of the advertisements, but the actual programs as well. These programs and the major networks they're on are all owned by only a handful of major conglomerates that control the majority of these influential systems.

I TELL YOU WHAT'S IN STYLE... I TELL YOU WHAT TO WEAR... I TELL YOU WHAT'S UGLY... I TELL YOU WHAT IS BEAUTIFUL... I TELL YOU WHAT TO BUY... I TELL YOU WHAT TO EAT... I TELL YOU WHAT TO THINK... I TELL YOU HOW TO VIEW OTHER PEOPLE... I ONLY TELL YOU HALF THE STORY... I LIE, AND YOU BELIEVE ME!

Media Mayhem

"*The media's the most powerful entity on earth. They have the power to make the innocent guilty and to make the guilty innocent, and that's power. Because they control the minds of the masses*." ~ Malcolm X

There are two sides to every story, and three when the truth is told. However, the syndicated mass media outlets only give us one side to the story, and the world believes everything they say, without even hearing the other side (or THE TRUTH). The mainstream media imposes disinformation that it wants us to believe, and most of the time it's malicious propaganda and negative content. They then try to justify this negative content by telling us it's what the public wants to see, and they're merely supplying this "demand" (which in turn just so happens to give them high ratings). I can pretend that my dog really likes dog food too if that's all I give him; you can even watch him beg and do flips for it as well. However, if I put a bowl of filet mignon and a bowl of Kibbles and Bits side by side, I wonder which one he'll choose? The truth is that we have no choices, just the same stale dog food they've been feeding us the entire time.

"The news stations don't report the news-they make the news!" ~ The World is (y)ours

It's not only the media outlets; it's also television shows, movies, and even cartoons that display violence and promiscuous content. Content that networks and producers justify airing by saying this content is the harsh truth to this world's reality and that it simply reflects the society that we live in. What if it was the very opposite? What if this force-fed content that's purposely being embedded into our minds and into our children's minds, are the very things we are absorbing and *projecting* back into our society simply because this is what we have seen, believe, and accepted as our

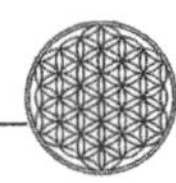

"consensus reality?" To discover the truth, we have to answer the following question in all earnestness. Is this content airing truly what the people want to see, or is this what *they* want the people to see?

"Television = Tell-Lie-Vision." A machine that tells lies to our vision!" ~ Laura Bruno

All of the aforementioned should at least prompt the question, "Why would they want to feed us constant negative content versus positive content?" By embedding negative content into our subconscious mind, this programs us to believe that the world in which we live in is chaotic and "dangerous". Therefore, we subconsciously maintain a fear-based internal belief system that allows our government to control us because we think the world is dangerous and that we need them to protect us. Think about it for a minute, how else is a small group of people going to control seven BILLION plus people? They need control over humanity's mind-not their bodies! If you capture the mind, the body will follow. They need us in fear so that we will always turn to them for aid. This is another example of how, and why the people continue to relinquish their freedom in exchange for a sense of "security".

"The government does not feed us, we feed the systems that feed the government" ~ THE WORLD IS (y)OURS!

The World's Best Security System

The world no longer remembers what real freedom is or what true freedom feels like. Instead of freedom, we seek security in life because the world is designed for us to choose security over freedom. In school, they program us to want security; in business and work, they encourage us to have security, and our government wants us to feel secure, not free. The more security society has, the more freedom we relinquish. We tend to confuse the two, when they are actually polar opposites.

When there are so-called terrorist attacks, what do we do? We externalize our power and turn to our government to save us; and in exchange for protection we give up our rights out of fear so we can feel secure. September 11th, 2001 (9/11) is just another example of how we relinquished more of our freedom and rights for this security/protection.

This Matrix of the world we live in locks us into these 'security systems' creating the illusion of freedom when in reality we are just being more closely monitored and controlled. Why do you think we put the world's most dangerous criminals in something they call a maximum "security" prison?

I recall a conversation with my mother and some of her colleagues (who were schoolteachers at the time). They were discussing their careers and I heard my mother say, "I have six years left", and her friend rebutted "I'm in for eight more", while another lady burst out in excitement followed by a quick handclap "I got two more years and I'm outta here!" They sounded like prison inmates going around the poker table during recess in the yard discussing how many years they had left in their "bid". I witnessed first hand how average middle-class citizens sacrifice so much of their freedom and happiness, just for this sense of so-called security.

The bottom line is that the people, places, words, images, and the energies that surround you the most are scientifically proven to affect your thoughts. You are a creator and your thoughts are your seeds of creation, so become aware of this power that you hold, because the forces that control the news and media content are more than well aware of this.

CHAPTER

13

HOW THEY REALLY PULLED IT OFF #GRIDLOCK

"*The general population doesn't know what's happening, and it doesn't even know that it doesn't know.*" ~ Noam Chomsky

The cult of secrecy is not the sole reason that the *Illuminati* have been able to control billions of people over the course of many years. They achieved this by utilizing the powers of the universe and its laws to their advantage. They suppress this vital information from the rest of humanity so it could never be used against them. With the power of thought, manifesting, attracting, and visualizing, the elite have collectively manipulated the universe's energy utilizing these laws to work in their favor. Remember, the universe cannot tell good from bad, bad from good, or right from wrong. It simply reacts to the vibrations and energy we collectively send out, while our freewill to deny or accept such cruel actions are what justify this.

This is why controlling the media and news-stations to feed the public their messages was so important. They found a way to control and manipulate the most powerful force all humans possess; not our eyes, not our minds, but our

EMOTIONS! By picking and choosing the content they want to air, what court cases they want us to follow, they found a way to sync the entire population's emotions based on the content they display to us. By controlling what we see, hear, and believe to be the truth, they were able to manipulate the most creative force known to mankind while overriding our freewill and forcibly initiating the law of attraction for us, without our conscious consent. Pretty slick! We just have to remember, they have the best minds, resources and technology that money can buy.

These elite had the patience and the willpower to carry out their plan, holding the same vision for more than two hundred years and channeling constant energy and action toward it. In short, they used our own powers of co-creation against us to create the world that they want, not the world that we would want. By manipulating the global consciousness grid to supercharge their manifestations, they have strengthened their systems of deceit and created a prison planet simply by using the laws of the universe to their advantage, unbeknownst to us. The name "Illuminati" actually stands for "enlightened ones". Although this group of elitists are far from what I would consider "enlightened", I would have to agree that they are a group of extremely spiritually educated individuals who possess some of the greatest secrets of this world. This is why humanity needs to spiritually awaken to these truths so they can *'get in the game'* and begin working smarter instead of harder!

To gain a greater understanding of how they are able to control our awareness and keep humanity from awakening, we must understand the power of "the grid". Before we probe into the power of the grid, we must first understand what this global *consciousness grid* is. Furthermore, we can only turn the tables and take over the grid once we hit "the hundredth monkey". This is where things start to get interesting!

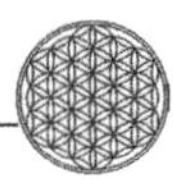

The 100th Monkey

The Human History Movie, part of a series by *Spirit Science*, does a great job of explaining our planetary grid and why it's vital that we know about it.

> *"A planetary grid is an etheric crystalline structure that envelops the planet and holds the consciousness of any one species of life. This grid does have an electro-magnetic component associated with the third dimension, but it also has a component for every dimension as well. These grids are geometric and science will soon discover that there is a grid for every species in the world. Each of these grids has its own unique geometry and there is not another one like it, just as the species themselves are unique. These grids give off light, and from space they can be seen as the source to the bluish green glow around the earth.*

In an earlier chapter I discussed global consciousness; what it is and how we all affect it, but I didn't explain the actual grid itself and how it monitors humanity's consciousness. In layman's terms, this grid is an invisible wireless-network database that encapsulates the entire planet. Strangely similar to Apple's i-cloud wireless-network software that stores every Apple user's apps, games, contacts, notes, calendars, e-mails, photos, videos, movies, and music (pretty much our entire life) into their database. Well, all of humanity's thoughts, emotions, revelations, and realizations are downloaded into this collective database within the global consciousness grid and stored as well.

In Dr. Michio Kaku's most recent book, The Future of the Mind, he mentions a study, which I quote below, that scientifically proves our thoughts can be recorded.

"In Los Angeles, scientists trained rats to perform a certain task. They tape-recorded the impulses in the hippocampus of the mind, of their brains, and then replayed these thoughts back into their brains, and sure enough they recall the task that they had learned. This is amazing; this is the first time in world history that scientists have been able to record a thought, a memory of something, play it back, and the mouse relearns the task."

To better explain how the collective of the global consciousness grid actually works, I will refer to the famous study of the hundredth-monkey effect from the original writings of Rupert Sheldrake, which you can read in the book excerpt here, The Hundredth Monkey, by Ken Keyes Jr.

"The Japanese monkey, Macaca Fuscata, had been observed in the wild for a period of over 30 years. In 1952, on the island of Koshima, scientists were providing monkeys with sweet potatoes dropped in the sand. The monkey liked the taste of the raw sweet potatoes, but they found the dirt unpleasant.

An 18-month-old female named Imo found she could solve the problem by washing the potatoes in a nearby stream. She taught this trick to her mother. Her playmates also learned this new way and they taught their mothers too.

This cultural innovation was gradually picked up by various monkeys before the eyes of the scientists. Between 1952 and 1958 all the young monkeys learned to wash the sandy sweet potatoes to make them more palatable. Only the adults who imitated their children learned this social improvement. The older and more stubborn adults, maybe of lesser consciousness, refused change and kept eating the dirty sweet potatoes. Then

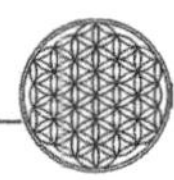

something startling took place. In the autumn of 1958, a certain number of Koshima monkeys were washing sweet potatoes—the exact number is not known. Let us suppose that when the sun rose one morning there were 99 monkeys on Koshima Island who had learned to wash their sweet potatoes. Let's further suppose that later that morning, "the hundredth monkey" learned to wash potatoes."

THEN IT HAPPENED!

"By that evening almost everyone in the tribe was washing sweet potatoes before eating them. The added energy of this hundredth monkey somehow created an ideological breakthrough!

But notice: The most surprising thing observed by these scientists was that the habit of washing sweet potatoes then jumped over the sea…Colonies of monkeys on other islands and the mainland troop of monkeys at Takasaki-yama began washing their sweet potatoes as well.

Thus, when a certain critical number achieves awareness, this new awareness may be communicated from mind to mind.

Although the exact number may vary, this Hundredth Monkey Phenomenon means that when only a limited number of people know of a new way, it may remain the conscious property of those people.

But there is a point at which if only one more person tunes-in to a new awareness, a field is strengthened so that this awareness is picked up by almost everyone!"

The scientists discovered that the monkeys seemed to be telepathically and unconsciously communicating in a way that affected the consciousness of other monkeys in geographically separated regions. The scientists became even more intrigued when the number of monkeys sharing the awareness affected the consciousness of that entire monkey species, which was located over several different islands. Since the scientist knew that these monkeys weren't 'tweeting' their new potato-washing method, the scientists needed to make sure this was no fluke. So their next experiment was to see if this would work on humans! If successful, this would reinforce the greatest human discovery in Bells' theorem that we are all one, and we are all connected.

> *"A research team made a picture out of human faces, about one hundred faces hidden within a single picture. But at first glance, you could only see about six or seven faces. They did several surveys with a few hundred people in Australia and said, "Alright, find the faces!" Most people could only pick out six, seven, eight, nine, or so, not many more. After that, the research team went to Britain and aired the picture on a closed cable BBC special that was shown only in England. They showed where all of the faces were, every last one. Then half of the research team, which stayed in Australia, did the study again with new subjects, and lo and behold, people were just naturally able to see more faces. After this experiment, they knew there was something that definitely connects us all, which the field of noetics is learning more about daily: it's mass consciousness…*
>
> *The consciousness grid is based on squares and triangles. Many governments around the world, especially the Russian and U.S governments were studying our grids back in the '60s, and probably earlier. When mapping out the grid on the planet, you'll find many little military bases on many of the notable points of the grid. There are tons of these bases way out in the middle of nowhere, like on the island of Guam. This couldn't be a coincidence that these government powers placed their military bases right*

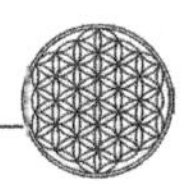

where the little spirals came out of the grid. They were trying to take control of the grid, because if you take control of the grid, you take control of human consciousness, and you control what we think and feel!"

~ The Human History Movie; Spirit Science

Aha! So this is how they have kept humanity in such a docile, sleeping state, accepting "the norm" for so long. How was humanity ever to try and reclaim Earth's human consciousness grid if we didn't know it was even taken from us in the first place? Or maybe you're reading this right now saying "This is crazy, there's no way this could be true", all while this very technology is being used against you at this very moment and is precisely the reason why your consciousness doesn't want to conceive that this could be possible in the first place. Pretty clever, isn't it? This is yet another reason the elite powers have been so successful in their ability to carry out such devious plans to enslave and control the population. But this is all about to change!

How to Reclaim "The Grid"

The scientific model says it only takes a small percentage of a population to affect patterns of changing consciousness. Recently, this theory even made it to the mainstream through an article posted on *NBCNews.com* that stated "*To change the beliefs of an entire community, only 10 percent of the population needs to become convinced of a new or different opinion, suggests a new study done at the Social Cognitive Networks Academic Research Center (SCNARC) at Rensselaer Polytechnic Institute. At that tipping point, the idea can spread through social networks and alter behaviors on a large scale.*"

"*With each person who awakens, the momentum in the collective consciousness grows, and it becomes easier for others.*" ~ Eckhart Tolle

If approximately 3-10 percent of the world's population can *awaken*, then we will be able to raise the global consciousness of humanity in order to reclaim our grid. This will trigger what I refer to as "The Event" and activate "The Plan", so that humanity can make "The Shift" and evolve into the true essence of our beings.

Soon all of the information provided in this book will have spread to the sufficient number of people required to spark the grid. With a critical mass needed, somewhere, someone will become that "hundredth monkey" that will trigger the awakening of the masses across the world! This person could very much be you by the time you finish this book.

"*I'm not saying I'm going to change the world, but I guarantee that I will spark the brain that will change the world.*"
~ Tupac Shakur

We are currently losing this information war because we don't even know that we're in one in the first place. We must first identify the problems at hand before we can do anything about them. All of their strategic plans and control mechanisms must be exposed so that their stealthy tactics can't be used ever again. Along with hijacking our consciousness grid, they have been force-feeding us disinformation that complements measures to control us and confuse us, in order to keep us asleep and from discovering these truths.

From the telephone poles in the ground, to the electrical lines that "grid" our cities, to the manmade clouds seeded in our sky, they are all multi-faceted technologies and strategies being used to prevent us from awakening; including other scalar weapon technologies that are being used against us right now that our consciousness can't even fathom. These technologies are so far advanced, it would make NASA's latest press release look like a *Toys R Us* flyer.

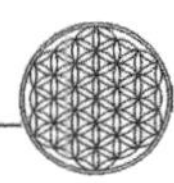

What in the World is Cloud Seeding?

This is the very reason you see those elongated clouds in the sky that have been strategically placed in our atmosphere. If you're not familiar with the term Geo-Engineering or Chemtrails, they are the stream of what seems to be white smoke or contrails coming out of the back of random airplanes. Yes, there are regular planes in the sky that leave "contrails" behind. But contrails dissipate in a matter of seconds and their tail, or streak, isn't very long. Chemtrails on the other hand, crisscross and leave "grid like" checkerboard patterns in the daytime sky. Why is this?

Well, it's exactly how it looks, they are creating an additional GRID around the planet by spraying toxic chemicals in our atmosphere that affect everyone; chemicals containing barium, aluminum, and other extremely hazardous elements to our planet and our bodies. These man-made clouds even have a term known as cloud seeding and were used as weather weapons in Vietnam in conjunction with a technology known as HAARP (High Frequency Active Auroral Research Program).

Our government's rebuttal on the allegations of these so-called chemtrails is for our protection against "global warming". However, they are not trying to prevent "global warming", they are trying to prevent something much greater and much more powerful; something I look forward to diving into in these upcoming chapters.

In addition to spraying these toxic chemicals in the air that block our sun's rays, these man-made clouds are blocking vital cosmic energies and LIGHT from hitting the surface of our planet, while reinforcing the grid and strengthening "The Veil". All of which might not make much sense for you at this moment, but it soon will!

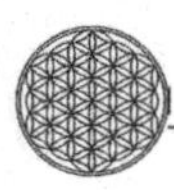

Lifting the Veil

"*Human beings are under the control of a strange force that bends them in absurd ways, forcing them to play a role in a bizarre game of deception.*" ~ Dr. Jacques Vallee

Earth is quarantined by advanced technology that constrains humanity from higher levels of consciousness, vibrations and frequencies that consequently limit the amount of energy that can enter our planet from the cosmos. What in the world does this mean? It means there is an electromagnetic field below and above the Earth's surface that stretches around the planet's circumference. In the world of metaphysics, this electromagnetic field is referred to as "the veil" that limits humanity's consciousness and is responsible for our feeling of separation instead of oneness. This veil is similar to an electric fence; a gigantic high-tech magnetic fence created with the sole purpose of distorting the space-time continuum here on Earth. This fence ultimately disconnects humanity from the source of higher levels of consciousness including our connection to one another. It's also the cause of humanity's chronic case of "amnesia", and is why every one of us has no clue where we actually came from or why we are even here. This is the same reason why there are so many different opinions/beliefs/religions of what, where, and who God is. These immediate beliefs that we adopt are usually contingent upon our geographical location and/or our parent's choice of religion at the time we are born, not necessarily the truth.

Currently, our dualistic thinking and ego is what makes us believe we are superior to one another. If this veil didn't exist, humanity would feel much more connected and able to experience the feeling of oneness previously discussed. Astronauts traveling into space that break past this electromagnetic field have reported profound spiritual experiences of connectivity and awakening. These intense

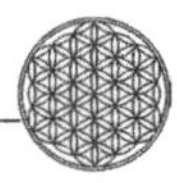

spiritual awakenings experienced by these astronauts even have their own phrase known as "The Cosmic Consciousness Phenomena/The Overview Effect"; a 'timeless' feeling of pure bliss and oneness that they've all reported.

Without this veil in place, humans would be able to absorb more energy and feel better connected to one another, without having to become an astronaut. If the veil were to dissolve today, everyone would noticeably feel this change and shift in energy; time as we know it, the ego, and duality would perpetually diminish as humanity's consciousness rose higher than ever.

However, this will only become a reality once the world reaches a critical mass of awareness through the collective consciousness. This is the only way we can dissolve the veil that entraps us in these lower vibrations. This is why you needed to know all the powers that you possess that were mentioned in earlier chapters. Lets really think about this; without these grids and veils in place that keep us "plugged into" the matrix, why else would we be perfectly fine with accepting the fact we're being robbed by bankers, bullied and spied on by corrupt politicians, ruled by corporate America, and improperly drugged by pharmaceutical companies? It's only when you fully awaken and unplug from the Matrix that you are able to see how crazy all this is, and actually care. However, some of us have cataracts and don't want to be unplugged because we fear the future, while others are more near-sighted and fail to see the bigger picture.

If someone were to break into your home and poison your food, drug your children, and steal money out of your pocketbook, you would do something about it, right? So we must ask ourselves "Why is it when our government does this to the world do we just accept this as "the norm? Yet we continue to be mad at the wrong people, care about the wrong situations, believe the wrong information, and react to all the wrong things. I know this all might sound a little hard to swallow, but the fact of the matter is that this is (y)our current reality.

In order to bring in the new paradigm, we must first dissolve the old paradigm. We do this by simply believing that there is more to life, and a better way of living. Just as our technology, computers, phones, and houses get updated and upgraded, we too must upgrade our consciousness and our quality of living. However, our economy continues to enslave us through our reliance on its systems (e.g. money and energy). These are the oldest systems best serving the people who made them, not the people who use them. It's time that we stop being bullied and upgrade our way of living, downgrade our government, and stop accepting our meager portion of a lopsided deal.

We're All Buzzed and We Don't Know It

Most of us don't realize that these grids and veils exist and that our minds and consciousness are being controlled. Nor are we supposed to know because it's specifically designed for us not to be aware of its stealthy presence. Compare this feeling of being fully conscious yet still not knowing the obvious effects of our actions, to one's consumption of alcoholic beverages.

I'm sure we've all had a friend, or two, who consumed a little too much to drink one night. When this friend was confronted about their level of intoxication and the fact that maybe they shouldn't be driving or drinking anymore, what was their immediate response? Nine times out of ten it was "I'm good! I'm not even drunk", or "Don't worry about me, I'm perfectly fine", when clearly they are slurring their words and stumbling to the restroom. But besides the fact that they are drunk, why do they feel and think this way? Well for one, it's because they really think that they are perfectly fine. What

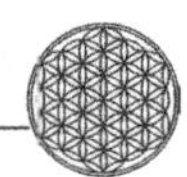

we must understand is that the main side effect of the consumption of alcohol is that it alters our perception and impairs our judgment.

So regardless of our intellectual comprehension of life, everything we say or do while intoxicated is coming from a standpoint of self-inflicting deception. Which is the exact reason why we think we're not drunk when we clearly are; why we make poor choices and decisions while we are drunk, why we sleep with that person we normally wouldn't even talk to, and why in some cases we actually think we can drive better than when we're sober. To a sober person this all looks and sounds ridiculous, but to the individual who has consumed one too many drinks, they are completely under the illusion that there is nothing wrong with them. This is simply because, well, they are UNDER THE INFLUENCE!

Being under the veil of the matrix is no different than being under the influence of alcohol. This is why we aren't aware of either its presence nor its power, because this is exactly its sole purpose and main side effect: to alter our perception of life, impair our judgment, and create separation from reality, all while making us think everything is perfectly fine and there's nothing wrong with us or the world in which we live.

This concept is very hard for the average person to grasp, never-mind the people with strong egos. However, no matter how smart or ignorant you are, there is no escaping the veils of the matrix. There is one thing, and one thing only that possesses the power to dissolve the matrix around you... THE TRUTH. The matrix's kryptonite is Absolute Truth, and your ability to accept these truths into your consciousness is what will restore your gifts and help the rest of humanity reclaim theirs. The power of these truths will then dissolve all the false limitations and doubts that have plagued you for all of your years on earth.

How to Sober Up

The Matrix can be broken for each individual, but the veil must be dissolved as a collective. Remember, the matrix is simply a system of many, but mainly a system of restraints, limits, rules, and beliefs; limits that can be broken, rules that can be bent, beliefs that can be changed, and restraints that can be eliminated! The quarantined earth created by the matrix is no different than a governor chip in an automobile. For those not familiar, a governor chip is a small microcomputer chip that's placed in just about every motor vehicle on the road today. They limit and control what the vehicle can or cannot do. They limit the fuel intake, gas mileage, MPH (miles per hour), and pretty much every major electrical performance component on the vehicle having to do with its functionality.

Just as every vehicle on the road has this chip in it; every single human walking this earth has a chip in them as well. An etheric chip affecting their belief system telling them what they're capable or incapable of doing on life's highway. A chip that has the power to run your life, but a chip that can be overridden and dismantled forever if you know how!

How to Override the Matrix Chip (Jailbreak)

In the 1940's, scientists stated that trying to run a mile in less than four minutes was impossible! Over hundreds of years, thousands of Olympians and athletes attempted this goal and failed. Experts stated that the human body reached its physical limit/capacity and that a four-minute mile wasn't humanly possible.

There was a man by the name of Roger Bannister who was determined to not only prove himself right, but to prove the world wrong. Bannister didn't just physically train like all the other athletes; he trained himself mentally. Ban-

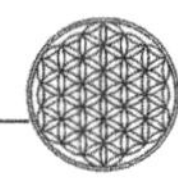

nister relentlessly trained using the power of thought, imagination, visualization, and the law of attraction. He even went to the extreme of celebrating the accomplishment of achieving this goal with his friends and family members. Then on May 6, 1954, Roger Bannister broke the four-minute barrier, running the distance in 3:59.4!

Here's where it gets interesting. After Bannister broke the record that stood for centuries, it was only a month later when another runner broke the four-minute mile mark. Followed by five more runners just twelve months after. Then, a total of 22 runners broke the four-minute mark over the next four years. Roger Bannister made the impossible possible in the consciousness of runners around the world by dissolving the mental programing that limited the human body from unlocking these abilities. Bannister was able to bypass the physical restrictions within humanity's collective consciousness and override his "governor chip", thus making the impossible possible for the rest of the world's runners to achieve. Today, the four-minute mile is the "qualifying" speed in the Olympics.

"Nothing is impossible, the word itself says 'I'm possible'!"
~ Audrey Hepburn

When you hear the story about the seventy plus year old lady that saw her grandson trapped under a two-ton car and lifted it up to rescue him, then you've just heard the testimony of someone who has overridden their governor chip and broken the constructs of the matrix. You may still be asking yourself, "Well, how in the world is that possible?" This is just one of many examples of how this human governor chip (the matrix) can be overridden. The elderly lady was able to lift the car because there was NO DOUBT or limitations that poisoned her mind telling her that she couldn't do it. She just did it because she knew she had to and that failure was not an option.

Our subconscious belief system and that little voice in our head derived from ego, is what prevents us from achieving the EXTRAordinary. The only reason we can't do something in this world is because we believe that we can't. As Henry Ford famously said, "*Those who think they can, and those who think they can't, are both right*!" Keep in mind that there's a difference between intending, and pretending to intend. Meaning, if all day you keep telling yourself "I can lift my car, I can lift my car", then you go outside and try to lift your car, but fail, this is because you truly did not believe you could do this with 110% complete and total conviction. Doubt was still present within the subconscious and the unconscious part of the mind; it is only when you can overpower all three aspects of the human mind (conscious, subconscious, and unconscious) that you are able to break the constructs of the matrix and achieve the impossible! For most, this only occurs when one is presented with a life or death situation.

"Everything's impossible, until somebody does it."

~ Bruce Wayne

The matrix and the dogma of this world subconsciously convince us that we are inadequate and powerless beings who are never truly in control. For far too long we have had the wool pulled over our eyes with pertinent knowledge and truths being kept from us that have the ability to break this pragmatic thinking and dissolve the matrix completely. This suppression of knowledge is similar to the days of slavery when blacks weren't allowed to have books so they couldn't read and educate themselves. This was a preventative measure to stop them from discovering how equally powerful they really were. The same tactics are true today. We are trapped in this forged illusion between our outer space and our inner space; a limited reality that continuously restricts us from discovering our extraordinary potential, the same way African Americans were suppressed from their abilities during slavery.

CHAPTER

14

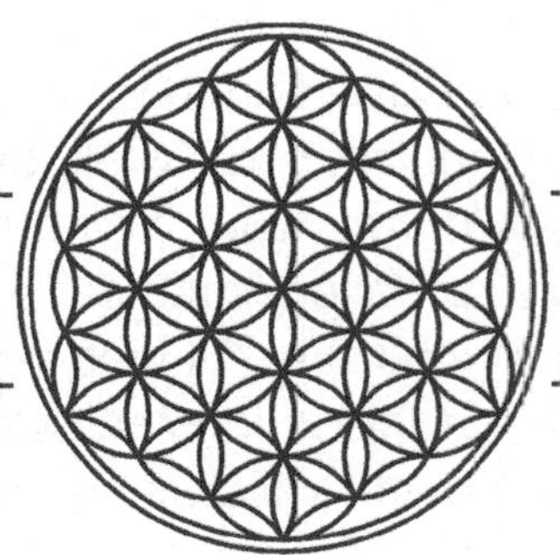

SO ARE YOU TELLING *ME* I'M A SLAVE?

"*Free people don't beg for rights.*" ~ Unknown

Do you really believe slavery was completely abolished or was it just reinvented in a clever way that we would fail to notice? "America-Land of the Free" is just a catchy marketing slogan that sounds friendly and inviting. Unfortunately, there is no land of the free on planet Earth right now; we are only experiencing the result of the best marketing campaign that money can buy. In all actuality, America has more of a stronghold on its citizens than anywhere else in the world, just Google the "NDAA Act" and you can look at just one reason why. These nifty marketing slogans are no different than the early 1900's Camel cigarette commercials when they had actual doctors advocating/promoting their new advertising catch phrase "Smoke as many as you want. They never get on your nerves." Soon we too will realize the irony behind America's illustrious marketing slogan as well.

"None are more hopelessly enslaved than those who falsely believe they are free." ~Johann Wolfgang von Goethe

Similar to slaves, humanity does not know their true power. If we did, we would not allow the world to be the way it is today. I had someone jokingly, yet half-serious, ask me once, “If this is all true, why haven’t they just taken us all out sooner, like during the Bush administration or something?” I laughed at their joke and replied, “Well, every criminal knows that they can’t get what they want if all they have is dead hostages; and every so-called “master” knows that dead slaves aren’t worth much, right?” I was being a bit too candid and brutally honest, but this is the reality of the elite’s plan, to keep humanity enslaved while using our human energy as mere “batteries” to power their profiting systems while advancing their global political agenda.

The harsh realization of this reality is knowing the moment you wake up and flick on your bathroom light you are contributing to these slavery systems. The moment you pull up to the gas station and pump gas into your car you are solidifying your enslavement, and the moment you pay your car or property tax you are funding your own enslavement. Why is this you may ask? Because paying unnecessary taxes and energy bills derived from the monopolization of so-called “natural resources” is corporate/government extortion. Especially when omissions of various alternative sources and more efficient means of FREE ENERGY are available for everyone.

For instance, in 1902, Nikola Tesla was working on a top-secret venture to create “wireless electricity”. When Tesla completed this project, he demonstrated the workings of his invention to the government and they were quite impressed with his discovery. When Tesla was allegedly asked, “So where is the meter?” Tesla proudly replied, “There is no meter, this is FREE ENERGY”. Eyes wide open; the government immediately confiscated Tesla’s plans and shut down his research indefinitely.

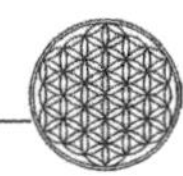

In 1954, the hydrogen engine (an engine that runs on pure water) was created and installed into an automobile and was ready for demonstration. The vehicle was brought to the Indianapolis 500, where it did a 110-lap presentation for a group of elitists, politicians, and investors. After witnessing such a fascinating display of pure innovation, it is said that Gulf Motor Oil was the company who wanted to heavily invest in this invention. After the paperwork was signed, the blueprints for the hydrogen engine were destroyed and the engine was never spoken of again.

In later years, a gentleman named Stanley Meyers created another water fueled car using slightly different "Water Fuel Cell Technology". Once again, the government, and multiple investors flocked to him. Then on March 20th 1998, Stanley Meyers was poisoned to death. His brother claimed that during a meeting with two Belgian investors, Meyer suddenly ran outside the restaurant saying, "They poisoned me!" right before he passed away.

This type of technology already exists and is waiting for us to demand its presence. The harsh truth of this world is that there's a new type of slavery upon us all: slavery of debt, obsolete energy/resources, and slavery to the corrupt and biased systems that work only to keep the masses under control and the elite wealthy. Small groups of so-called elitists have made a mockery out of humanity and don't even care to hide it anymore.

Take out your pocket change for a quick example. In this order (from left to right), line up a quarter, a dime, a nickel, and a penny all facing head side up. Does anything stand out to you besides the penny being the only colored coin? Notice the direction that each head faces. Do you see how President Lincoln's face is the only head facing in the opposite direction? Could this be just a random manufacturing oversight from our government? Or could it be because Abraham Lincoln was the only president who decided to free

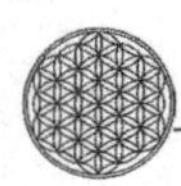

the blacks and abolish slavery? Could this be the reason they "turned their backs" on him because they felt he turned his back on them? Could Lincoln be the only "colored" coin in our entire U.S currency because he's the one that stood up for the slaves, so they decided to make him one of them by putting him on the only brown coin? Is it also just a coincidence that this coin happens to be the most devalued coin we own? Or is this all just a big conspiracy theory like President Lincoln and President Kennedy's assassination?

"There's a plot in this country to enslave every man, woman, and child. Before I leave this high and noble office, I intend to expose this plot." ~ President John F. Kennedy (7 days before his assassination)

U.S President Kennedy boldly warned us of this evil plot to enslave our race, yet for some reason-no one listened. Although Abraham Lincoln accomplished a quantum leap towards humanity's liberation, slavery itself was never abolished, just reinvented in clever new ways. Such clever ways that humanity doesn't even know whom their new master is, or how their minds and beliefs are imprisoned by the very "systems" that control this world. The irony is that our programmed mind and 'governed' consciousness is the very thing that's being manipulated. Therefore, this double-edged sword is also a catch-22 that not only prevents us from coming to such a revelation, but has us programed to immediately dismiss and/or ridicule anyone who makes such an outrageous accusation.

"The search for truth and knowledge is one of the finest attributes of man- though often it is most loudly voiced by those who strive for it the least." ~ Albert Einstein

For the majority of humanity, most won't even know that they are slaves—until they are freed. Or will they? The famous Greek philosopher Plato explained this best in his allegory of the cave.

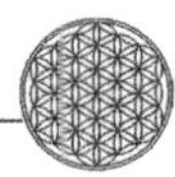

Are We Still Slaves or Cavemen and Don't Know It?

"I freed a thousand slaves. I could have freed a thousand more if only they knew they were slaves." ~ Harriet Tubman

Plato knew that human beings are naturally resistant to change. He knew that human beings were so reliant on the existing conditions and the ethics of society, that it would be hard for them to break free from their current paradigm. He knew that human beings eventually become complacent living a known, superficial life, even if deep down they feel that the status quo is not in accordance to their beliefs.

Plato's Allegory of the Cave is the story of human prisoners chained inside a cave, who are unaware of any reality of the outside world. With no knowledge of a reality other than their cave, they remain content walking along a known paved path questioning little to nothing. They have no desire to live a meaningful life or to seek truth, because it has never occurred to them that another reality exists beyond what they can see.

This continues for generations until one day, one prisoner decides to question this existence and breaks free from his chains. He escapes the cave and begins to explore the "strange" new reality of the outside world, which is the real world. Yet, when he returns to the cave to share his experience with the others, he is met with disbelief and treated as a liar and an outsider.

"The further a society drifts from the truth, the more it will hate those that speak it." ~ George Orwell

Plato's Allegory of the Cave is extremely relevant to our present day. Most human beings are either content with or dependent upon the current circumstances within their society. People tend to adopt whatever is handed down to them by their predecessors. However, if there were more awakened souls amongst us awakening other souls, the status quo would not be accepted as it is today. Humanity would be freed from its shackles, mental bondage, and prefabricated illusion of reality. We would crawl out from the dark and follow the light, and finally see the world as it truly is, not what's only being shown to us.

This might just seem like an ancient analogy I'm referring to, but this is the reality to how humans react. You can go on YouTube and see footage capturing the end of World War II when U.S soldiers went to concentration camps to free the prisoners. They opened the cells that contained these hostages and none of the prisoners would come out. The prisoners were accustomed to such horrible conditions of enslavement, that the reality of freedom became so far-fetched; they retreated back into their cells when freedom finally came to liberate them.

Plato's analogy is parallel to us living in a dark cave our entire lives and knowing no other reality. This is what makes it quite difficult for someone to convince us there's an entirely new world for us to discover, if we just care to take a look. This is why we tend to ridicule things out of ignorance without even doing our own research to see for ourselves. This conditioning is what makes it difficult for someone to convince us there's a beautiful new world out there when all we have known is darkness and deception. It's hard to convince someone their entire life has been based upon a foundation of highly strategized lies. This is why we must experience the truth for ourselves rather than have it told to us. Deep down, we must first realize that we are prisoners to well-oiled and manufactured systems. Then, we must raise our consciousness and break these shackles so that we can seek the truth, and share this truth, as the prisoner in Plato's allegorical cave did.

Once the critical mass of humanity awakens and

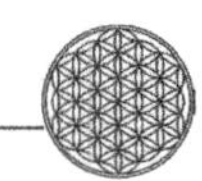

these current systems of enslavement are exposed, humanity will collectively reclaim its sovereignty and put an end to the deception. However, as Plato exemplified in his allegorical cave, awakening the others is no easy task. No matter how obvious things may seem, or how excited one may be to share great information, there will be some implications that may arise.

Awakening The Others

"You can lead a man to knowledge, but you can't make him think." ~ Unknown

It is the importance of this critical mass previously mentioned that I wish to emphasize to you now. Since we aren't quite sure how many are already awakened or need to be awakened, it is essential that we share this information and help spread the awareness in order to reach this goal. You don't have to call out of work and go picketing on the front lawn of the White House; start by researching as much as you can and talking to the people closest to you. If you don't feel comfortable reiterating this information then you must recommend this book to your close friends and family members or at the very least let them borrow this copy so they can read and discern these truths for themselves. By doing this you will at least feel confident that you tried your best to awaken the people you care about the most (if all else fails). If you do choose to assume the much needed leadership position of awakening others, kudos to you, but there are a few things you must know beforehand.

"*True leaders don't create followers, they create more leaders.*" ~ Unknown

Although the mental programing for teenagers and young adults (via music and television) has been much more potent than previous generations, you will notice that the older the person that you are trying to awaken (40+), the harder it may be. This is due to the amount of mental conditioning and mind programming they've undergone over the years. It's quite hard for them, or anyone in this sense, to accept the fact that their entire life has been based on a slough of lies, so you must not only be conscious of this, but also gentle and considerate. Keep in mind that the portion of humanity that is still sleeping is not at fault. This could be your mom, your uncle, your aunt, your spouse, your cousin, your teacher, or your boss. Remember, this was you at one point, and this was myself at some point as well. You also have to remember what everyone is up against. These small groups of people who are running the world have the best minds including all the resources and exotic technology that money can buy. So quite frankly, if you were to think about it, the job of awakening people is probably the hardest job on the planet! With that said, if you can awaken just one or two people who are close to you, then congratulations! You just went up against a billion dollar a day operation, hacked the matrix, and won the hardest game ever played!

"Don't be in such a hurry to condemn a person because he doesn't do what you do, or think as you think. There was a time when you didn't know what you know today."

~ Malcolm X

You will notice that trying to awaken someone who isn't ready will be like showing them all the answers to the exercises in the previous chapters (e.g. man's liar face, bird in the bush, etc.), but they still can't see it. This feeling of "how can they not see this when it's right in front of them?" is the same feeling you will have when you can't get someone to awaken to the reality of this world. So be sure not to get frustrated when you find your friends and loved ones not awakening as fast as you want them to.

One thing you must realize as you start to awaken

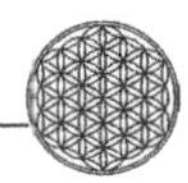

others to their powers is that it's impossible to awaken some-one with only one conversation. Even though you are trying to help them and pull them away from a mountain of deceit, they will still cling to this mountain cliff for dear life. And if you try to rip them off they will just hold on tighter. You must slowly pry one finger off at a time until they realize the drop they feared their entire life was only but a few feet from the ground. You must learn to let their consciousness absorb small doses of this information and digest it until they're ready for more. Treat them as infants, you must spoon feed them slowly. If you try to force feed them, they will only spit it back in your face and never want to eat it again.

This process is similar to how baby chickens are born. The baby chick needs to break through its shell on its own in order to develop the proper muscle strength for its survival. As much as we want to help, and as much as we see them struggling, if we try to help break their shell for them, the chick won't develop properly and will most likely die within the first week of birth. Meaning, we cannot expedite any-one's awakening process; this is a natural process that must happen on its own and at their own pace. All we can do is assist them with resources of information, plant seeds, and be there when those seeds blossom into questions. Never jam anything down anyone's throat. When all else fails, just restructure the points you are trying to make in the form of a question, instead of a statement. Try it! All you have to do is get them to think, they will get curious on their own.

You must also understand that some people just don't want to wake up yet and get ready for school. We all know it's far easier to go back to bed than to wake up in the morn-ing and go to work. Some people aren't ready to unplug from the Matrix just yet. These people don't even know that they are dependent upon these systems, and you will find them desperately fighting to protect the very systems that are enslaving them. When Plato's truth seeker tried to show the prisoners the way to freedom, not only did they say no, they scorned and ridiculed him while defending their illusion. Just like Plato's truth seeker, you too will notice that some people just won't be able to see the truth. They will not only do or say anything to remain asleep and plugged in, their doubts and lack of truth will do everything to convince you that you're crazy in their unconscious attempt to try and plug you back in! But you mustn't let them!

Fighting the Truth

Do you remember when you first found out Santa Claus wasn't real? Your first reaction might have been that the person telling you this was a lying fool. You probably didn't want to believe them, and were in denial, so you tried to hold on to your beliefs for as long as you possibly could. Then eventually when your close friends and classmates awakened to this fabricated fairytale for themselves, you finally decided to accept this as your truth.

"*As our consciousness raises, our truth changes.*"

~ The World is (y)ours

We've all seen where the fat lady singing in the Opera hits the high note and all the glass in the building shatters. This is because high sound vibrations can cause certain glass to crack and break into pieces. Depending on the size, shape, and resonant frequency of a leaded crystal wine-glass, high sound vibrations can cause the glass to bend and stretch—in a way, trying its hardest to hold on to its old form—before it eventually can't hold its form any longer and these high sound vibrations cause it to shatter. Similarly, humans try to stretch and hold on for dear life to the reality that they know best, even if it's based on lies. The truth always holds a higher vibration (literally), which is why you've always heard the phrase "The truth shall set you free." We must learn to "let go" and allow the higher vibrations of truth

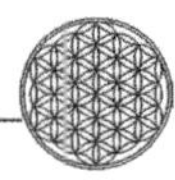

to break us free of old beliefs that don't serve our highest and greatest good any longer.

How to Break The Shackles

If you want to break the shackles that bind you, you must first accept these truths into your consciousness as your reality. I must continue to emphasize that we're playing a game in which we do not know the rules. You see, the other team has the playbook and they know all the rules to the game that we play. So when I present you with some of the many rules to this game, it's only because they are the cardinal rules that we must know. One of which is...*never give up your power!*

Since childhood we've been forced to verbally surrender our sovereign freewill every morning, five days out of the week, and 12 years of our life. Every morning in school we announced an *affirmation* out loud that pledged our loyalty and allegiance to a specific flag; a flag owned by the very people enslaving us.

The full definition of allegiance in Merriam-Webster's dictionary is defined as "the obligation of a feudal vassal to his liege lord". The definition of *Pledge* is "a binding promise or agreement", "The state of being held as a security or guarantee". Pledging an allegiance affirmation is considered a sacred vow in the playbook. The most devastating repercussions of pledging our allegiance to a flag, a country, or a nation that's "under God", is that we automatically accept all the foul rules that our politicians have created for this one "indivisible nation". We automatically give up our sovereign freewill when we inadvertently agree to all of their malicious plans they've created to control us. Which is why you must reverse this right now by stating the following affirmation, "I NOW RECLAIM MY SOVEREIGN FREEWILL" three times out loud.

This is just another example of the sneaky and sly ways these elite groups have been able to manipulate the laws of the universe against us and use these rules to override our freewill without us knowing. This is yet another tactic used to divide us and make us think we are separate. By having us send out these affirmations to the universe every morning and surrender our loyalty to a specific country, we unconsciously create "borders" in our mind that separate us from the rest of the world merely according to our residence and race.

"*Race, religion, ethnic pride and nationalism, etc. does nothing but teach you how to hate people you've never met.*"

~ Doug Stanhope

The more pride one has for a country or a flag, the easier it is to justify wars with other nations. The easier it is to use propaganda to control the people so they turn on one another. These divisions and created borders are the sole reason why so many neighboring countries dislike each other. Why Americans make fun of Canadians, why Dominicans and Puerto Ricans rival each other, why Pakistan and India despise one another, why Cape Verdeans don't like to be mistaken as African or Portuguese, why the French dislike the Germans, the Chinese dislike the Koreans, and the list goes on... If everyone displayed this same type of loyalty to humanity or planet earth, the world would be an entirely different place right now.

Now, someone who doesn't understand the power of their words, affirmations, or the universe's ability to communicate with us through affirmations, might read this and feel that I am unpatriotic or disloyal to my country; and they would have a decent argument. However, my loyalty is with no country, no nation, or no man. My loyalty lies with our Creator, Planet Earth, and humanity as a collective. Where my loyalty stands today is where my loyalty will stand for eternity, not where I was born in this lifetime.

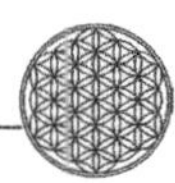

"*I have no country to fight for; my country is the earth. I am a citizen of the world.*" ~ Eugene Debs

But there is still an unfair game being played, and if you wish to play your part in this planetary shift, then you must read the playbook now and get back in the game!

Playing the Game

"Millionaires don't use astrology; billionaires do!"
~ J.P Morgan

We are all playing a tiring game, yet an extremely significant one. Our bodies are equipped with the most advanced technology in the world, and the universe is the most sophisticated intelligence we know of, and both are here to assist us. We have been given the most powerful tools known to man, but purposely haven't been told how to use them. It's like giving an iPhone to a caveman with no instructions or training. They're not going to know how to use it, and will most likely misuse it and do all the wrong things with it. Although there are many pertinent truths embedded in various religious scriptures, the real instruction manuals have either been destroyed or hidden from us. It was the utmost importance to constantly come up with clever ways to distract humanity so that we never discover the real game that's being played, or how to play it. It was critical to the people in power that we never figure HOW to utilize our gifts and use the forces of the universe to work in our favor.

The hard truth is that you're playing a game that you were never taught how to properly play. A game that you do not know the rules to, but your opponent does. You're a good person, a good player, hustling your butt off every day and you're never late for practice. On game days you're playing full court press, sprinting up and down the court, dribbling, crossing-over, and outperforming your opponent on every play. The only problem is that you and your teammates are shooting in the other person's hoop, scoring points for the other team, and we can't seem to understand why we're losing the game. No one is telling us how to play; they're just enjoying their courtside seats watching us look like fools. This is assuming that we're even aware that we are playing a game to win or lose in the first place.

We must know that this is no ordinary game; this is the most important game of your life with everything you could ever imagine (and more) on the line. Earth's previous generation was playing the playoffs for us so we can make it to where our generation is today; which is the Universe's Super Bowl of cosmic events being played right here in the Planet Earth Arena! This once in a lifetime event will be fully disclosed in the very next chapter because there is no more time to waste, you must know the game you play and know the rules to play it.

Training For The Cosmic Super Bowl

"*Isn't it funny how day by day nothing changes but when you look back, everything is different.*" ~ C. S. Lewis

Before we discuss the details of this long awaited Cosmic Super Bowl event, we must first begin your training by discussing change in and of itself in order to prepare the psyche. The truth is, that most people resist change. No one actually enjoys the process of change, because change means doing something different than the norm, and we're simply accustomed to the norm. The norm is comfortable for us, while change is a hassle, because change means learning how to do something all over again. If it isn't broke, don't fix it, right? The obvious problem is, most don't know or don't care about humanity's broken society and what's really going on in the world. Many people ask for "change" then complain when change never happens. There's a difference between

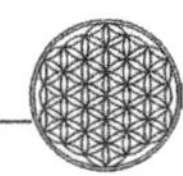

wanting change, and demanding change! Our time has run out wanting and wishing for change to occur in the hopes of another man's hands, it's time we now take command and demand for this change, once and for all!

Dealing with change isn't easy, but change is necessary and healthy. Old ways must die and new ways must be birthed. We must start digesting and discerning these truths now, so that when the inevitable and wonderful changes become obvious, they won't seem so shocking, and the transition will be much easier for all of us.

Change is gradual, yet it happens right before our eyes. It's like waiting for your child to take their first steps. Then what seems to be in the blink of an eye, they're enrolled in dance class or in Little League softball. We tend not to see things coming, but it's much more noticeable after we see them pass. In the same way, our planet and humanity are changing right before our eyes and we're not even realizing it.

We may think that some things are permanent or will never change, but they always do! Look at the millions of people who get married or get tattoos in their young adult years. Whenever they decide to make such a commitment, at that time they know it will be for the rest of their lives, and they accept this reality. But this doesn't end up being the case when they decide to get a divorce or a laser tattoo removal.

I recall having a conversation with a group of friends around 2006 about the probability of our country electing a president with a different ethnic background than what we've previously experienced. This conversation soon turned into a debate as we discussed whether we would ever elect an African America or Latino President in our lifetime. For the majority in the room the answer was "No way, Jose." Clearly, we were proven wrong. This just goes to show that change indeed happens right before our very eyes! What we may think seemingly impossible, against the odds, or unimaginable can very well become our reality, and a lot sooner than we think!

What we thought would be the way of our existence forever is about to transform. For most, this will come as a huge culture shock. But this change has been long needed, and is long overdue. The interesting thing is, as crazy as you might have found any of the content in this book, the positive change that awaits us is far more mind-bending than anything you have read thus far. The new world that is emerging is so amazingly beyond belief that my only concern is that you might not believe me if I tell you! But here it goes...

The Moment You Have Been Waiting For...

What if I said that YOU and this very planet you live on are simultaneously evolving and ascending into an entirely new and unimaginable world right now? What if I told you that this is indeed the sole purpose and the very process that the opposing forces have been trying to directly prevent for many, many years; while going to great lengths to suppress all information relating to the very possibility of such a planetary shift?

"*Fear is not real. It is a product of thoughts you create. Do not misunderstand me. Danger is very real. But Fear is a choice.*" ~ Will Smith, After Earth - The Movie

You must know that there won't be mass destruction or a World War III as they want us to believe, so do not buy into any of that, no matter what. The only war to come is the truth war that we are already in. This is a much greater war with a much greater opponent because it's a war with one's self. A truth war from within that no one can fight for you but yourself. This is the reason I have told you to fear no one, and fear none of what's to come; because you should never

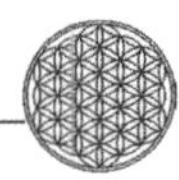

fear someone who feared you first and who fears you more. All the money, time, knowledge, and technology used to prevent you from awakening and discovering what you are about to read in this next chapter, is highly indicative of how much they fear you because of what you're capable of once you realize the powers that you have and what's to come.

An unstoppable and inevitable cosmic cycle known as "The Big Shift" is evolving and fulfilling our planet's destiny as you read this very sentence; this is the most anticipated cosmic event to ever occur in the history of the universe and is affecting and will continue to affect ALL of humanity in the most astounding unimaginable ways. Just don't be surprised if you never studied about this shift in your history textbooks, watched it on the news, heard about it from a friend or family member, or read about it on NASA's website.

This approaching transformational shift is similar to that of a caterpillar. Caterpillars consume and consume and consume until they eventually get so bloated that they fall asleep and form a cocoon. Humans are caterpillars of information. We have consumed so much disinformation that we have fallen asleep and lost our connection to the real world and our true identity. Once we digest this old disinformation and decide not to consume any more, our collective consciousness and our intent will show that we are truly ready for a new way of life. Only then will we burst out of this cocoon of darkness and transform into this beautiful new being that we've never imagined we could be, just like the caterpillar. In this darkness of hard times do not be discouraged; as the famous proverb goes, "*Just when the caterpillar thought the world was over, it became a butterfly.*"

The tiny seed knew that in order to grow, it needed to be dropped in dirt, covered in darkness, and struggle to reach the light."

~ Sandra Kring

We have come full circle in human evolution, and the time is upon us to finally understand all that we have consciously and unconsciously pondered for all these years: our connection with other people, our universe, and ourselves. It's time that we understand our planet, our purpose, and the direction in which humanity is heading, rather than just continuing to live in oblivion.

As we approach our final destination, we have reached a dire time where truth and transformation is essential. It's a glorious time that all religious scriptures and sacred tribes have foretold about for centuries. The time of this inevitable event and mass awakening has finally come to make Earth's planetary liberation a reality.

This rapidly approaching planetary transformation I speak of is not only inevitable, it's just around the corner! Unfathomable transformations that we weren't able to discuss in previous chapters can now be disclosed. Strap your seat buckle extra tight, because you are about to enter a world that's far beyond Never-Never Land!

CHAPTER

15

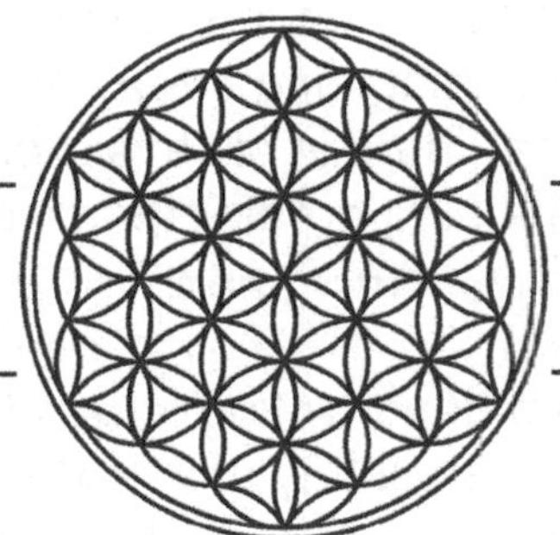

THE SUPER BOWL OF HUMAN EVOLUTION

"*You are radiant beings of magnificence and power. You are One with the Oneness. You are motes of Source. You are beautiful and brave. You have been through so much to be where you are. And now you stand on the cusp of a choice to decide where you will go next. Be true to yourself. Choose with your heart. Choose with Love. Release the fear. Become everything that you already truly are. Now… choose*"
~ Adamu

The global elitists have been suppressing humanity's evolution for centuries. Yet one may think, "How could this be true if our technology has been evolving faster than ever?" It is not our technology that's being suppressed, it is us! Technology and humanity must evolve together in order for this world to be harmonious. Although this harmony has not been the case, we have reached a point where there is no time left, and no other option but to evolve as a species together.

"*It has become appallingly obvious that our technology has exceeded our humanity.*" ~ Albert Einstein

We know at a point in time humans traveled by a horse and carriage. At that time, they had no clue that the next form of transportation would be a train. They also had no clue the next form of transportation to follow would be the automobile, let alone imagining the airplane or the jet at that time. This proves that there is always room for improvement, and it's usually something greater than we ever expected! Can you guess what's coming next?

We went from hand writing letters to composing e-mails; to creating a completely new text-messaging *slang* language in just years. Our advancements in technology are speeding up at an insane pace, and that's just the technology that's available to the public, never mind what's being kept from us. If you look at our history, more significant technological advancements have been made in the last fifty years than in the last five hundred years altogether. Time, what we know of it, is speeding up and people's expectations and attention spans are getting shorter and shorter. We want things faster and faster, almost instantaneously; and we're receiving these technologies and speeds as fast as they're coming out. This 'microwave society' of wanting more and more, faster and faster, is what makes the people reliant on these technologies. If our broadband, Bluetooth, 4G, Wi-Fi, or LTE were to be cut off and replaced with dial-up right now, we would probably all go insane and either throw our electronic devices out the window, or ourselves. People's need for speed is at an all-time high and the rate of our evolution is speeding up so fast, indicating that a major breakthrough is about to occur. So what will the next quantum leap in our evolution be? Well, the time is now, the place is here, and you are about to find out firsthand!

Do you ever wonder why you have two arms, two legs, and all the other functioning body parts that are fully useful, yet use less than one-third of your brain? Why is this? We have finally reached the point in the human evolution

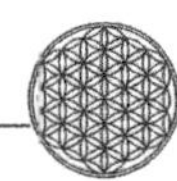

cycle where we will be able to use ALL of our brainpower, not just one-third. Does this sound too good to be true?

Have you noticed yourself dreaming a lot more and actually remembering your dreams in the morning? Have you noticed yourself becoming more psychic lately? Do you call or text friends who respond with, "Hey, I was just thinking of you." Or do you notice when your phone rings that you know exactly who it is before you even look at the caller ID? You may even find yourself finishing someone else's sentence for them, or thinking the very same thing at the very same time. These are the telltale signs that you are feeling the effects of the higher vibrations from the new "energies" approaching. This is the prelude to the new paradigm in which humanity enters a higher frequency of consciousness. It may seem gradual now, but what if I told you we are evolving at such a rapid speed, in such an amazing way, that we don't even realize the marvels of what's about to happen?

December 21, 2012. What Was Up with This Date?

This specific date never reflected the doomsday, or end of the world that was hyped in Hollywood movies and mainstream media. The Mayan calendar didn't mark the end of civilization as most of us thought it might. It marked the end of civilization, as we know it, and the birth of a new age, emerging within a new world.

Every religious scripture and prophecy has foretold these ages. Some refer to these times as *The Golden Age, New Earth, State Zero, The Shift, Ascension, Heaven on Earth, Armageddon, The return of Christ, The Rapture, The 144,000, Judgment Day,* or *"The End Times".*

The mystery around this enigmatic date prompted me to analyze more than a thousand hours of research to give due diligence to the topic. When I decided to delve into this area of interest, I had no idea that I would be opening a can of worms. The more I researched and tried to understand the subject, the more confusing it became. I ended up consulting with scientists, shamans, philosophers, astrophysicists, tribal elders, and New York Times best-selling authors from across the globe. I attended workshops and traveled the world searching for answers to make sense of what I thought was just a date. However, the date wasn't just a date; it was a pleasant warning from an ancient civilization foreshadowing what was to come. It was a message that has been suppressed and purposely misinterpreted to describe a doom-and-gloom event in order to keep humanity in the dark and in a state of fear.

This is yet another reason why the pyramids were so important. The civilizations living in ancient times had to find a way to pass along important information to future generations without it getting destroyed. They knew that scriptures would get burned, tablets would get broken, and anything else could be damaged or stolen, but carving hidden coded symbols, messages, and prophecies into stone—would last for centuries.

The Prophecy

The Hopi tribe is a respected tribe of elders that have brought forth many findings and prophecies of our age. An ancient Hopi prophecy states, "When the Blue Star Kachina makes its appearance in the heavens the Fifth World will emerge". This will be the day of Purification. The appearance of this Blue Star Kachina will mark the beginning to the end of time, while the Red Star Kachina will mark the end of time. The "end of time" refers to the end of third-dimensional living and the beginning of fifth-dimensional living. What is the difference between third-dimensional living and fifth-dimensional living? It is something so remarkable and extraordinary that I will only touch upon it and urge you to research it for

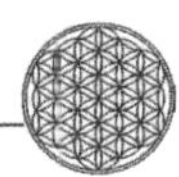

yourself. What I will say is that you will be amazed beyond your wildest dreams. So where is this Blue Star Kachina and what does this have to do with the new world emerging and this great cosmic event?

Interestingly enough, on October 24, 2007, Comet 17P/Holmes, a short-period comet first discovered in 1892, shocked astronomers with a spectacular and unexpected eruption in the sky. In less than twenty-four hours, the comet brightened by a factor of nearly a million and was illuminated a bright blue becoming visible in the evening sky with the naked eye. Within a few weeks, the expanding corona of the comet expanded several times the size of our sun.

The Blue Star Kachina is said to mark the times of a great purification period beginning prior to 2012 and would last for seven years. It just so happens that comet 17P/Holmes travels in an orbit around the sun with a period of about seven years. Coincidence? Some spiritual leaders have accepted Comet 17P/Holmes as the Hopi Blue Star Kachina, while others disagree and say something much greater than Comet 17P/Holmes awaits us that can happen any day!

More than thirty different ancient cultures and ancient philosophical systems all over the world have been encrypted with information advocating that history repeats itself in extensive cycles. These same ancient cultures, religions, and prophecies that have clashed over their differences, now agree that some big cosmic and/or spiritual event is about to occur in our lifetime. I've always told myself that if I get three compliments or comments from three different people on the same day about the same thing, then chances are they're probably all right. So, if more than thirty ancient cultures, tribes, and religious groups that have disagreed for thousands of years are all finally agreeing on something, I think we should at least listen to what they're trying to tell us.

Wouldn't you think so too?

We are currently living during the rarest cosmic cycle in the history of our planet—a cycle that only occurs once every 25,920 years. What does this mean, exactly? Well, these same religious groups that have disagreed for centuries now all agree that a great event *is* near.

The events that are about to unfold all seem to be intersecting at the same point, time, date, and place: HERE AND NOW! Many have interpreted these prophecies to promise some sort of worldwide cataclysmic event involving mass chaos and death. However, this is a great misunderstanding in use of negative metaphors to describe what's actually a very positive event. Due to the mainstream media's false hype of the connection between the end of the Mayan calendar and the end of the world, many thought the phenomenon was just another Y2K scare, while others wondered whether the Mayan civilization was so insightful after all.

It's a fact that the Mayan calendar is evidence of a highly advanced mathematical system of timekeeping. A system that has been so precise in determining the timing of major celestial events that it has been able to predict every equinox, solstice, and eclipse for the last five thousand years without error! This legendary and highly respected calendar is more accurate than our Gregorian calendar. So, ask yourself: is the most important astrological event to occur in the past 25,920 years just a fluke in the Mayans' immaculate system of timekeeping?

To all the skeptics who ask, "Well, why don't I see any of these changes you talk about and why didn't anything happen on December 21, 2012? The answer is simple. First, one must truly understand the calendar and what change it actually represented and predicted.

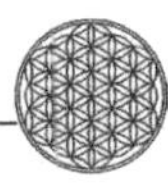

Understanding the Calendar

The Mayans set their calendar back to 3,114 BC, five hundred years before their civilization even existed, and they ended it on December 21, 2012, the winter solstice. So we must ask ourselves, why would they date their calendars back to a time before their civilization even existed, and end it on a seemingly random date far into the future? What's interesting about this is that the Mayan calendar didn't necessarily measure time; it tracked and monitored the evolution of humanity and human consciousness through cosmic Earth cycles translated in linear time. The specific date of December 21, 2012, marked the "end of time" and the beginning of a new cosmic cycle; a cycle that occurs only every 25,920 years along with several other rare cycles, including a solar cycle as well a major pole shift of the Earth's magnetic field, all of which occur around the same exact time. There is scientific proof that Earth's magnetic field is drastically shifting as we speak.

For example, look at this cycle of change the same way you might look at the cycle of four seasons in a place like New York City. Each season is very distinct and different from the others. In the Autumn, leaves change colors before they fall and the Winter brings snow and frigid temperatures. Spring brings new life and flowers, while the Summer brings heat waves and scorching temperatures. The cycle of change the Mayans refer to is no different. This isn't just an earth cycle that takes only months, it's a cosmic cycle that takes thousands of years. And it just so happens that our generation is going to be the generation that experiences this beautiful new cycle. We are exiting the Piscean age (old paradigm/third dimension) that's been dominated by the masculine for thousands of years, and we are entering the Aquarian age (new paradigm/fifth dimension) that will soon bring balance to the masculine and feminine energies on our planet.

Just as we slowly see the signs of Spring approaching as Winter ends, we will slowly see the signs of this new cycle approaching as the old cycle ends. Then before we know it, we will be living in an unrecognizable world that's the polar opposite of the world we've been living in all our lives. The transformation from this new cosmic cycle is already happening and has been scientifically confirmed. Except it's not the weather that is about to change, it is us!

Law of Gender: The law of gender is quite simple to understand, but is difficult for many to accept. As we already know, the universe is about balance, not domination. It is the forces of both the masculine and the feminine energies that are the foundation of creation within this universe—the yin and the yang.

The most powerful, charismatic, and advanced souls on this planet right now are the souls who are androgynous (possessing both feminine and masculine qualities). When a soul is too dominant masculine, or too dominant feminine, it lacks the emotional intelligence of its *twin flame* (their other half of different gender). Masculine and feminine energies are present in both men and woman and can only be developed through one's self-awareness. You develop these energies by first acknowledging them, embracing them, then appropriately allocating them in certain situations when they are called for. Someone who is homophobic and tries to deny or suppress these energies is only sabotaging his or her own powers and abilities while stunting their soul growth.

The Hip Hop/Rap industry has embedded in our children's minds that having feminine qualities or being "Gay", is absolutely the worst thing you could possibly be in this world. This thought pattern and belief system has suppressed our youth from obtaining 50% of their powers, while robbing their Yin from their Yang without them even knowing.

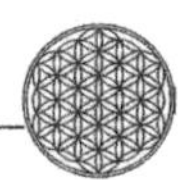

This has to do with why I believe rapper/poet Tupac Shakur was one of the most influential souls in not only the music industry, but on the planet! Tupac was a powerful androgynous soul that personified the law of gender by embracing both his feminine and masculine qualities, and even profiting from them.

Tupac is a good example to use because he not only embraced both these divine energies, but was the embodiment of duality in this world as well. Tupac's emotional spectrum was vast as his pendulum swung heavy in both directions. He was the only rapper that could make a song filled with pure hatred and anger that would make an honor roll student want to buy a gun and shoot up his fifth grade bully's house. Then on the same album, on the very next track, Tupac could make a song about women's empowerment that would make the coldest criminal in the world call his mother just to tell her that he loves her and make him want to start treating women better. In the Tupac documentary film, the gangster rapper candidly admits that he's an extremely sensitive and emotional individual that adopted many feminine traits being raised by women his entire life. This acceptance of both the masculine and feminine energies is what allowed Tupac to be so diverse and passionate within his poetry. This is the reason why the "thugs" loved Tupac and the women adored him.

"*Ladies love me long time like 2Pac's soul*" ~ Sean "Jay-Z" Carter - I Just Wanna Love You (Song Lyrics)

The same way The Cabal/Illuminati have manipulated every one of the universal laws to work against us in their favor, they have manipulated the Law of Gender by suppressing the feminine energies and using tools like the Bible to reinforce this by marginalizing the women of that time (e.g. Virgin Mary, Mary Magdalene, etc.). This is quite obvious in such a patriarchal society where only male figures have graced the face of our entire U.S currency.

Masculine energies have dominated planet earth for thousands of years now. The Golden Age of Aquarius is now awaiting the critical mass of our population to awaken and acknowledge it, so it can restore these powerful feminine energies to bring balance back to planet earth. As the world awakens, you will notice this shift and you will witness many women beginning to speak their truth, step into their power, and assume more leadership positions. Even newborn female babies are coming in with more wisdom than ever before. If you research the most popular baby names you will see that the name "Sophia" has been the most popular name for the past three (3) consecutive years (2011, 2012, and 2013). If you Google what the name "Sophia" means, you will discover that the name means "Wisdom".

The signs of humanity's evolving consciousness are already showing in many ways. People are awakening across the world, rallying for peace, protesting for fairness, and reclaiming their independence. This is the foreshadowing of great transformational planetary change to come, and the unimaginable evolution of our human race that is near!

How Are We Evolving?

Although there are a few theories on human evolution, we're taught in school that we evolved from apes/primates. Did you ever stop and ask yourself how we evolved from primates to grunting cavemen banging sticks together, to intelligent beings using cell phones to fly fully equipped drone aircrafts with heat-seeking missiles across the planet? Studies have been done that proved Chimpanzees are four times stronger than the average college football player. If the evolution of Chimps to Man story were true, you would have to ask yourself, "Why would we lose all of our strength in this evolutionary process?" If humans eventually became more

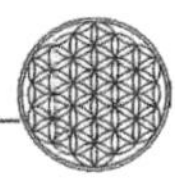

physical and started building large structures and moving large boulders, wouldn't we need all the strength we had? As a certified ISSA (International Sports and Science Association) fitness professional, I know that 95% of my clients come to me to gain more muscle mass and burn fat. We live in a society where we are constantly trying to become faster and stronger at everything we do. So why is it that we would just lose our strength when we were becoming more physical?

The realization that humans 'evolved over time' is very vague and only half true. It is not the passing of "time" that is responsible for our evolution; it is what's happening while time is passing that is significant. If anything, time would do the opposite. Isn't time the phenomena responsible for making us become old and grey? Isn't time what slows us down and causes us to become ill, weak, and eventually die? This is because time is not what causes us to evolve. Time is just the process which we measure our stages of evolution. So, if time isn't what makes us evolve, then who, what, why, when, and how in the world did we all evolve?

Evolution of Consciousness

It is the increase of personal and planetary consciousness that is responsible for the adaptation in our survival awareness and our species' spiritual growth; a process referred to as...evolution! It is the awakening and rising of one's consciousness and awareness that contributes to humanity's collective consciousness, which is the epicenter that regulates our evolution.

The awakening and the raising of ones consciousness is best described using the analogy of climbing up a mountaintop. As you climb higher and higher you start seeing the world in a whole new perspective. Your views change and so do your truths, therefore your reality changes as well. As your vantage point increases, you see everything you were before with much more clarity. The higher you climb the more you broaden your horizon. But, it's only when you reach the top of the mountain that you can become fully enlightened. This process is referred to as ascension and this is where all of humanity is heading, up to the top of the mountain. Now it's just a matter of deciding if you choose to commence this journey now, or decide to start climbing once you see everyone else climbing because you don't want to be left behind.

This mountain analogy is nothing new. In fact, this analogy was a science to the Mayans and their calendar. Instead of a mountaintop, they used a pyramid, where each of the nine platforms of the pyramid represented a higher level of consciousness. The top four levels of the pyramid were categorized as National Consciousness, Planetary Consciousness, Galactic Consciousness, and finally, the capstone of the pyramid, *Universal Consciousness*, which is where we currently are today (the all-seeing eye).

Experts who studied the Mayan calendar show that the Mayans were not only able to measure human consciousness over the years, but they were also able to predict significant dates within the calendar by pinpointing these influxes of consciousness, which inevitably resulted in major turning points for humanity including the discovery of fire and the birth of the internet, just to name a few. The invention of the Internet is a good example. According to their calendar, the introduction of the Internet triggered the Planetary Consciousness stage in our evolution by allowing us to explore and interact with the rest of the world from the comfort of our computer chair with no geographical constraints.

So what does this dusty calendar made of rocks mean to us today? Well, each level of the pyramid not only represented the nine different levels of humanity's consciousness evolution; it also represented the speed/rate of our evolution as well. As cycles/levels of this pyramid calendar completed,

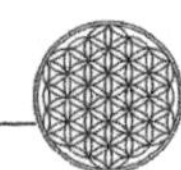

the next level up on the pyramid started a new cycle, and so on. As each cycle completed, the speed of our evolution process accelerated as well. Eventually leading us up to the capstone of the great pyramid where human evolution would be at it's fastest. This is where humanity is today! What would normally take us hundreds, or even thousands of years to evolve, is now happening in just days!

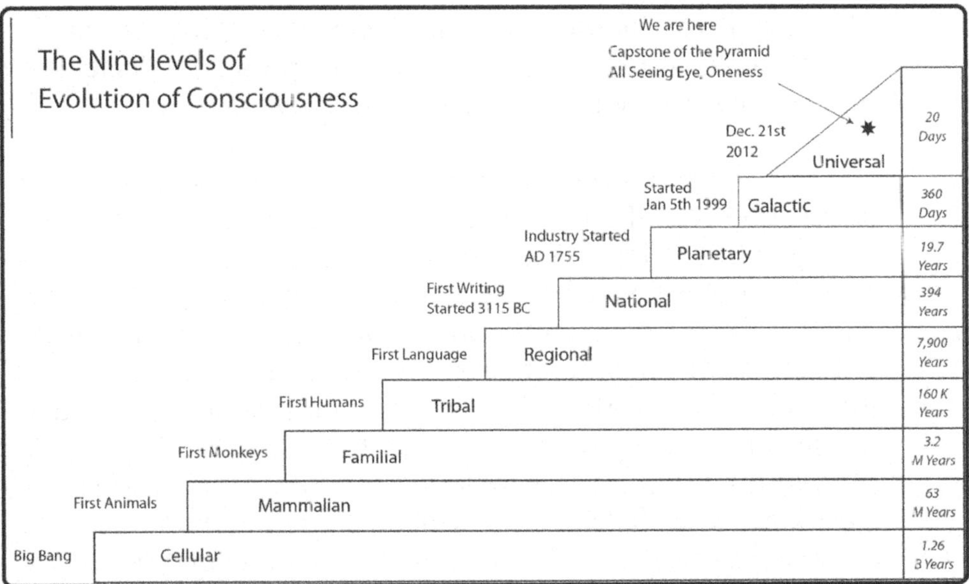

The date December 21, 2012 was never intended to be an apocalyptic event. This date marked a massive influx of energetic surges from the cosmos to our planet, which opened up a portal to multidimensional realms, which ignited a consciousness metamorphosis like never experienced before. What does this all mean?

It means right now we are experiencing the most powerful enlightening and positive energies ever to reach the surface of our planet in history. These new energies are hitting the Earth from the cosmos and expanding human consciousness at a ridiculous rate. Humanity is becoming more aware of what's really going on in the world than ever before. With our awareness at an all-time high, more truths are coming to light because it's much easier for us to see through the lies.

You will find yourself becoming more curious and asking yourself more questions. You will start to notice things that you've never noticed before, you will start caring about things you never cared about, and you will find that people and events will become much more transparent to you. Things that you thought made perfect sense before will no longer make sense as you watch the old paradigm dissolve and new cycle emerge right before your eyes.

The mass awakening is already happening, and here's some proof. On the next page you will see a screenshot that was generated from *Google Trends*, a sophisticated search engine application that tracks trending data recorded from all Google searches worldwide. If you type "Spiritual Awakening" into this search engine, the search results will display the "trend" from 2008 - 2014, which is calculated into a graph by the amount of searches conducted using the key words "Spiritual Awakening". What's interesting is that it displays a significant spike in "Spiritual Awakening" right around the date of December 21st, 2012, the same day our planet crossed the galactic plane and a massive influx of cosmic energy raised the world's consciousness and activated humanity's "Junk DNA". Coincidence?

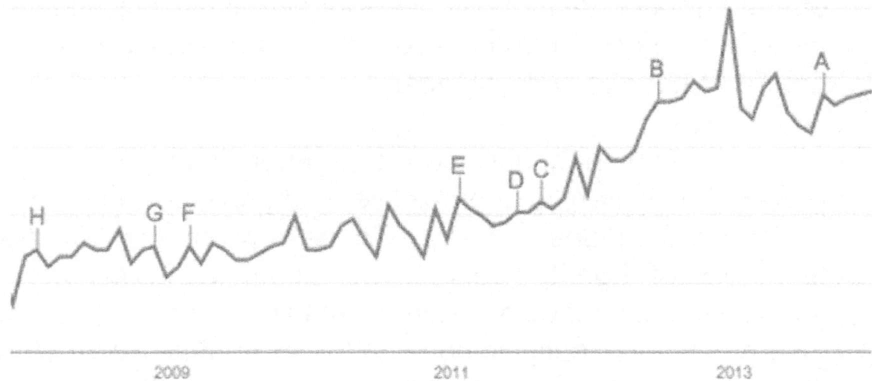

Image credit: www.Google.com/trends "Spiritual Awakening"

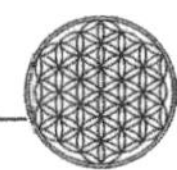

How This Rapid Consciousness Influx is Affecting Us

Technologies, events, and experiences are responsible for the raising of humanity's consciousness levels. Events such as the Wall Street scandals, Monsanto, Wiki leaks, and the Snowden case, just to name a few, have put the awareness of these corrupt events in our collective consciousness. It is now common knowledge that the largest corporations are in bed with our government, our banks are ripping us off, robbing us blind, and our government is spying on all of us. It's not that these events are new, these events have been going on for some time now. It's the increase in our consciousness that's making us say, "Hey, wait a minute...", as we all experience that awkward moment when one realizes they've been lied to and getting ripped off the entire time. The sad part is that these groups don't even try to hide it anymore; all the answers are hidden in plain sight. Take the artificially intelligent personal assistant known as "Siri", on Apple's famous i-phone model. What is "Siri" spelled backwards? I-R-I-S. What is an Iris? An iris is an eye! Hence, "i"-phone. Could this mean they've always been spying and had an "eye" on us all along? *Iris* is also the name of the personal navigator software on Google's famed Android phones as well. Coincidence?

Consciousness Cleanse

Many people are seeing very cruel, unconstitutional, and animalistic events going on in the world at this time. This might seem like an increase in crime, poverty, and unrighteousness, but this is not true. In fact, since we crossed the galactic plane on December 21, 2012, negative energies and the probability of negative timelines has drastically decreased. But why does it seem like the world is in total chaos and disorder more than ever before?

Well, it goes back to the saying: you cannot find a solution to a problem without knowing what the problem is in the first place. Therefore, these unfolding events and experiences are playing a significant role in humanity's awakening during such pivotal times of our planet's consciousness evolution.

These negative worldwide events you see happening are not the increase of negative events; it's the awareness of these events finally coming to the light. Darkness and negativity already exist and this is merely the purification that is taking place, not an increase in violence and crime. In fact, take for example New York City; it would seem to be common sense to make the assumption that when the economy is bad, or when there is a recession, the crime rate goes up. Yet, as of 2013, the New York City murder rate is at a 100-year low. So don't be fooled by the media making you think the world is in total chaos when this is merely the exposing of all negative events that's already been going on. These matters need to be brought into the light so humanity can heal and transform these issues by first recognizing them. Something I refer to as... *The Consciousness Cleanse.*

All the deception and lies are finally coming to the light and being exposed. It's like changing the light bulbs in your kitchen. When you replace the old burnt-out bulbs and put new ones in, what's the first thing you notice when you flip the switch? You notice that your kitchen, which you thought was clean, is actually a mess now that you can see every nook and cranny from all the new light. Humanity must first see and recognize these events, deception, and inhumane cruelty so we can change it. Quite frankly, any problem, no matter how big or small, must first be identified and brought to the light before it can be cleansed, healed or transformed. We must know about the problem and address it before we can fix it. Our planet is no different, and this is the cause for this illusion of increased destruction and chaos.

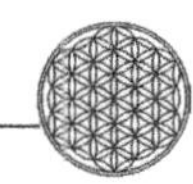

There is a purification that's taking place. This purification is due to the amount of positive energies currently hitting the surface of the planet, which is causing the "agitation" of these negative energies to erupt. We can compare this purification process to the washing of an old, dirty glass that has been sitting in the back of the cabinet collecting filth and dust over countless years. When we first pick up that glass to clean it, it will "kick up" all that old dust and filth. As we begin to rinse the glass in the water, we notice the glass becomes even more scummy, cloudy, and dirty than before because we've agitated the gunk that has settled in it. However, we know that the glass must get dirtier before it gets cleaner. Soon, all the filth is finally washed away from the glass, and as long as we take care of that glass from now on, the filth will be gone forever. This is exactly what is happening to our planet right now. The floating debris of negative energy that has polluted Earth for so many years must first be cleansed and purged before it can be gone forever.

Although there is a lot of negative energetic debris on this planet, the good news is that positive energy is much stronger than negative energy; love is far more powerful than hate, good is far more powerful than evil, and the light is far more powerful than the dark. The light represents love and truth, while darkness represents lies and deception.

We must ask ourselves, where is the only place darkness can exist? The only place darkess can exist is where the light is not! We must know that light will always outshine darkness when the two forces meet because darkness cannot survive whenever light is present. You cannot walk into a room filled with light and turn on the darkness, but you can always walk into a dark room and extinguish the darkness by turning on the light.

"Happiness can be found, even in the darkest of times, if one only remembers to turn on the light."

~ J.K. Rowling, Harry Potter Series

This is why all the lies and deception being force fed to us will eventually come to light; so we can allow the light to expose these truths and show us the way. This battle of duality, light and dark, good and bad, is the cause of our fluctuating mood swings, random sense of hopelessness, stress, fatigue, depression, and lack of self-worth lately. However, with the amount of positive energies anchoring on our planet at this time, negativity can no longer hide from the light and victory of the light forces will soon prevail. These are just a few notable changes occurring from this shift, slowly but surely.

This process is synonymous to the process of flipping a light switch in a giant commercial building. When the light switch is flipped, do all of the lights come on immediately at the same time? No, some begin to turn on right away; some don't turn on at all at first, while others flicker then slowly brighten as the lumens increase. Planet earth is experiencing this same process right now. Earth's light has been activated and the switch has been flipped. Now, it is time to watch all the powerful light-beings begin to brighten to their maximum capacity and LIGHT UP THE DARKNESSS once and for all!

A more interesting phenomenon that many are feeling the subtle effects of, but would never 'in a million years' question the possibility of its extinction, is Time. Most people look at the concept of time as linear, when time is more cyclical than anything. It's like a never-ending giant train track that goes in a continuous circle of cycles, not from point A to point B in straight timeline like we think. But what if I told you that "Time", as you know it, is about to change? The veil that quarantines Earth is what keeps humanity trapped in lower vibrations, dense matter, and is what's responsible for what we call "time" here on Earth. We will soon see time disappear as we move into higher dimensions (something I delve into shortly). Soon everyone will finally know what it's like to experience the timeless feeling that the astronauts experienced.

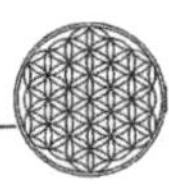

The Death of Time "As We Know It"

"*People like us, who believe in physics, know that the distinction between past, present, and future is only a stubbornly persistent illusion.*" ~ Albert Einstein

The death of time! What in the world does this mean? Trying to explain what it feels like to experience the absence of time is virtually impossible and is something that one must personally experience. Attempting to explain this feeling would be the equivalent to trying to describe a kaleidoscope to a blind person; good luck! The only reason I have any idea what this timeless experience feels like is from my Ayahuasca journey to Peru that I previously shared with you.

This rarely experienced and indescribable timeless feeling is exactly what the astronauts were experiencing when they pierced the veil that encapsulates earth. This is also what the Mayans were referring to as the end of time; not the end of humanity's time on Earth, but the end of time itself. This is why they ended their calendar and stopped recording time on that specific date of December 21, 2012. They knew cosmically that Earth would be making a quantum leap in her transformational shift when crossing this galactic plane. We are now just waiting for the critical mass of humanity to awaken to make this our reality.

If you wish to explore this timeless phenomenon further, I recommend researching "The Cosmic Consciousness Phenomena", or "The Overview Effect" via YouTube. The astronauts who are interviewed do a great job of explaining this emotional feeling on video better than I can with words.

Their "Time" has Come To an End

Have you noticed linear time passing more and more swiftly, or better yet disappearing? Days, weeks, and months fly by and you just can't seem to get enough things done in a day, which stresses you out even more. You look at your clock or at your calendar and you have no idea where the time went. This is because we are shifting into a higher dimension in space where time, as we know it, becomes irrelevant. This is also the reason why people just don't want to go to work anymore: time is what regulates "work" on this planet and many are feeling the effects of time slowly dissipating while we move into a unified consciousness. Many are just realizing that they need a career change because they're now feeling the presence of the void that comes from not living in alignment with their true passion and soul path. The "death", or diminishing of time, is what is responsible for this phenomenon.

I know the concept of expanding and collapsing time is hard to comprehend, because this "stubborn illusion" is what regulates our lives; it is what keeps humanity slaving in the corrupt systems we call work, while continuing to chase and save something (time) that never existed in the first place. This fabricated illusion is probably one of the more difficult concepts to understand, never mind to explain. However, at least having this concept seeded in your consciousness will help expedite the dissolution of this faux life regulator.

"Time doesn't exist, clocks exist!" ~ Unknown

While the world awakens to such unfathomable truths, there are many shifts taking place simultaneously. Every soul on this planet is currently evolving into a new dimension, a higher dimension, where anything and everything is possible. You're probably asking yourself, "Well, what the heck is a dimension anyway?" Just as the concept of time is one of the more difficult concepts to understand, the understanding of living within multiple/higher dimensions is probably even harder to comprehend. But let's take a crack at it!

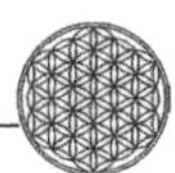

Experiencing Different Dimensions

There is approximately 7.3 billion realities happening simultaneously on this planet right now; but there should be only one reality that matters to you—YOURS! The United States Census Bureau estimates the world population at 7.328 billion people as of 2014. Which means there are currently 7.328 billion people on this planet each living out their own realites within their own minds. Although our perceptions and belief systems determine the reality we choose to live, it is our levels of consciousness that determine if we are capable of living in the higher dimensions.

A dimension is another name for an alternate reality, but is a bit different than the reality most are familiar with (the third dimension). The only comparison I can use in attempting to explain this alternate reality within another dimension would be similar to what you experience in your dream state. Every night while you are sleeping, your brain's pineal gland releases DMT, the naturally occurring compound that's responsible for making you dream. Whenever you dream you are accessing multiple dimensions while your consciousness is literally teleported to all types of places and spaces that you created with your subconscious mind. Every night you are traveling through many planes of existence and experiencing life in multiple dimensions; it's just hard to remember these experiences upon awakening. However, when you are dreaming, does it not feel 100% real? Yet, 99% of the time you do not know you're dreaming and you cannot tell the difference between your two realities (dreaming and awake).

During that 1% of the time when you do realize that you're actually dreaming, you experience proof that you have the innate ability to 'consciously' travel and experience life while coexisting in multiple dimensions. In all actuality, we are coming to a point in human evolution where we won't have to be sleeping or dreaming to experience limitless life within higher dimensions. Multiple dimensions are always present and can be accessed at anytime if we were only taught how to do so. Many yogis and monks have the ability to do this while in meditation via astral traveling. This pretty much feels like you're dreaming, but you are completely conscious and awake. Every one of us has the ability to do this but most of us are completely unaware and can't exercise this gift. This is simply because it's extremely hard to recognize and practice something that we have no previous knowledge of.

The best way to describe the understanding of dimensions would be using the analogy of radio stations. Lets pretend that the Earth is a giant radio and our "Dimensions" are its stations. As we know, there are multiple radio stations available on any one radio and that many stations can all exist at the same time and place simultaneously. Each station has its own specific "frequency", and if we are just one decimal off, or a slight frequency too low or too high, we will get nothing but static or distortion when seeking our desired frequency.

Dimensions are no different. They each have their own specific frequency and until you reach that exact frequency, you will not be able to access that dimension. Fine-tuning yourself to a higher frequency and attempting to consciously experience reality in higher dimensions is like manually tuning your radio's knob until you hit that exact frequency. Since Earth is one of the lowest vibrational planets in the universe that operates in the lowest density (third dimension), one will always have to raise their frequency in order to access higher dimensions. It is only the veil and the constructs of the matrix, which suppress our vibration/frequency, that make this difficult to accomplish at our current level of consciousness. However, once one is educated on the Ascension process, they will then be able to raise their vibration and fine-tune into the exact frequency of whatever station/dimension they desire, and access all that it offers.

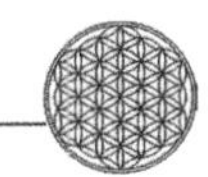

Just as every radio station plays different songs, offers different shows and various entertainment options, each dimension in this universe has its own ways of living as well. And for the most part, the higher the dimension, the better!

This is why humanity has been pushed away from spirituality and metaphysics. This knowledge has been suppressed and has forced us into lower third dimensional living where we are more easily controlled. Meditation, the usage of crystals, obtaining truth, and eating live organic foods, all help to raise your vibrational frequency. Using these tools will eventually give you better access to these higher dimensions and assist you in your ascension process if you are diligent in your practice.

However, the times we are living in now are a bit different than ever before. The entire world as a whole is about to experience this shift into a higher dimension. This is why it is crucial that we awaken the critical mass needed in order for this to manifest and trigger the events that will make this possible.

Making This New Dimension a Reality

Earth has been rapidly raising its vibration and frequency for the last five or so years. As humanity begins to rebuild its systems, we will move from living in the third dimension to living in fourth/fifth dimensions. As you conduct your own research, you will notice some sources will say that we are moving into the fourth dimension while others will say we are moving into the fifth dimension. I refer to it as the fifth dimension, but just know both sources are talking about the same thing. In all actuality, there are many different dimensions present here on earth (as exemplified with the radio station analogy).

The times we're living in now are all about raising our individual consciousness high enough so we can contribute to the raising of humanity's collective consciousness. We will not be able to ascend individually; we have to ascend together as a species. Before we are able to reach this higher-dimensional living and make "the shift," humanity must first help purify Mother Earth and create a new world in order to be ready for this state of bliss. This will not happen on its own, or overnight. Change is a result of action. We won't change the world until we first identify the problems, unite, and find nonviolent ways to fix them.

I recommend the following book/movie that illustrates this enlightenment very well: James Redfield's The Celestine Prophecy. In it, the characters are on a quest for the truth of an ancient prophecy while experiencing planetary changes similar to what we are about to experience.

"In the old paradigm the sky was the limit, in the new paradigm there is no limit." ~ The World is (y)ours

The topic of Ascension is by far my favorite topic to research and discuss. However, less than 3% of the population is even aware of this reality, never mind the fact they're actually ascending this very moment completely unbeknownst to them. They have no clue that they are currently living out their most significant lifetime in the most prophetic era in all cosmic universal history.

There is nothing more mind-bending and awe-inspiring then being able to absorb the knowledge, wisdom, and truth of ascension into one's consciousness. If you are not yet aware of what this nine-letter word truly represents, then please give me the honor of introducing the most significant evolutionary topic known of human existence.

CHAPTER

16

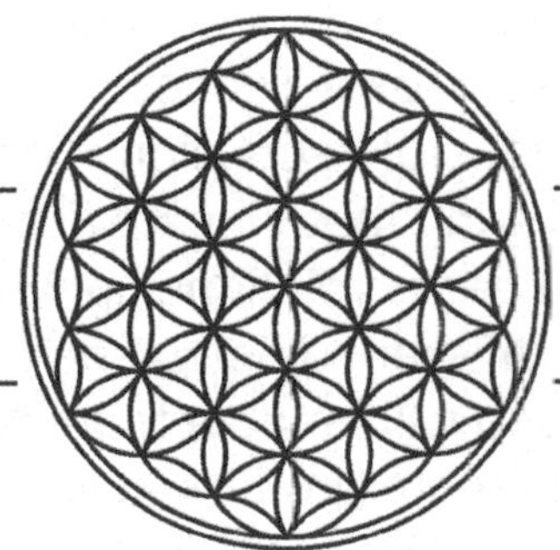

ASCENSION-WHAT IS IT EXACTLY?

"*The evolution from human to divine consciousness involves healing duality and its legacy of karma and disease at the cellular and atomic levels.*" ~ Sol Luckman

Many refer to this shift as "Ascension". Ascension can happen in many ways and this process is not what people expect. Some think ascension will be similar to the Mayan's mass ascension whose civilization just vanished off the face of the earth because they were able to reach higher levels of consciousness during their great cosmic event. This will not be the case for humanity at this time, because it's not just our bodies that are ascending, it's our consciousness! In fact, it's the opposite; all the highly evolved souls of higher consciousness are needed here more than ever. These individuals will be our future leaders and teachers that will help us during these ascension times to help bring in the new paradigm. Ascension is an individual process that has already started for many; just know that no one is going anywhere right now until we all liberate this planet for the highest and greatest good of Mother Gaia (Mother Earth) and humanity. This earth needs to be rebuilt so there can truly be heaven on earth as all the prophecies and religious scriptures have predicted.

This ascension process into higher dimensional living through the rising of human consciousness and removal of suppressed emotions is different for everyone. The process of ascending is solely based on the individual's level of consciousness, life lessons experienced, soul path, and spiritual growth during the times of ascension. The hardest part about ascending is discovering that you are. The second hardest part is developing a better relationship with yourself so you can distinguish the difference between your soul and your ego. By doing this you will be able to release the heavy suppressed emotions that are grounding you in lower levels of consciousness on 3D earth. Let me explain.

How To Ascend

I will use an analogy and compare your ascension to a hot air balloon. We know that a hot air balloon is anchored to the ground with numerous sand-filled bags, and in order for a hot air balloon to raise and take off, all of those heavy bags first need to be released. This same process is required if you wish to ascend into higher levels of consciousness and vibrations. Unfortunately, humans similarly tend to let their heavy emotions, doubts, fears, and limiting belief systems act as their sandbags and weigh them down in life, thus preventing their ascension. So the question is, HOW do we release these sand bags filled with those heavy emotions and unhealthy belief systems that are being anchored by the lower functioning aspects of our ego personality?

Although the answer may sound simple, "*Just release and let go*", this process is actually quite challenging because it's only through deep self-realization that sincere forgiveness can take place. Only unconditional forgiveness will release you from the energetic cords that bound you to those heavy energies found in those sand bags. Once you truly start forgiving the people that hurt you and disappointed you in life, including the most important person of

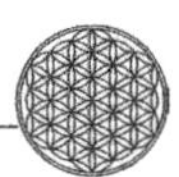

all (yourself), this is when you will be able to dump out that 'emotional baggage' from your vessel. As you release these grudges and heavy energies one-by-one, you will literally begin to feel yourself become more buoyant, lighter, and free of karmic debt. Next thing you know, you'll be soaring in the clouds viewing life through entirely new vantage points and perspectives that you never imagined, changing the way you look at EVERYTHING. These new perceptions on life enable you to start experiencing higher levels of consciousness while triggering many profound transformative realizations and life-changing epiphanies. Once one finally learns to forgive and come from a place of pure unconditional love, one really starts to take off on his or her ascension path.

The Final Battle

Our ego tends to tenaciously hold on to all the pain, grudges, resentment, doubt, fears, guilt, and shame from the past. This is what anchors us in lower levels of consciousness and prevents our ascension. That aspect of us (ego) fears ascension because it's afraid that it will be abandoned, or much worse, annihilated! As the higher functioning aspects of yourself (higher-self) wait for you to heal and release the lower functioning aspects of yourself (ego), life can become quite difficult and bitter sweet if you aren't aware of this process within your ascension.

Your soul must always be in control of your vessel (thoughts and actions), and your co-pilot (ego) should always be in the passengers seat. Unfortunately, your ego is the *control-freak* who constantly tries to get behind the wheel and steer your ship. Although a co-pilot is much needed on this life journey, there can only be one captain on your ship. Therefore, it is imperative you avoid "the takeover" and become aware of this battle taking place so you can maintain control of your vessel (thoughts and actions) at all times. Remember to never let your ego *justify* your wrongdoings;

this is something the ego has MASTERED and will fool you every time if you let it. To avoid this you must be brutally honest with yourself and always put yourself in the other person's shoes in order to eject the ego out of the driver's seat.

This internal *Soul Battle* over your vessel is a battle that everyone must undergo in order to ascend. In fact, this is the final battle of *Armageddon* that every religious scripture has spoken of for eons. However, many don't know that *Armageddon* is an individual process that is happening inside each and every one of us, and it's happening right now!

Who Will Survive Armageddon? (The Ascension Roster)

"Religious people are afraid of going to hell, spiritual people have already been there." ~ Les Brown

Many religious people believe "their people", the anointed ones, will be the only people who will make the shift and be saved, but this is not true. This shift does not label or discriminate based on status or religious beliefs. One only needs to hold 50% light or more to qualify for ascension. Chances are that your soul holds this amount of light and has already made the decision whether you are ready or not to make this shift. If you made it to this part of the book, then simply your curiosity to continue reading indicates that your soul has already decided that YOU ARE READY!

There's no way you could have ever made it to this part of the book if your soul was not ready. There are actual trigger mechanisms that monitor our consciousness and act like barometers when we are starting to awaken. These triggers occur when we begin reading or watching something that our current reality and consciousness' doesn't agree with (similar to how our brain reacted to the Bird in the Bush exercise). Except in this case, these awakening triggers will make you feel extremely tired or extremely fidgety all of a

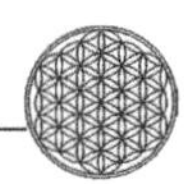

sudden, causing you to stop watching or reading whatever material that's awakening you.

If you haven't noticed by now, this is the exact reason why this book was written in layers. Each chapter slowly prepares the reader for the next chapter, and the next, as the information becomes deeper and more profound as he/she reads on. So just know that there's no way you would have made it to this part of the book if your soul wasn't fully prepared for what's about to occur.

It was not your mind that decided to read this book; and it was not your ego that decided to read this book either. Your soul is what called this book into your life! As our egos continue to diminish, our souls are becoming more operative within our physical bodies. This means that our egos will not be able to reject and ridicule these truths for much longer. People will start listening to their soul's intuition, rather than their mind (where the ego dwells). This was the gift of Dr. Martin Luther King Jr. He had the innate ability of speaking directly to people's souls, not just to their minds. This is the ability needed to start such a movement. How else would an African American male be able to gather 250,000+ people of all races and places to the steps of the Lincoln Memorial to March on Washington in the 1960's?

Our soul's decision to experience living in the fifth dimension and higher, is so mind-bending and amazing to our current reality that I choose to discuss very little on the details of what this life will be like. I don't want to derail you, my reader, by what may seem "unbelievable," so I urge you to do additional research and come to your own conclusions. The ascension energies are here, you can feel them, and they're coming in stronger and stronger with each day passing. Maybe you can feel it or you cannot; but know that this is happening, and here are some of the signs:

It's Already Happening, and Here's How…

Animals are usually more sensitive than people are to energies and Earth changes. When natural disasters are about to occur, animals are often the first to sense those energies. Within hours of a coming tsunami, animals are barking, meowing, or fleeing to safer ground because they sense what's coming. They can all feel it. There is a sense of collective consciousness within them when these catastrophic events are about to unfold.

Creatures within the animal kingdom are already experiencing the effects of this coming Earth change and are responding to the loving fifth-dimensional energies of the approaching Golden Age. We are already seeing examples of predators and prey playing together, and mothers of one species nursing babies of another species. These aren't just stories, this is actually happening!

The effects of planetary changes are much like the development of a newborn baby. In the first couple of years, you really don't get to see too much growth in personality. However, after a couple of years that baby starts to walk and talk and you start to see the unique personality traits and characteristics of that baby develop. Soon you start to see all of Mother Earth's new gifts and talents unfold as you realize what an amazing *being* she really is. This is what our planet is currently experiencing!

You're Not Going Crazy! (Ascension Symptoms)

Large amounts of new cosmic energy are reaching the Earth's surface that science can actually measure. Since 2007, these fifth-dimensional energies have been arriving toward Earth gradually, allowing our bodies to absorb these new energies over time. It is important that we receive these energies over time and not all at once. Too much of these

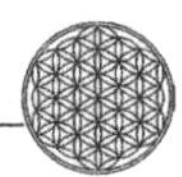

high energies at once will destroy our bodies, whereas smaller bursts of these energies will trigger fewer side effects. In 2012, this energy had tripled from the previous year and is intensifying on a daily basis.

The effects of these energies over the next few years will be different for everyone. The unfolding changes will be changes that you will feel rather than see. As these high energetic light pulses (unseen by the naked eye) intensify on the planet, our consciousness and spiritual awareness increase as our initiations and the dissolution of the ego commence. Some of these energetic effects are physical, mental or emotional, while others are etheric and spiritual.

Physical

Due to increasingly high energetic vibrations and the immense amount of light (positive energy) coming from our cosmos, many people are experiencing conditions such as weakness, disorientation, light-headedness (vertigo), forgetfulness, random headaches, heart palpitations, changes in appetite, heightened sensitivity, feeling uncomfortable in their own bodies, random aches and pains, decreased or increased need for sleep, sudden energy surges between the hours of 2:00 AM and 4:00 AM that awaken them, extreme fatigue, and other random sensations. Depending on how sensitive one may be, they might experience seeing or hearing things that others don't. Something I've noticed with myself is my new unpredictable sleeping habit. Sometimes I only need four hours of sleep and will be fully energized for the entire day. While other days I'll sleep for eight or nine hours and be completely exhausted the entire day no matter how much I sleep or how many naps I take.

These physical effects are simply because we are experiencing the most energy our outdated third dimensional bodies have ever absorbed, and they don't know how to handle it. If you find these symptoms persist and bother you, try taking a pinch of sea salt and placing it under your tongue; this will help you absorb the energies better and allow them to flow throughout the body with minimal side effects.

Know that these intense physical changes are normal. Your body is fine-tuning itself to these new energies while recalibrating and rebooting itself daily. Therefore, it's important to listen to your body. If you feel the need to sleep, then sleep. If you feel you need to eat more, then eat. Our body speaks to us and knows best, so be sure to provide it what it needs for this transition. Once these energies are integrated, many will feel the urge to start eating healthier and exercising more.

Emotional

In the upcoming years, the influx of these new energies will have peaked. Many people have already been experiencing the effects of extreme fluctuating mood swings, loss of identity, feeling like they don't belong here, crying spells, and random feelings of happiness along with sudden bouts of depression. These enlightening energies are forcing people to really look inward at themselves. It is bringing all the negativity and fear to the surface that for years have been buried deep inside us. These symptoms are to be expected with the increase of energies reaching the planet. For this reason, I urge you to take this information into consideration when discussing the possibility of taking antidepressants with your doctor.

You will notice old patterns, belief systems, and behaviors are being pushed to the surface. Deep suppressed emotions are emerging so they can be dealt with and released.You will see people cry whom you have never seen cry before. You notice people whom always seemed so closed off beginning to open up more, and you will see feuding families forgiving one another and reuniting.

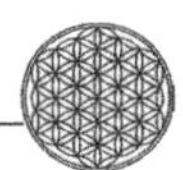

As your vibrations rise, you will notice yourself gradually separating from certain friends, events, and situations that don't suit your new vibration. Sometimes feeling so introspective that you just want to go into solitude. You simply won't feel like being around certain people or places anymore, and you won't have any excuse for these new ill feelings. This will be energetic and will happen naturally since like energy attracts like energy on life's highway.

Spiritual

As the intensity of the energies increases daily, and as the veil thins, the law of attraction and what you manifest will be magnified like never before. These intense higher vibrations are supercharging our manifestations—whether good or bad—at record speeds. This is why it's important to stay positive minded more than ever because the law of attraction is in constant SUPERCHARGED MODE!

Many people will begin seeing specific repeating numbers such as 11:11, 4:44, and 12:12, just to name a few. Additional spiritual awakening signs occur in the form of random sightings of feathers, pennies, and hummingbirds. Some people will experience strange unexplainable connections to foreign places such as Egypt, as well as historical eras such as the Renaissance era or the medieval times.

The nostomania within many has been occurring more frequent lately as well. Many people are beginning to feel like they don't belong here (Earth) anymore and they just want to go "Home". This sense of home sickness is actually a form of awakening that is reminding these individuals that the universe is much bigger than just one tiny planet.

Many will experience random physic abilities and positive paranormal connections with their loved ones who have crossed over by feeling their presence. The remainder of the population will notice that they are remembering their dreams with much better clarity than ever before, as dreams will start becoming more vivid and lucid.

Soul Level

Whatever religion one might be, I think there is one clear consensus that we should all agree upon: we are not just our bodies or our minds; we have a soul, a higher self, which lives on after our physical body dies. Whatever one might think the soul does after death is one's belief, but the commonality of beliefs should be that there indeed is an immortal soul that exists within all of us.

The soul is actually said to weigh approximately 21 grams, which has been proven by science. In 1901, Duncan MacDougall, a doctor who tried to prove the existence of the human soul conducted a famous study. He measured the weight of a person at the moment of death and closely monitored the weight down to the gram. He used six test subjects, all of whom experienced an immediate weight loss averaging 21 grams, giving merit to his study that the human soul exists, and actually weighs 21 grams.

"*To the well-organized mind, death is but the next great adventure.*" ~ J. K. Rowling, Harry Potter Series

We are merely a soul experiencing a body, not a body experiencing a soul. These energetic changes occurring aren't just affecting our physical bodies, they're also affecting us on a soul level, and here is how...

These increasing energetic differences are intensifying as many individuals are feeling a strong 'urge' to make a major change in their life. Whether it's seeking a new career/job, ending or starting a relationship, pursuing a new major of studies, relocating to a new area, or visiting a far

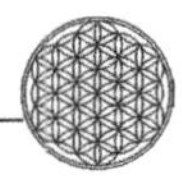

off place they have a sudden desire to visit. I'm not talking about irrational impulse decisions; I'm talking about becoming increasingly aware of YOUR SOUL CALLING. That growing sense of urgency you had lately to act upon an idea that has been simmering in your mind is your soul speaking to you. To most this might feel like your life is falling apart as you start to question your own existence and purpose here on this earth plane, and sometimes even feeling a sense of depression and the need to "run away" and start over.

When we live out of alignment with our soul's divine purpose, we are committing spiritual suicide! How little or how much money we make will not make a difference either. The only way to live in alignment with your soul purpose is to face your fears, follow your heart, take risks, and explore new paths. It is only when we venture outside of our comfort zone that we are able to find comfort in our discomfort. It is only when we let our passion navigate us into the unknown that we discover abilities and gifts that we never knew we had.

"If you want something you've never had, you must be willing to do something you've never done." ~ Thomas Jefferson

Some people are feeling as if they are being pushed out of their current job or career, and the irony of this is that's exactly what the universe is doing! Yet the fear of losing money and job security is what's grounding them, keeping them stagnant. Don't be afraid of this change! This is your soul awakening to its divine life purpose. Old belief systems and current situations begin to fall apart; so new ideas and new opportunities can take their place without you rejecting them. Life is only hard when we are working towards goals that aren't in alignment with our true soul path. When we are in alignment with our divine purpose, the universe opens up the world for us and everything we want comes with grace and ease. You must pay attention and recognize opportunity when opportunity is presented, so you can take action when action is needed.

The strongest of souls that have not awakened to their power soon enough, could possibly be going through something called *The Dark Night of the Soul*. This is by far the hardest initiation into remembrance (awakening) that one can experience. Someone who awakens and becomes aware of their purpose will then seek their power once they know they're capable of it. However, a powerful soul who has yet to awaken and accept what they're capable of, will have their power seeking them! This is when *The Dark Night of The Soul* steps in; a dark phase in one's life that only the strongest of the strong souls can endure, where the only way out, is in! Embrace this; do not be afraid of your power.

Our Bodies Are Changing Before Our Eyes

"*You are more than your thoughts, your body, or your feelings. You are a swirling vortex of limitless potential who is here to shake things up and create something new that the universe has never seen.*" ~ Dr. Richard Bartlett

These energetic changes that I explained are affecting people all over the planet in many ways. One of the most profound ways is the genetic mutation (upgrade) of our etheric DNA. What I learned from my research is that currently our bodies are made up of carbon-based cells made mostly of hard, dense matter and very little light. But this is changing: the carbon-based cells that make up our body are transmuting and evolving into crystalline cells. As our bodies adjust to cellular changes from carbon to crystalline, our bodies will be composed of less matter and will be able to hold more light, hence, "Light body". This is the same part of our DNA that scientist have previously referred to as "Junk DNA". But do you really think God made humans with DNA made of junk? Last time I checked God didn't make junk. But

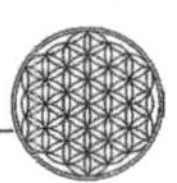

it doesn't necessarily matter if you believe this or not, what matters is the rate of our vibration is speeding up daily within each of our cells so fast, indicating that something amazing is about to happen!

Why Now, Why us?

Look around. Look at the world. Can't you see that things can be better than they are? Can't you feel something in the air? That much needed change is coming? Perhaps you're asking yourself, "If this is all true, why in the world is this happening now?" Well, this change must happen; it is this planet's destiny. Just as we must love our bodies, we must also love our planet; it is as alive and conscious as we are. We tend to forget that our planet takes care of us; we don't take care of it. This clearly shows which is the more conscious, responsible, and loving entity.

I will admit that I was a person who took the planet for granted and never really sat and thought about how generous and loving our planet has been to us despite all the damage and abuse that she has absorbed from us. It never struck me as to what was really going on around me. Yes, I knew about pollution, littering, and the ozone layer, but did I really think that would affect me personally? What would be the worst that could happen? For years I failed to see the obvious bigger picture, just like a fish that fails to see the water in which it swims. A fish doesn't realize that it is swimming in water, the same way we are blind to the fact of what's really at stake and in jeopardy on our planet.

Planet Earth is ALIVE!

The same way that a plant, an animal, or a human can die, so can our Earth. So why does humanity think it's impossible to kill a planet? Our Earth is a living and conscious being, just as we are. The same ways a human and a plant can be killed-so can our Earth. This isn't the first time this has happened. If you were to research the real history of our universe you will find similar stories of humanity's negligence leading to planetary destruction with the fall of *Lemuria* and *Atlantis*. These are not fairytale stories, these stories are as real and significant as the life you live.

We are closer than ever to extinguishing all life on our planet. If Earth were to die, it would have an irreversible adverse effect on all the planets in the solar system. It's simply not possible for this planet to sustain itself anymore with more than 7 billion people occupying and consuming all of Her natural resources. We cannot continue bleeding Her for oil, polluting Her seas, disrupting Her ecosystem, and pumping toxic gases in Her lungs. Mother Earth is completely out of balance, which is causing humanity to become out of balance as well—because we are all one! We wouldn't treat our biological mother this way; why do we continue treating our Mother Earth this way? Mother Earth is our real mother. She has endured our torture for countless years, yet out of pure, unconditional love, she still keeps giving us our every breath of oxygen we've inhaled, every drop of water we have ever swallowed, and every meal we have ever eaten. She provides us a home, our only home! Most humans can't imagine life without a planet because this is something their consciousness can't fathom.

"*The thing we take for granted more than anything else in this world-is the world itself.*" ~ The World is (y)ours

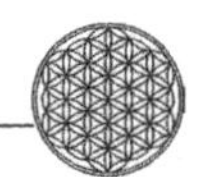

This is what ascension is all about: humanity must make the conscious decision to awaken to the problem and start creating the solution. So what's the solution exactly? Well it's not the 7 billion people consuming Earth's resources that need to be extinguished; it's the systems that offer these resources to the people that need to be eliminated. Energy resources that involve burning coal, drilling for oil, and *fracking* natural gas have been obsolete for decades. The descendants of the elite groups who first created these bias systems of profit keep them alive with the illusion of scarcity versus abundance. They force the world to use their products and services by making us believe that these are the only options available to us. But when will enough finally be enough? When will humanity say "NO MORE"? And if we do succeed and are able to unplug from the matrix and these systems, how will we manage to survive then?

Law of Relativity: The law of relativity is how we deal with the relevant problems in our life at any moment in time. This law works with the decisions we make when we are facing difficulties or obstacles that could result in a major turning point in our life. To understand this law you must first understand that the universe gives every person many life lessons to learn throughout the course of his/her life, and every person's lessons are different. It is how we manage our thoughts and deal with the emotions that arise when these challenges occur that's significant. The universe does not care how long it takes you to learn a lesson! It is up to you how you deal with these obstacles and how long it takes you to learn the lesson.

TIP: Refrain from feeling self-pity or powerlessness. Embrace all challenges and obstacles by accepting your life lessons as learning opportunities for personal and soul growth. Keep in mind when we fail or try to run from any life lesson, it only prolongs the inevitable and that same lesson comes back tenfold, disguised with new faces and places to fool you. You must accept the fact that there is no escaping a life lesson. None! So learn now, learn fast, and move on!

No Need to Worry

"*In the middle of difficulty lies opportunity.*" ~ Albert Einstein

Earth has been around for billions of years and science has proven that there have been many pole shifts, evolutions, and planetary changes thus far that have benefited humanity greatly. So why would it be so hard to believe that we are the ones to experience this next great change? Many souls have signed up to experience this event at this time, and YOU are one of the lucky ones who get to witness this amazing transformation firsthand. We have a big responsibility here on this Earth at this time. But I assure you that only the strongest of the strongest souls are here now to assist in this transformation, and if you are here on this planet and reading this very sentence, then, yes, that is you!

"*Our deepest fear is not that we are inadequate. Our deepest fear is that we are powerful beyond measure.*"
~ Marianne Williamson

We all have a divine purpose on this earth. We are all just as important as the next person, and our role is just as significant as anyone else's. We must understand that there are no extra souls on this planet and that every single human being who walks this Earth is here for a specific purpose for a much greater cause. Too much of the population lacks confidence in their talents and attributes. When in fact, each one of us is born with a special gift, which we can use to assist humanity and earn a living doing so. There is not one soul born on this earth plane without a gift, not one. Humanity must learn to search within and find their gifts, and believe they are worthy and capable of having such amazing gifts.

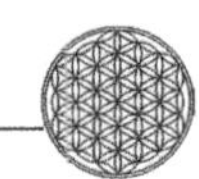

You are far more mystical and powerful than what you've been told, taught, or led to believe.

Your journey has already begun and it's time to awaken your soul, the place where all your powers lie. You must start thinking differently, asking different questions, and making different choices. If you cannot figure out what you should or shouldn't do while making any decision(s) that could potentially alter the course of your life, just remember to ask yourself this simple question, "What would love do?" and that answer will be the correct choice-ALWAYS!

FEAR NOTHING! The universe is designed for your survival and you have ample tools for this expedition. There is a new world emerging with more powerful energies and benevolent beings that are assisting you in your evolution, so know that you are not alone on this journey. Discernment, intuition, and spirit will guide you through these times

How Will We Know This Is Happening?

The prelude leading up to the approaching chain of events will occur in our dreamtime. People worldwide will notice that their dreams are becoming more vivid and lucid than ever before. They will also notice the messages and events happening in their dreams are bleeding into their real life. Following this realization will be a series of global synchronized dreamtime events that will affect everyone on a global scale.

An example of this awakening event for the more-awakened individuals would most likely occur while they're at work, school, or lunch. They might find themselves talking to a friend trying to articulate how amazing and realistic their dream was the night before; when someone nearby overhears their conversation and chimes in to say that they had a very similar dream the night before as well. The others will find themselves experiencing sporadic cases of déjà vu in some similar fashion.

These frequent dreamtime experiences will be undeniable to these individuals and they will just know that something is going on. These dreamtime events will be the first telltale sign that something amazing is about to occur on this planet; something we have been long awaiting!

You should also try to pay more attention to the skyline if you can. You will notice subtle shifts in its appearance such as "strange clouds", odd colors, and many peculiar things to look for that's to come.

When Will All of This Happen?

"You cannot put a lid on a volcano." ~ Unknown

We must know that this long anticipated inevitable event is not a one-day event predicted to happen on any specific date. It is a process that has now been fully activated, and it is now up to us how quickly it manifests. When the light forces finally take over the consciousness grid and dissolve the veil, it will result in drastic improvement of the planet's vibrational frequency and there will be a *MASS AWAKENING* felt all around the world. People will feel much lighter and happier overall and it will be very visible and evident to everyone. People will not be so depressed, they will not be so concerned or afraid, and they will simply be able to feel that something has changed. This big shift in energy will be felt by almost everybody and will be one of the first physical signs that this emerging new world has begun. If you ever watched the movie *The Giver*, starring Jeff Bridges and Meryl Streep, the very ending of this movie gave us soft disclosure of exactly what humanity will feel at the time of this *Galactic Pulse* (the big shift).

We will know this change is upon us once we see a series of shocking and amazing events begin to unfold right in front of our eyes!

CHAPTER
17

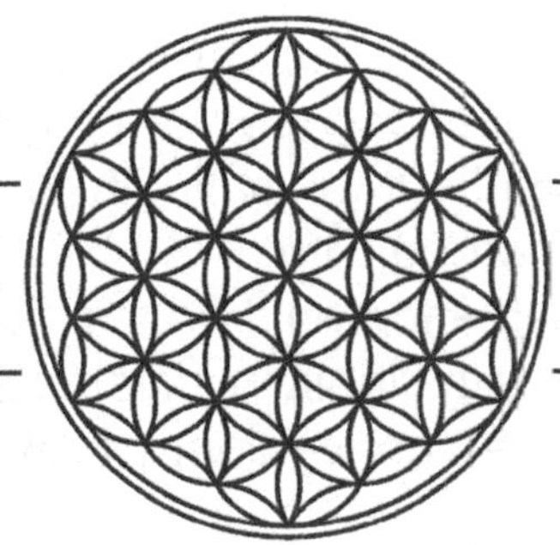

THE EVENTS

1). Mass Arrests, "The Trigger Event"

"Injustice anywhere is a threat to justice everywhere."
~ Martin Luther King

One of the first and most important events that must happen in order to trigger the collapse of our unjust systems is the global liberation and long-awaited mass arrests of culprits considered the "untouchable" elite. These individuals include those behind the pharmaceutical companies, corrupt government officials, investment bankers, corrupt church leaders, large conglomerates and corporations, and those involved in war crimes and crimes against humanity.

The names of some of these culprits are going to shock most people, but once the crimes they have committed are exposed, their household names will no longer be as highly respected as they once were, to say the least. Nevertheless, these arrests must happen, otherwise these people of high power will continue to hold humanity hostage and prevent the following events from occurring. Some of these arrests have already taken place, but since the Cabal still controls the mass media outlets, these arrests won't become public until the remaining mass arrests occur and the Resistance Movement (Light Forces) finally overtake the media outlets as well. Many people may not believe all the truths mentioned in the previous chapter titled "Exposing their Plan" until these mass arrests occur before their eyes. When these arrests take place and humanity finally sees what these elite figures are being charged with, it will be a rude awakening that no one will be able to deny! This is the moment where the majority of humanity finally *wakes up* and realizes that the airline they've been conveniently flying their entire life, has been hijacked!

NOTE: *The Resistance Movement* is a group of positive light-beings who have infiltrated all the corrupt systems worldwide with the single mission of making these arrests when the time comes. They consist of a large group of individuals around the world, each member of which plays a significant role in the plan of planetary liberation.

2). The Reset Event (New Financial System)

"It is well enough that people of the nation do not understand our banking and money system, for if they did, I believe there would be a revolution before tomorrow morning." ~ Henry Ford

They say the only two things in life that are guaranteed, are death and taxes. Well, they're going to have to come up with a new punch line! The next major sign will be the complete collapse of our financial system and stock market. Now, you might look at this as a bad thing. But consider this: What if the new system were to provide a completely transparent form of open-source banking for everyone that offered debt forgiveness from predatory lending, eliminated interest rates, eliminated income tax, and allowed people to pay a flat rate sales tax in order to maintain the state?

Before long, we will understand that the current economic systems are no longer salvageable, and never served

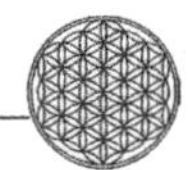

us well anyway. They created a system that forced us to have to work 40 plus hours per week, for 40 plus years of our life, only so we can retire and make 40% of an amount that was never cutting the mustard in the first place. The systems were rigged and the odds were always against us.

The Rothschild gold that currently backs the worldwide monetary banking system is just a façade. This gold is no longer in their possession as states and countries are starting to ask for it back, and will soon find out for themselves. Several major countries are already bankrupt and on the verge of collapse, and these old systems are literally just hanging on by a thread. You can compare our economic financial systems to a bunch of “Banksters” playing the classic puzzle video game Columns/Tetris, where you have to stack certain shapes where they belong in order to create an even playing field and win the game. Anyone who has played this game knows that when mistakes are made in the beginning, even if you find a way to maneuver through the chaos that was caused from these mistakes, you eventually will have to fix those mistakes you made. Our financial system is at a point where too many mistakes have been made and the blocks are piling up way too quickly to fix. All the players are now panicking, making desperate last attempts to save what’s left. Ultimately they know that their inevitable “End-Game” is near and the only way to fix the system is to let it all crumble and start from scratch. This is what humanity has been waiting for! Once we are freed from the current slavery of debt, money, and power, status will no longer define us, and we will see each other as the equals we are.

There will be no public warning when this happens; it will just happen. If you have money in the stock market or in a large bank, consider taking it out and investing in commodities such as gold, silver, and so forth. If you do wish to keep your funds in a bank, just keep in mind you will still be supporting the very ‘Banksters’ robbing you and funding their operations as they can legally borrow money in multiples based on the money you let them borrow.

"I believe that banking institutions are more dangerous to our liberties than standing armies." ~ Thomas Jefferson

If you wish to unplug from their matrix and stop funding the bad guys completely, then extract all funds from your bank account, or at least place your money in a small privately owned bank, such as a local credit union, if you can not invest in pure commodities or something tangible such as land/real estate.

NOTE: Before this system resets, it would be wise to stock up with at least a two-week supply of food, water, and gas. Do not do this out of fear; just be responsibly prepared as if a big storm were coming. The reason for this is when the systems reset and before the new financial system is in place; banks will be closed, credit cards won't work, and all the grocery stores will be wiped out within 45 minutes once people realize what's going on. As far as the gas, anyone who lived in New York City or New Jersey when Hurricane Sandy hit will completely understand how precious this valuable resource really is when it's scarce.

3). New Election Dates

"*Politicians and diapers must be changed often, and for the same reason.*" ~ Mark Twain

In conjunction with the planetary liberation and the financial system reset, we will see the rebuilding of our current government. New leaders will emerge within six to twelve months after these events occur, and this process will weed out all the corrupt politicians from the system. If you've always wanted to be a politician, but didn't want to walk into a cesspool every day, then this is going to be your chance. A new type of governance will emerge that will really be for the people, by the people.

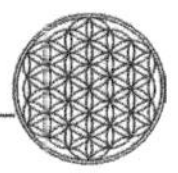

4). Losing Your Mind

"*The truth will set you free. But first it will piss you off.*"
~ Gloria Steinem

Over the years I've developed an insatiable appetite for knowledge and wisdom regarding the topic of awakening. I'll never forget the day I asked my mentor to tell me everything she knew, even things above my level of consciousness and comprehension. She then told me in a sarcastic, playful voice, "Be careful what you wish for." I smiled and asked, "Why's that?" She then shifted into a more serious manner and told me, "If you wish to learn these truths, you really have to be willing to lose your mind." Lose my mind? I wasn't sure if that statement was literal or metaphorical, but either way, I soon realized that she couldn't have been more accurate.

"*You must unlearn what you have learned.*" ~ Yoda, Star Wars

You cannot fill a cup that's already full. In order to be capable of learning these truths, you must first forget all that you've been taught and truly "lose your mind" before you can digest these truths properly; truths that also have the ability to make you feel like you're losing your mind once you learn them.

The "De"programming

The awakening is something everyone will experience in his or her own way. There is no escaping this mass awakening. The only way to prepare for what is to come is to seek what we have been deprived of our entire lives: The Truth! This deprogramming event will most likely happen when the mass-arrest public trials commence. When this happens, all barriers will disappear, the invisible divisions created by religions will be revealed, all lies will be exposed, and truths will surface.

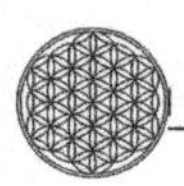

As the veil lifts and the blindfold comes off, the mind deprogramming will be quite difficult for some. Those of us who are unprepared for these changes ahead of time will most likely not be able to cope with the rapid changes taking place in our psyches. Some will not be able to grasp the fact that everything in the world has been built on a lie. The groups that this will be the most challenging for will be life-long scientists, born-again Christians, or any religion extremist or teacher who believes "If it's not in their book, then it's not true." This is mainly because they feel they've done everything right by fully devoting themselves to God; which would be very much true, and this is exactly why it will be hard for these wonderful people to accept such truths that shatter their core beliefs, because they are indeed good people who believe they are going against the word of God.

5). The Disclosure Event

"*I don't laugh at people any more when they say they've seen UFO's. I've seen one myself.*" ~ U.S President Jimmy Carter (Washington Post interview, 1975)

Once the majority of the population is deprogrammed and safely unplugged from the matrix, then the world will be ready for its greatest disclosure. Among the undisclosed truths to be revealed to the public worldwide following the collapse of the old systems will be proof of the existence of extraterrestrial beings. Yes, you've read this correctly! There will be undeniable proof for everyone that we are not alone and we never have been.

These beings I speak of are here to help us, not blow up our planet like the Hollywood movies have depicted. In fact, these beings have helped minimize the collateral damage from the new energies Earth is experiencing, numerous natural disasters, and from our own destructive nature, which has nearly wiped out the planet quite a few times. To

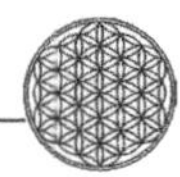

be quite candid, if it weren't for these intelligent higher consciousness beings, humanity would have nuked each other a long time ago.

I know that the official disclosure of ET's might sound a little too farfetched to be true, but why is it that every alien film that hits the big screen these days becomes an instant blockbuster hit? Well, according to U.S. News & World Report and a survey conducted by National Geographic, 36 percent of Americans believe that aliens have visited Earth, and nearly 80 percent believe that the government has kept information about UFOs secret from the public. Maybe the idea of life on other planets isn't so farfetched after all. Maybe our generation will be the lucky ones to see firsthand, that we are not alone!

If people were to actually spend time researching the truth about these extraterrestrial beings as I have, they would be shocked after realizing that many of these beings look more human than possibly imagined. In all reality, there are many stranger looking creatures right here on Earth than there are in outer space. I know personally if I saw a 50 foot slimy creature with 50 arms and hundreds of tentacles trying to suction my body and squirt a mysterious liquid into my eyes that could temporarily blind me, I would be scared to death! Yet we call that an Octopus, or a giant squid, and we're perfectly fine with that because we're told it lives underwater on Earth. But if we were to see a tall humanoid looking being that breathes the same air as we do, has two arms and two legs like we do, with maybe slightly tinted bluish skin who just so happens to live on another planet, we would freak out and head for the hills. It is the limiting of our consciousness and the human ego that doesn't want us to fathom that there are other beings out there, more intelligent and advanced than we are. If people only knew the amount of divine intervention that our star brothers and sisters have done in order to keep us safe, and that the majority of our favorite everyday technologies originated from these races, we would view these benevolent beings with much less fear and much higher regard.

As worldwide disclosure on extraterrestrial existence nears, don't be surprised when you hear about an astounding number of UFO sightings and stories of personal encounters. This will happen just before complete extraterrestrial disclosure, which will take place only after ALL the aforementioned 'events" occur. Until then, you will slowly see some significant political figures peppering this full disclosure to come. It's already happening now, you can Google articles about President Bill Clinton admiring the microbial life discovered on Mars (life on other planets). You can also YouTube both Princess Nakamaru of Japan and former Canadian Defense Prime Minister, Paul Hellyer, publicly admitting to not only ET and UFO existence, but the U.S government's involvement and interaction with these ET races over many years.

Russia's Prime Minister, Dmitry Medvedev, has already disclosed their top-secret folder containing truths regarding Russia's contact with ET races. A Ministry of Foreign Affairs (MFA) report on Prime Minister Medvedev's agenda at the 2015 World Economic Forum (WEF) states that "Russia will warn President Obama that the "time has come" for the world to know the truth about aliens, and if the United States won't participate in the announcement, the Kremlin will do so on its own."

"Why is it that the world wants us to believe that Santa Claus is real but aliens are fake? How is it that countless pilots who have seen UFO's with their own eyes isn't enough evidence for government disclosure, yet on our U.S currency the government puts "In God We Trust" with far less evidence?"

~David Wilcox

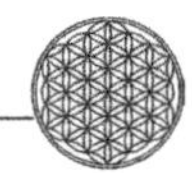

Although, there are many political figures coming forth, disclosure will be a gradual process, so there is no need to worry about a mother ship landing on your front lawn any time soon. However, you must believe that this time will come, and it will come much sooner than you think. The knowledge of life on other planets will soon be solidified into the collective consciousness of humanity. The majority (critical mass) of the surface population will finally have to accept these truths when the evidence is too great to deny. Then, whether you're ready or not, "they" will uniquely 'reveal' themselves starting with the people who's consciousness have been conditioned (awakened) and are ready for this type of realization. I emphasize the word 'reveal' because many think that "they're coming"; but trust me when I tell you, THEY ARE ALREADY HERE! I make this statement boldly because I have personally seen evidence of their existence with my own two eyes, on several occasions since August of 2012. Ironically, I happened to share my ET/ UFO experience in the same location where a few of the guys from the History channel's hit television show *Ancient Aliens* did as well. And yes, one of them was the guy with the crazy hairdo (Giorgios Tsoukalos). The irony behind this story is that Giorgios was speaking at this conference (*Contact in the Desert 2014*) that I attended in Joshua Tree, California, and someone directly asked him the question that everyone wanted to know, "Giorgios, have you ever seen a UFO in real life?" To everyone's surprise, and to his disappointment, he answered, "No, I wish I could say yes, but no I have not". Little did any one know that later on that very same night there would be an exotic UFO light-show in the sky that not a single person could deny it as anything less than a cosmic phenomenon.

What's even more exciting than these first hand experiences, is what will happen on the day these beings remove their cloak of invisibility and reveal themselves to the mass population. The same way any good guest would arrive and exhibit their hospitality, I promise you that when they do come, they will not come empty handed!

6). NEW Technologies and Cures

In the new era about to emerge, free energy, suppressed/new technology, and cures for disease will be introduced, including cures for cancer that have been hidden from the public for countless years. There will be free and proper health care for all. There will be soothing chambers of light and sound that will heal all illness and injury in the human body while removing all impurities that have imbalanced us over the years. In the very near future, the days of filling up at the pumps at more than four dollars per gallon will be obsolete. Among the new technologies to be introduced will be a device that can be installed by your mechanic to make your car run FREE of gas and run on just water (hydrogen engine) or vegetable oil (100thgreasemonkey.com).

NOTE: Please visit www.IamAwakened.com and sign up for our newsletter so you can get live updates on "the event".

How Should I Prepare?

"*All learning is simply recollection*." — Plato

The good news is you don't have to do any type of training or preparing for anything. Just like Matt Damon's character in the movie The Bourne Supremacy, we already have all the knowledge, training, and skills that we need to know inside of us. When certain matters arise, just know that you will have the answer and you will know exactly what to do without thinking or doing, but by just being. The questions of how and why this is possible are irrelevant; have trust and faith, as this is all you'll need. The same phenomenon of how an adolescent child can be thrown into a pool for the first time and know how to swim; The same phenomenon of how a baby sea turtle born in the sand knows it has to crawl

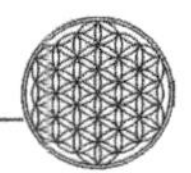

to the ocean and it somehow already knows it can swim; Our DNA is encoded with this information within every cell of our body. All the knowledge we need in this world lies within the cellular memory of our soul, our DNA, and inside our sub-conscious mind.

Fear nothing, have faith, and believe that there are no coincidences in life, because there are none. Know that where you're currently at is exactly where you are supposed to be, and where you are supposed to be is exactly where you are!

We truly are more than just our physical bodies. Our soul has all the answers we need; if you can just accept this as your truth, you'll never have to worry about anything ever again. The only preparation you need at this point in time is to decide 'when' you are going to fully wake up! During your new quest for answers and truth, you will be presented with many earth-shattering discoveries, some true, some not. So how do you discern what's true and what's false?

Who Should I Believe?

"*Many people, especially ignorant people, want to punish you for speaking the truth, for being correct, for being you. Never apologize for being correct, or for being years ahead of your time. If you're right and you know it, speak your mind. Even if you are a minority of one, the truth is still the truth.*" ~ Gandhi

Old traditions have been passed on through shamans, psychics, channels, whistle blowers, and visionaries over time. Many of these way-showers started mystery schools underground to pass along their teachings. These same philanthropists became outlawed, tabooed, ridiculed, stigmatized, ostracized, and sometimes even killed. Take for example the accused "witches" in Salem, Massachusetts (1692) that were publicly crushed to death just for having natural psychic/metaphysical abilities.

There's a 99.9% chance that if you were living in the 1920's-1940's you would think cigarettes were healthy, asbestos was safe, and lead paint was harmless. If you were living in the 1800's you would most likely be racist since slavery was considered "the norm" back then. And what about all the people who previously thought the Earth was round versus flat? Those people were the true "crazies," right?

This is simply how the evolution of our consciousness works; when our consciousness raises, our truth changes. No matter what times we are living in, there is always going to be those who bring forth new truths that are mocked and rejected by the mainstream. What is common sense to us now might have seemed like fairytales back then, which is why it's important to keep an open mind when faced with new material, even if it seems to be a bunch of hocus-pocus and phony baloney.

"*If we value the pursuit of knowledge, we must be free to follow wherever that search may lead us. The free mind is not a barking dog, to be tethered on a ten-foot chain.*"

~ Adlai E. Stevenson Jr.

I have presented many personal opinions and viewpoints, along with examples of the scientific studies and research I have found over the years, throughout these chapters. If one cannot accept such truths revealed to them, it is not the power in these truths that are being denied, it is the power within them that is not being recognized. A few bold people usually ask me, "Why should we believe what you say?" I say to these individuals, "Don't believe what I tell you! But don't believe everything that anyone else tells you either." That's how we got in this mess in the first place. Trust what I am telling you is my truth, but don't accept it as your truth if it doesn't resonate with your soul.

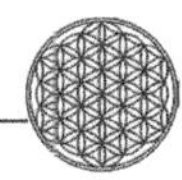

"*Believe nothing, no matter where you read it, or who said it, no matter if I have said it, unless it agrees with your own reason and your own common sense.*" ~ Buddha

Go out as I did and ask as many questions as you possibly can, and research any material and topics you feel most curious or unsure about. Anything in this book that seems too unbelievable or too farfetched is exactly where you should start! Search for truths that resonate with your soul, not just satisfy your mind.

Google: Your New Best Friend

"*The revolution will not be televised*" ~ Gil Scot Herron

Many say that the Internet isn't always a credible source for information, but this is merely to deter us from seeking the truth. The controlling powers want us to turn to the mainstream media as our primary source of information because that is what they control, unlike the other content providers online, whom they cannot control. Of course not everything you read on the Internet is true, so you must use discernment, just as you should anything else presented to you in life, or in a book—even this book.

"Trust nothing but your intuition, your intuition will tell you who to trust." ~ Unknown

We must not allow ourselves to be aware of only what these global elitists want us to be aware of. We need to get into the habit of conducting our own research and using our internal discernment of truth that resonates within our souls, not what spikes TV ratings. We need to take control of our thoughts and emotions and choose to be the sovereign beings that we are, and not the gullible puppets they want us to be. If you truly wish to see all the madness and corruption in the world, don't turn on the news, go on *change.org* and read all the petitions people have posted. At least there you are able to take action and make a change!

Facilitate your own research and discern everything for yourself, because at the end of the day, you believe what you choose to believe; and what you choose to believe is what ultimately becomes your truth and shapes your reality. Trust your gut, listen to your heart and intuition, and don't let your conditioned mind, logic, and reason get in the way. Don't be a follower, be a student! Only take in and digest what resonates with you, and leave what doesn't to be revisited another day. Never toss out something just because you don't want to believe it.

"The day you think you know it all, is the same day you never learn anything new again."

~ Linda J. Cole

If any of the information presented to you has made you feel upset, uneasy, or even angry in any way, know that this is normal. You have every right to be upset, but you must use this energy in a positive, non-violent manner. Transmute this anger into righteous anger, or "tough love", and use this energy to motivate yourself to learn more and to awaken the others. The emotion of anger is actually an upgrade from feeling victimized, hopeless, or powerless. However, it is important to move on from this space fast so you don't attract its like energy. You must springboard to the next higher vibrational tier on the emotional spectrum in order to progress your spiritual awakening (see ascension chart on www.IamAwakened.com).

During your new journey, it is imperative that you always remain the student and avoid the gurus. As the great philosopher Socrates stated, "True knowledge exists in knowing that you know nothing." You will soon see, as did I, that the more you research and learn of these truths, the more you will realize how much you never knew in the first place.

CHAPTER

18

THE BEST ADVICE EVER GIVEN TO MAN

"*And no message could be any clearer, if you want to make the world a better place, take a look at yourself and make a change.*" ~ Michael Jackson, Man in the Mirror Lyrics

Every day that passes and every new person that becomes aware of the ideas presented in this book brings us one step closer to the final liberation of our planet. The new paradigm is already here, just waiting for us to acknowledge its presence so it can be welcomed in. Under universal law, the new paradigm cannot usher itself in until it is invited. So what are we waiting for, right? The timing of the big shift approaching is solely contingent upon the awakening of humanity as a collective, by reaching the critical mass needed. However, this change will happen in our lifetime, in this generation, and probably sooner than you think, as long as everyone participates in the awakening process. This doesn't mean you have to jump up on a soapbox and preach to the choir, if you wish to fix this world you must first focus on yourself before you focus on anything, or anyone else.

"*If you want to awaken all of humanity, then awaken all of yourself. If you want to eliminate the suffering in the World, then eliminate all that is dark and negative in yourself. Truly, the greatest gift you have to give is that of your own self-transformation*" ~ Lao-Tzu

Like Gandhi says, "Y*ou must be the change you wish to see in the world*." In life, we can only hope that our children learn what we teach them, but we can be sure that they learn what we SHOW them. Humans need to be shown what to do, not told what to do. We must lead by example and be that example that others want to emulate. For example, when we are faced with an unfamiliar word or difficult math equation, it's one thing to be told what the word means or how to solve the equation, but it's only when it's explained or demonstrated using examples that we are best able to understand the problem at hand. We need to be these examples not just to our children, but also to our fellow neighbor. Leading by example isn't just one-way in my eyes; it's the only way! We must not only talk the talk, but we must walk that talk to encourage all the talkers to want to be walkers.

United We Stand, Divided We Fall

"*None of us is as smart as all of us*." ~ Ken Blanchard

One of the most intense and moving speeches I have ever heard in my lifetime came from Charlie Chaplin, in The Great Dictator. Chaplin plays dual roles; one, that of a dictator who resembles Adolf Hitler and another, that of a Jewish barber. After a series of peculiar incidents, the dictator gets replaced by his lookalike barber, and is transported to the capitol, where he is asked to give a speech. The barber is extremely reluctant to get in front of this massive crowd, but after being urged by his military personnel, the barber hesitantly makes his way to the podium in bewilderment. As he stands in front of four giant microphones, looking confused

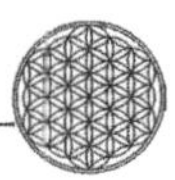

and intimidated by the immense crowd thinking that he is Hitler, he apprehensively begins to utter nervous words of uncertainty that soon transform into the most empowering and electrifying words that shocked the world forever. Chaplin's words about uniting humankind gives me chills every time I watch this movie clip. If you have not seen it, I strongly urge you to take the time to watch it. Although this movie is more than seventy years old, the speech is as relevant today as it was then.

"*A man who stands for nothing will fall for anything.*"
~ Malcolm X

If you were to take a note out of a symphony, it would lose its significance. Humanity not only needs to stick together, we need to know that sticking together is the only way we can create the amount of change needed to liberate our planet. We must understand that humanity doesn't just need change; we need each other to make this change and we simply need each other in general. Take people who are incarcerated in prison for example. When an inmate gets in some sort of trouble while incarcerated, the most severe punishment they give that inmate is placing them in segregation or solitary confinement by removing them from the other inmates, correct? Now let's think about this for a second. If you were to imagine being in prison and constantly surrounded by cold criminals—maybe even rapists, murderers, and drug lords—wouldn't you think you'd want to get as far away from such people as possible? Yet instead the authorities isolate inmates from other human interaction as a form of reprimand or torture.

This act is actually the cruelest punishment they administer because humans need to be around other humans to survive or else we go crazy. Take Will Smith's character in the movie <u>I Am Legend</u>. We need one another to grow, evolve, learn, and love, regardless of the circumstances; it's just human nature. We must realize that we the people have and always had the power to make this world a better place. We were meant to live in community, a "common unity"; this is where our greatest dominion is.

"*Snowflakes are one of nature's most fragile things, but just look at what they can do when they stick together.*"

~ Vesta Kelly

It is no coincidence that the trees on Earth breathe in the carbon dioxide that humans just so happen to breathe out; and it is no coincidence that we humans breathe in that same oxygen that the trees breathe out. Just as the bees need the flowers to survive, the flowers need the Earth to survive, the Earth needs the sun to survive, the sun needs the universe to survive; and humans need all of the above to survive, because ultimately everything on this planet is divinely interconnected and dependent upon one another. From the tiniest cell in our body, to the vast sun in our sky, everything on this planet is dependent upon something else for its survival.

"In deep and lasting ways, when we heal ourselves we heal the world." ~ Mark Nepo

Law of Correspondence: The law of correspondence is where all the laws in the universe exist. It is the spiritual web that interconnects all things in life and is the cosmic life force that perpetuates oneness within the universe. The law of correspondence is the glue that holds oneness together so all planes of existence are in harmony (physical, mental, and spiritual). All changes that occur in one plane of existence affect the other planes, and the law of correspondence balances these planes so all things in life can function harmoniously for their survival and/or evolution.

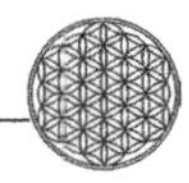

"When the power of love overcomes the love of power, the world will know true peace." ~ Jimi Hendrix

Once humanity realizes that our issues aren't separate from one another, that we're not alone in this battle, and that we are all in this game together, humanity will remember the power we have as a whole to change the world. We already have the divine blueprint within us; we don't have to learn anything, it's just a matter of remembering. In a world where we are born into bondage and taught that we are separate from one another, we must break this belief and come into remembrance of who we really are and why we are here. Keep in mind, that the word "dismember' means to divide into parts and pieces, and the word "remember" means to become whole again. Therefore, I am neither your teacher nor your guru; I have not taught you anything new and you have not learned anything new. You came into this existence with all the answers inside of you already. You are now learning how to extract them by *unlearning* what you've previously learned (false belief systems). I have merely initiated you into remembrance by assisting in your awakening that has activated higher functioning aspects of yourself, which are now being remembered.

We Are Who We Have Been Looking For!

"*The world will not be destroyed by those who do evil, but by those who watch them without doing anything.*"

~ Albert Einstein

They say if you are not part of the solution to a problem, then you are part of the problem. This is very true and congruent to earth's current crisis. The remaining people who are sleeping and still plugged into the matrix are the 'enablers' who are actually anchoring the rest of humanity in lower levels of consciousness and preventing the events from triggering. In other words, there will be no planetary liberation of any kind until the critical mass of humanity is fully awakened. Keep in mind that there is no cavalry coming to save us. WE the people are the ones we've been waiting for; yes, that means YOU! So if you are awakened and you know of these truths, there is no more time to be a cheerleader on the sidelines, its time to get in the game and help awaken the others. It was never "us against them" to begin with; we can only blame ourselves for allowing and accepting these conditions of life.

"*We must stop blaming society, when WE ARE SOCIETY.*"
~Unknown

Together, we can completely change the world by uniting humanity's collective thought through meditation or by simply visualizing a better world in everyone's mind. This is the most powerful ability humanity has as a collective. Knowledge is true power, and this knowledge is our weapon, it's our golden key for peace, prosperity, oneness, and paradise on Earth. The time is now; celebrate now! If we each play our part, together we can literally achieve the greatest accomplishment and accolade in the history of the universe!

Like Steve Jobs famously said, "*The ones who are crazy enough to think they can change the world, are the ones that do.*" Just by raising your awareness to your surroundings and using your emotions and thoughts to shape (y)our reality, YOU are the one who now has the ability to help awaken the world, become or awaken the remaining 100th monkey, activate the grid, and literally save our planet! You now fully understand the true power of "knowing", and what to do with it. Just like our childhood friend G. I. Joe always said, "Knowing is half the battle." This is why YOU are a pivotal, key player in this process. As children, we all had a superhero we looked up to, but you must realize that you are the superhero now, you are the Jeti Master. Yes, YOU! I know, who would have ever *thunk* it, right?

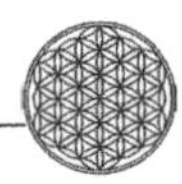

We Have Everything We Need

"*God, grant me the serenity to accept the things I cannot change, the courage to change the things I can, and the wisdom to know the difference.*" ~ Reinhold Niebuhr

In *The Wizard of Oz*, Dorothy's journey comes to an end when the Great Wizard is finally exposed. After a long journey filled with many obstacles, Dorothy and her companions finally find this Great Wizard, who is merely a man with a bad case of Napoleon complex hiding behind a giant curtain. As Dorothy and the Scarecrow start to confront the fake wizard for tricking them into believing he existed and could fulfill all their desires, the wizard finally cracks under pressure and confesses he never had any powers to begin with.

The Wizard then convinces the brainless scarecrow of how smart he already is and gives him a fake diploma. The Scarecrow is ecstatic and all of a sudden starts shouting out algebraic and calculus equations.

Then The Wizard tells the Cowardly Lion that he's confusing courage with wisdom and calls him a hero and gives him an old rusted Medal of Honor. The Wizard then initiates the Lion into a fabricated elite group called the "Legion of Courage" and suddenly the Lion feels like a king again.

The Tin Man was still missing a heart. So The Wizard gives him a big red clock that ticks to put inside of him. Everyone is pleased as Dorothy is told all she had to do is click her heels three times and she will already be home.

The journey and deception revealed in this plot is what humanity is now experiencing and will soon discover, The Wizard being our government, while Dorothy, the Lion, the Tin Man, and the Scarecrow represent humanity.

Although The Wizard was lying and they all believed they lacked something that only The Wizard could provide, he still changed their perception when he finally admitted that they've always had everything they needed all along, they just didn't believe it. The same will happen for humanity once the mass-arrests occur and the curtain comes up during the public trials, which will reveal all the lies and deception used to suppress us from discovering the truth.

"*The Revolution is inside yourself.*" ~ Osho

Once humanity finally decides to confront our own political party of fake wizards, we too will see the curtain come up and the puppeteers come scurrying out when the smoke starts to clear. Soon we will realize that we had all the tools and gifts we ever needed in this journey all along and that WE and no one else, are the ones with the power that we've been seeking the entire time.

The final scenes of this movie that we are all starring in are about to play out. As *The Greatest Show On Earth* approaches the climax of its season finale, there are many wondrous surprises that await us. Unfortunately for the bad guys all 'good things' must come to an end. Even they know that the good guys always win at the end of the movie.

CHAPTER

19

IT'S (y)OUR TIME!

"*I am only one, but I am one. I cannot do everything, but I can do something. And I will not let what I cannot do interfere with what I can do.*" ~ Edward Everett Hale

The content of this book is not intended to highlight the problems we face, but more so to highlight the solutions that most of us aren't even aware we're facing. The intention is to shine light on these dark areas and expose truths that should prompt you to at least think, "Maybe, just maybe, there is more to the story than I've been told." As I've persistently suggested, you must research and decide this on your own. I have merely provided a vehicle of information that you can now take down any road you wish, as fast or as slow as you please.

If at any point while reading this book you feel your switch was flipped, your internal flame was lit, or your spark was ignited, just know it will be much harder to go back to sleep now that your light has been turned on. Therefore, I apologize in advance, but you will thank me in the long run. Just know that from this day forward your life will never be dull or boring again now that you have initiated yourself into The Awakening! Your "misinformation meter" has now been upgraded, and you will notice it will be much harder for anyone to lie to you again. You will identify and transcend everything that was intended to fool you and you will see obstacles and deception coming from a mile away now.

"Once you see the magic, you'll never miss the trick."
~ Ronnie Donnelly

We must understand that we are all sovereign beings who are equal and all connected regardless of race, religion, or country borders that have separated us. We have to realize that we are all here with the same goal, just playing different roles, but all starring in the same movie. We all come from the same source of creation living on this free-will planet where everything and all is possible. Life isn't supposed to be this hard. It's time to be who we need to be, say what we need to say, and do what we need to do, so we can live the way we wish to live.

"If not us, then who? If not now, then when?" ~ John Lewis

We must learn to speak from our heart, not from our mind, listen with our soul, not with our ears, and start seeing each other as the equally powerful co-creators that we all are. I can't emphasize enough how mind-blowing and amazing this world can and will be. Trust me when I tell you that you would fight tooth and nail for this new world if you had only a glimpse of what's around the corner. You must believe!

Amazing feats are only considered to be miracles when we achieve the things we believe we couldn't achieve. Once we come to the realization that THE WORLD IS OURS, we will have the power to change any outcome we wish. Only then will we realize that the act of a miracle was

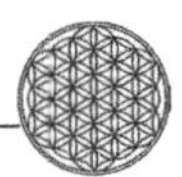

only considered miraculous to the people who thought those miracles were unattainable. Once enough people awaken to these truths, the veil will lift, the earth will shift, and everyday will seem like a miracle here on earth.

It is imperative that we expand our thinking, raise our consciousness, dissolve unhealthy belief systems, and eliminate the barriers that have separated us from uniting into our power. We must open our minds and our hearts to the infinite potential and endless possibilities here on this planet. This is the only way we can unplug from their matrix and break the constructs of this forged illusion of reality; a reality created to control us by fooling us into believing we're anything other than powerful spiritual beings with amazing abilities and extraordinary gifts.

Choosing Your 'Perception Lenses'

"We can complain because rose bushes have thorns, or rejoice because thorn bushes have roses." ~ Abraham Lincoln

Even though we all have the innate ability to attract certain events, people, and circumstances into our life, we must understand that "ultimate control" is an illusion. We rarely have any control of *when* or *how* any of the aforementioned can play out. This is also the beauty of manifesting because we forget that situations can manifest far better and much faster than we could ever imagine, if we simply believe that it can and set this as our intention.

As for the things we never asked for, the unexpected events, unfortunate circumstances, and the things we do not have any control over, there is only one way to deal with these perceivably negative situations in a positive manner. By exercising our choice of perception we are able to shift our perspective, which allows us to deal with any situation that life may bring us. It is only through our choice of perception that enables us to control the uncontrollable.

"When life hands you lemons, make lemonade."
~Elbert Hubbard

Our perception of life is the lense we choose to view our reality. We just have to remember that we are the ones who prescribed these "perception lenses" and that we can swap them out for a new pair at any given time. Know that it's normal and okay when other people cannot view life the way you perceive it. Your only job is to be sure you avoid being overshadowed and pulled into their reality through self-doubt. So stand firm in your truth and protect your beliefs. If you can control your perception you can control your reality, and once you can control your reality, you have mastered life and graduated from *Earth School*.

"When you change the way you look at things, the things you look at change." ~Dr. Wayne Dyer

Image credit: Russian cartoonist Igor Vorobyev found on http://johnelkington.com/2007/02/

FINAL WORDS

Now that the stars are literally aligning, everything that we thought was impossible in the old paradigm is now possible today. The systems you see today are already crumbling

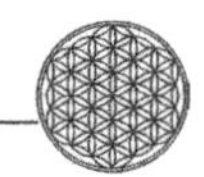

beneath us; yet the media isn't talking about it. Life is about to get a whole lot easier than life as we know it. Some might view the destruction of the old systems as chaotic and earth-shaking, but what these people fail to see is the bright future that lies behind the walls of deception. Yes, there might be a bit of a bumpy road when these old systems and old ways begin to crumble, but whether we know it or not, this is what we have all been waiting for! As Mayan elder, Grandfather Don Alejandro says, "*The very walls you will see falling down in front of you are only the walls that kept us imprisoned all these years*." We will witness the death of the old world order, not the Earth, the death of the beliefs and prejudices of ignorance, and the corrupt social structures that upheld them. We must stay positive and be sure not to mistake humanity's destiny for anything less than beautiful.

Positive thinking is a prime ingredient for resurfacing ourselves from within. We must stay focused and positive minded in order to be able to deal with anything that comes our way. Positive thinking can promote the shedding away of our problems and worries while manifesting a new life for us. Using the tools I've shown you, you can create, destroy, or preserve any reality you want by what you *choose* to focus on the most. As you now know, "energy flows where attention goes", so you must realize that the key to successfully co-creating within this world is to focus all of your energy on the present moment and visualize exactly what you want while remembering to <u>never</u> focus on whatever it is that you do NOT want.

I have shown you that your thoughts and the thoughts of others have been 100 percent proven to change outcomes of certain events and circumstances. The effects from these consciously powered thoughts not only have the power to change one's life, but also have been proven to change the world! We must realize that we are participants in the outcome and creation of our own lives and of the world. We co-create within this universe, a universe that not only allows for

our participation, but requires it! Every day in every way, with every thought and every emotion that you emit,
you are not just living out your life; you are creating your life!

REMEMBER TO REMEMBER

"*May the force be with you.*" ~ Master Yoda

Now that you are aware of your gifts that were disclosed in chapters 1-9, when you start to use them, you will begin to notice that certain like-minded people will enter your life unexpectedly, certain events will start to unfold in mysterious ways, and you will begin to see that the almighty and powerful universe is on your side and ready to assist your every thought and desire. Just be sure to use your powers wisely, and then be sure to awaken others to theirs.

"New definition of a Billionaire: Someone who positively affects the lives of a billion people!" ~ Jason Silva

In life we are either a creator, or we are a part of someone else's creation. Once you fully accept the true power that you harness as a creator, then, when you don't like a certain event or situation in your life, you can change it! The paintbrush is always in your hand, so masterfully create any scenario you envision. Whether you consider your life to be your canvas, your play, your movie, or your book, know that you are the author of your story and you have the power to create any beginning or ending you wish.

Being the author of your own story isn't the hardest part of creating whatever it is that you want; the hardest part is simply REMEMBERING that you *are* the author throughout your entire story. Remembering that you are always creating and always in charge, every minute of every day, all the time. You are in constant creation with every thought, every vision, and every emotion that you have. All you have to do is simply

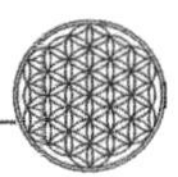

REMEMBER to REMEMBER that you possess these great powers. Once you master the art of *remembering* that you are always in control, it will be the equivalent to that feeling you have when you're dreaming and suddenly *awaken* to the fact that you're dreaming and have the ability to control your dream. This is the power you have if you choose to evoke it.

"*Row Row Row Your Boat, Gently Down The Stream, Merrily Merrily Merrily Merrily, Life Is But A Dream.*" ~ Alice Munro

My personal journey into the awakening has been a dream and a movie both wrapped in one. There have been many nights when I laid my head on my pillow, closed my eyes, and just waited for the movie credits to start playing behind the blackness of my eyelids. So I understand that for some it may feel like this book has turned your world upside down, but in reality, your world has just been turned right side up! Just know that the light at the end of the tunnel is far brighter than you could ever imagine and that you are much more than what you think you are. I know that I can tell you these things, and I understand that they may just be words that you'll read (for now). However, once you can accept the fact that maybe there's more to life than what you've been told, shown, or read in one ancient book, then you will experience these truths for yourself, I guarantee it! It's all out there for you to discover, and it's out there for everyone, but only if you begin to take notice. Although it may seem a bit of a paradox, I promise you that you'll start seeing it, as soon as you start believing it.

You must start right here, right now! Let this book be the catalyst that propels you to discover the secrets within your universe and all the immense powers and amazing hidden abilities of your most valuable asset in life... YOU!

THE ~~END~~ BEGINNING!

CONGRATULATIONS!

You now know what it truly means to be *Awakened* and what *The Awakening Movement* stands for. Now that you're awakened, you can start wearing your *Awakening Gear* and begin identifying with other Awakened souls around the world! If you do not have your Awakening products yet, you can visit www.IAmAwakened.com and get yours today!

Personal Request: If you could please post a short review on Amazon.com for me, I would greatly appreciate it. Also, please tag me and share this book on your social media pages (@ManFromTheStars); and please recommend this book to people you know who will either "Get it", or to people you know who really "Need it".

P.s. You are now officially eligible to join *THE AWAKENERS!*

Namaste,

~ Kurtis Lee Thomas

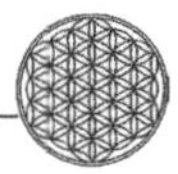

WANT TO JOIN THE AWAKENERS?

The Awakeners™ are a group of people, like you and I, who are awakening to their purpose and are now on a mission! Our mission is to awaken the rest of humanity to their gifts, talents, and abilities. This mission involves gathering an army of like-minds to help enlighten humanity and raise worldwide consciousness by shining light on global crises using various means of media, blogs, vlogs, special events, charitable drives, and various educational workshops.

Awakeners "think different" and wish to share their vision with the world. It is our vision to lead the world into the Golden Age of peace and prosperity by sharing suppressed truths, showing new ways, and providing the most accessible and comprehendible information of TRUTH, regarding human affairs, while unifying all races and religions.

... AND HAVE FUN DOING IT!

Visit www.IamAwakened.com for NEW Book Releases, tour dates, or to Donate to *The Awakening Foundation.* Anything and everything counts!

Contact The Author:

Kurtis Lee Thomas
PO BOX 19628
JOHNSTON, RI 02919
www.Facebook.com/ManFromTheStars

ABOUT THE AUTHOR

Kurtis Lee Thomas is a successful entrepreneur, motivational speaker, and business intuitive who has dedicated his life to following his passion and paying it forward. his mantra of "First you must LEARN, then you should EARN, so eventually you can RETURN", led Kurtis to become a philanthropist and certified Life Coach. Kurtis adamantly believes that the harmonious communion of the body, mind, and spirit is the key to living a happy and healthy life. THIS thought pattern and diligent lifestyle choice are what eventually led Kurtis to becoming a certified Reiki Master, certified Hypnotherapist & Neuro-linguistic programming practitioner, as well as a certified International Sports Sciences Association fitness professional.

In 2011, Kurtis had an amazing and eye-opening spiritual experience that changed his world forever. Kurtis discovered amazing abilities and mysteries about himself and the universe that he not only felt compelled to share with the rest of the world—he felt obligated!

"It is a rare author who can take the complexity and beyond-words aspect of spirituality and put it into simple english. Kurtis Lee Thomas is one of those rare finds."

~ *New York Times* Best-Selling author G.W Hardin